Tales from Tennessee Lawyers

TALES FROM TENNESSEE LAWYERS

⚖

WILLIAM LYNWOOD MONTELL

THE UNIVERSITY PRESS OF KENTUCKY

Publication of this volume was made possible in part by a grant
from the National Endowment for the Humanities.

Editorial and Sales Offices: The University Press of Kentucky
663 South Limestone Street, Lexington, Kentucky 40508–4008
www.kentuckypress.com

09 08 07 06 05   5 4 3 2 1

Library of Congress Cataloging-in-Publication Data

Montell, William Lynwood, 1931-
Tales from Tennessee lawyers / William Lynwood Montell.
p. cm.
Includes bibliographical references.
ISBN 0-8131-2369-0 (hardcover : alk. paper)
1. Law—Tennessee—Anecdotes. 2. Law—Tennessee—Humor. I. Title.
K184.M664 2005
348.768—dc22
2005018319

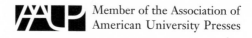

CONTENTS

INTRODUCTION

Drive anyplace across the beautiful state of Tennessee, ask for the names of good storytellers, and you'll always be provided with the names of several persons, including many local lawyers and judges. In doing this, beginning in May 2001, I came up with the names of certain legal professionals who truly know how to tell a good story, whether it is an honest-to-goodness description of a case in which they were involved or simply a universal tale that has been passed along across the years around the state and nation.

When I began this Tennessee lawyer project, many of the storytellers I contacted quickly expressed a willingness to participate. They were interested in helping to preserve a portion of the history of the Tennessee legal profession. They kindly set aside time from their busy schedules to recount stories for me and to describe interesting aspects of the legal system then and now. These professionals recounted wonderful, absorbing tales, some of which were humorous, frightening, insightful, thought provoking, or filled with sorrow. Most of these stories were told as personal experiences, or about things that happened to the storytellers' friends in or out of the courtroom. Like lawyers across Kentucky, who are featured in my earlier book, those I talked to in Tennessee were willing to trust me once they learned of my academic background. I explained that now, as during my years as a university professor, I am not interested in writing about kings, queens, and presidents; I am much more interested in writing about local life, history, and culture.

The primary criteria established prior to contacting potential storytellers were their age, gender, and geographic location. I primarily selected storytellers who were middle-aged or older, although some young attorneys were intentionally chosen. And while many of them are affiliated with larger legal firms, some were chosen because they practice alone or as a member of a small firm. The rationale for choosing older lawyers and those who work in small firms was that these individuals typically have many interesting memories from which to draw. Younger attorneys typically practice in larger firms around the state and thus tend to specialize in a particular aspect of the law. Many older lawyers work as general practitioners rather than handling cases in such specific categories as domestic relations, homicides, and bankruptcy, and many of them are excellent narrators. So, too, are many of those who work in more specialized areas, but their excellent stories are often not as universal as those told by the others, especially by lawyers and judges who live in small rural towns and villages. Legal practices in such locales tend to serve a greater diversity of clients, with varying social and economic backgrounds, and a wider range of interesting and illuminating cases.

This book includes stories told by female attorneys, as it should, given that in Tennessee female lawyers are almost as numerous as males. I was told that approximately half of all students in law schools these days are female, which has been the case since about 1970. Larry Rice, an attorney from Memphis, stated that "female attorneys are just as honest, tricky, underhanded, above board, devious, cooperative, and friendly as male attorneys. . . . But all lawyers are lawyers, and our common experience pretty much brings us to common ground, and being a female doesn't affect that." In Tennessee, female attorneys do have their own bar association.

Female attorneys were extremely few in number before the 1950s. Two of the early women lawyers included herein were Claude Swafford and Judge Shirley B. Underwood, whose stories were recorded by interviewers affiliated with the Tennessee Bar Foundation, Nashville.

Thanks to the Tennessee Bar Foundation and to the references and frequent contacts made by other lawyers and judges in my behalf, I was able to record stories told by both male and female lawyers in every geographic region of Tennessee, comprising West Tennessee, Middle Tennessee, and East Tennessee. The persons who provided stories lived and/or practiced in the following cities and towns: Memphis, Covington, Somerville, Dresden, Jackson, Clarksville, Waverly, Columbia, Fayetteville, Nashville, Gallatin, Lafayette, Celina, Smithville,

Livingston, Cookeville, Murfreesboro, Pikeville, Jasper, Chattanooga, Maryville, Dandridge, Bristol, Knoxville, Johnson City, and Kingsport.

The stories chosen for this book fall within seventeen categories, all chosen on the basis of the oral accounts provided by persons interviewed. These categories consist of viewpoints, courtroom blunders, legal humor, divorce and adultery, homicides, lawyers and judges, sexual and physical abuse, courtroom incidents and jury justice or injustice, illegal sales, political elections, thievery, executions and race relations, bad words spoken in court, animals in court, domestic relations, bankruptcy, and miscellaneous. Some of the categories contain numerous accounts, while others include fewer stories. Humor, divorce, homicides, lawyers and judges, courtroom incidents, and animals in court are the most popular categories, appearing again and again in many of these interesting, insightful verbal accounts.

Notably, personal accounts, rather than points of law, are central to most of the stories. These accounts may deal with certain legal themes, but the focus is always on people. Academic folklorists emphasize that people everywhere build their lives in accordance with beliefs, customs, practices, and frequently heard stories. Thematic stories and tales assist people in organizing their daily lives along meaningful lines. Many stories in this book illuminate this point.

In gathering the stories, I interviewed numerous active and/or retired lawyers and judges, working without any set script. I eagerly contacted these prospective storytellers, set up a time and place to sit down with them to record their stories, then drove to meet with them. Each interview typically lasted about two hours. To put the interviewees at ease prior to recording their actual stories, I began with questions such as the following: "What are the chief differences in the legal profession then and now?" "Is there a noticeable difference in the legal systems in the three chief geographic areas across the state?" "Was there a time in bygone years when lawyers would sit around and share stories?" "If so, how do you account for the fact that it isn't that way anymore?" "How do you feel about lawyer ads on television?" "What is one of your favorite memories about another lawyer or judge?"

Each of the interview sessions was recorded on either a battery-powered or an electric tape recorder. I then transcribed the tapes at home. Transcription is time-consuming and not an easy task, given that one must listen carefully enough to understand every spoken word. The bulk of each interview has been incorporated in this book, although not every story and/or descriptive commentary has been included.

In addition to accounts told to me personally, this book includes numerous stories provided by the Tennessee Bar Foundation, directed by Ms. Barri Bernstein. In 1999 the foundation initiated the Legal History Project, an intriguing oral history interview commemorative. An explanation in the spring 1999 issue of *Points of Interest*, the newsletter of the Tennessee Bar Foundation, provides the rationale for instituting the project:

> In order to preserve a part of the record of the legal profession in Tennessee, the Fellows of the Bar Foundation have begun a Legal History Project. The purpose is to interview, on video tape, senior attorneys about their lives and experiences in the law. The individual interview tapes will be kept by the Foundation for viewing and use by scholars, historians, and colleagues of the interviewees. . . .
>
> Once the interviews were completed, a collage tape was created using the "best of" moments. The final product, entitled "Tennessee Legal Traditions 1999," was professionally compiled complete with titles and music, and it premiered at the Fellows' Dinner in January.
>
> "The wisdom and reminiscences of Tennessee's senior attorneys are a valuable resource which the Fellows intend to preserve," said Scott N. Brown Jr., of Chattanooga, chairman of the Foundation. The stories that are included in "Tennessee Legal Traditions" are amusing and instructive to all members of the bar. (p. 2)

The present book includes some of these stories and viewpoints recorded by the Tennessee Bar Foundation as told by ten lawyers and/ or judges across the state, whom I chose primarily because of their geographic locations; in other words, in some instances I had not recorded stories from anyone else in their locale.

Many people in the general public assume lawyer stories to be essentially humorous accounts. However, in reading these stories, it will immediately become apparent that the accounts are not just a compilation of jokes. They describe serious court proceedings in which humor occasionally may spring forth. Humor is a natural gift to human beings that is utilized in numerous situations, including those faced by attorneys, often just to help relieve tension and deal with life's problems.

The first category of stories in this book consists of tales that are indeed humorous, but most of the other accounts are more serious—sometimes poignant, painful, or horrifying, as well as insightful. In Tennessee, as elsewhere, the courts and legal systems may not always see people at their best. It is apparent from reading the stories herein that by the time an accused person enters court, the plaintiffs and defendants are often having a difficult time with the case at hand. If the problems they are facing during a trial in court could have been solved without much difficulty, a satisfactory precourt ruling or solution already would have been accomplished. Unquestionably, lawyers and judges often deal with persons whose lives are deeply troubled, and they try to find, or effect, solutions to problems that are basically unsolvable. Working in such situations, lawyers frequently encounter periods of stress while performing their legal duties.

Although most of the stories in this book describe actual occurrences that happened somewhere in Tennessee, some recount events that occurred elsewhere. Everyone, lawyers and judges included, likes to tell and/or hear a good story. And no one appreciates a good story better than a small-town lawyer who relies on narrative skills and an ability to influence and move a jury along positive lines. It will also be apparent to readers, especially trained folklorists, that a few universal narratives—such as those dealing with adultery and theft—can be found in this book.

Folklore consists of more than universal narratives; it also focuses on stories about local culture, life, and times, both past and present. The same is true of oral history, which is both the method by which verbal information about the past and/or present is collected and recorded, and the body of knowledge that exists only in people's memories, which will be lost when they and other members of their generation have died. The body of knowledge about the past that is conveyed through oral history is different from the information typically contained in formal written documents. For example, formal records of a court case typically include only names, legal charges, and the final verdict. Oral history accounts of courtroom actions, such as those included in this book, provide similar information but also describe personalities, the use of occasional bad words in court, disagreements among lawyers, and emotional responses by the persons charged. Thus, orally communicated history can supplement written records by filling in the gaps in formal documents or providing an insider's perspective on momentous events.

Researchers interested in the history of families, communities, ethnic groups, gender differences, professional legal activities, and countless other topical categories find that too few written documents are available to permit reconstruction of the past from formal sources. In the legal profession, for example, when newspaper files, court records, and other written sources normally utilized by historians have been destroyed by fire, flood, theft, political chicanery, or simple neglect, the only remaining source materials may be the oral recollections and personal reminiscences of local lawyers and judges. More and more academic scholars now realize that oral tradition is often the only available source of historical information. Some of my academic history friends, who laughed at me during the 1960s and 1970s for writing books based on oral history interviews, now incorporate this methodology in some of their works. They realize that meaningful history can be written only when oral sources are as adequately researched and documented as thoroughly as are written ones. Orally communicated history is increasingly recognized as one of the most useful tools for conducting research on specific topics, whether local, statewide, or nationwide. Were it not for the publication of the present book and similar ones written by local lawyers and judges, an insightful understanding of the legal profession in Tennessee and of the lives of the persons involved would be less possible. Thus, there is little difference between the methods used to collect oral history and those employed in obtaining verbal folklore materials with historical content. Consequently, there is a great deal of overlap between these two fields of study.

One of the prominent, recurring themes in the lawyer and judge stories included here focuses on the changes in the Tennessee legal system over the past few decades. Some of this information was provided by individuals who perhaps believe that some practices from earlier times should have been retained. Lawyers who feel this way seemed to truly appreciate how things were during "the good old days." I cannot verify whether their attitudes are correct; it is possible that they recall a more rosy past because they are uncomfortable with some aspects of the current legal systems.

Many of the persons I interviewed prompted my desire to help preserve the legacy of Tennessee small-town and small-city trial lawyers so that their cultural and professional past would not be forgotten. Some lawyers who fit into this category are perhaps an endangered species or have already passed from the scene. I believe that their stories needed to be included so that future generations might know how the contemporary legal system came into being. The fact that these are the stories that lawyers recount to outsiders, as well as to themselves, proves that the storytelling tradition is important, providing insight into how lawyers view themselves. Their storytelling legacy can be appreciated by readers of many ages, backgrounds, and professions. I find that recording and publishing these meaningful oral accounts is the greatest satisfaction I derive from this type of academic work.

This book of Tennessee stories, like *Tales from Kentucky Lawyers*, which was published in 2003 by the University Press of Kentucky, gives credibility and recognition to the persons who told the stories and to the legal profession as a whole. I hope that scholars will read this book with as much interest as individuals who read it primarily for pleasure. I also hope that this book might motivate other older lawyers to share their stories with younger attorneys who, in turn, will pass them along to their peers. For all readers, these stories should convey the importance of lawyers and judges who have devoted much of their lives to the well-being of local people in the areas they serve.

I want to express my deep gratitude to the men and women of the Tennessee legal community who took time to share insightful memories from their distinguished careers. While doing research for this book, I developed special respect for these and other members of the Tennessee legal community who have devoted so many years to the practice of law and work to guarantee that all clients receive fair representation and treatment in court. They are community-wide and statewide building blocks who will not be forgotten in the forthcoming years.

1

VIEWPOINTS

The following accounts in this chapter are not stories per se; they are commentaries on attitudes within the legal profession and court systems, then and now. These accounts provide commentary about present-day judges, the rising cost of court fees, the lack of appropriate trial time, the lack of socializing among lawyers these days, the presence of fewer visitors in courtrooms in recent times, and commercial advertising.

Favorable commentary is found in several instances in these accounts, especially in relation to female attorneys, who began to make inroads into the profession in the mid-twentieth century, lawyers and judges who reach out to help local people, and lawyers who continue to practice in rural, small-town areas.

The following viewpoints were provided by lawyers and judges across the state of Tennessee.

1. "THINGS ARE NOT THE WAY THEY USED TO BE"

I was very brash as a young lawyer. I could stand up and try a lawsuit from my hip pocket almost, and have no fear. But the longer I have practiced law, the more unsure of myself I get. I became conscious, so to speak. I wasn't ready to take on every windmill that came along. And with that growing maturation as a lawyer, our ethics and board of responsibility have become more strident, in my opinion. We have to put up with so much from a disgruntled, upset client because of a bad result. And the pendulum has sort of swung the other way now, and I don't like that part of the law.

I'm very fortunate in that we don't have any tyrants as judges here in this area. But I've been to other counties where there is a robe fever. They've never done any real practice; they've never been in the real pits. What I wish is that our judges had more trial experience, more human experience in the law and its effects, as opposed to maybe being a district attorney for several years and then decide they are ready and qualified to be a judge. I just wish that we had a better system related to the judges. But where I practice, we have some good judges, and I'm very proud of them. They've given me a hard time over the years, but I probably deserved it for being too forthright or straightforward with my clients many times. Judges could be a lot better at streamlining, or cutting to the chase, as opposed to waxing eloquent, which is what they think they are doing.

Raymond Fraley, Fayetteville, September 20, 2001

2. "Lawyer Practice and Court Fees"

Money was not my god when I was a lawyer. I never made a lot of money. I'm thankful for that now because I'm retired. I've had lawyers that's made more money in one year than I've made in a lifetime. And today, they wish they had what I had. They wish they had retirement, but they're still hitting the pavement because money is like water. It will seek its own level. The more you make, the more you spend.

I never charged big fees, and I never sued anybody over my fees. It was more of a ministry to me. I felt like I was helping some people out. That's why in my practice of law I never really practiced law; I couldn't make the money. So, therefore, I worked for the state and the city.

Fees today are probably ten times more than when I practiced in the 1960s and when I practiced in the 1970s, compared to what they are today. Court fees and court fines are astronomical, as are what the lawyers charge. In my opinion, I don't think the lawyer is worth that much. Of course, I don't think plumbers and brick layers are worth what they get either. Everything has gone up. I think a coke still needs to be a nickel! So, I live in the past.

Don Dino, Memphis, January 7, 2004

3. "Significant Changes in the Legal System"

There have been different changes in different areas across the years.

However, the most visible change is the increased acceptance of minorities and females in the legal system. But on an individual basis, over the last fifty years the biggest change is that we've become more and more paper pushers than we are litigators. My career has been what I have to wade through to get ready to go to court.

I love going to court! Trying cases is my favorite thing to do. Trying a case calls upon more of me and is more satisfying to me than any other event in which I participate. I had to go through law school to get to try cases, then after I got out I have to wade through more and more and more and more paperwork. It's to my clients' advantages for us to settle cases, but the discovery we have to wade through, the motions we have to wade through, the documents we have to wade through consumes us. I'm a trial-oriented lawyer; I don't think I spend over 20 percent of my time in trial. The rest of my time is spent getting paperwork done, going through depositions, briefs, discovery memorandums, mandatory filing, all those kinds of things. But given my preference, I'd rather spend most of my time in trial.

The opportunity for the trial lawyers to exercise their skill keeps getting smaller and smaller.

Larry Rice, Memphis, January 7, 2004

4. "Needed Changes in the Contemporary Legal System"

I have two things to suggest, but they are highly technical. One is that lawyers be required to exchange discovery in electronic form [digital] so that they don't have to type it over again.

The other thing I want to see is for the Judicial Selection Commission to have divorce lawyers on the commission. Half of all the civil litigation in state court is domestic relations. But like lawyers feel, everybody picks on them. Divorce lawyers are the redheaded stepchildren of the bar. They are left off of commissions, and people need to realize that half of the civil litigation, half of the citizens that deal with the civil cases in circuit chancery, are divorce cases, and we need to do a better job with that.

Other than that, I spend a lot of time learning how to adapt, fit in, and make the system work.

Another thing I'd like to see is what California adopted and Mississippi almost did, to get what is known as a strike. We've got twelve different judges hearing divorce cases here in Shelby County, and you're stuck with whomever you draw. In California, where they have a multiple jurisdiction, where you've got more than one judge, you can strike one judge, and you don't have to have a reason; you don't have to do anything. All you have to do is move your strike, which means that particular judge does not hear your case.

One of the things you get are personality issues, especially in divorce cases, because there is an emotional level to divorce with which a lot of judges are not comfortable, and they don't help having their personalities to intrude on the process. A lot of things about a divorce are personality based. In other words, who is a good custodian? You are going to be affected by which one of your parents took care of you. You're just going to bring that to it when you come. A guy who stays out and drinks all night is not going to be particularly sympathetic to a woman who appears in front of him and says, "I want a divorce because my husband stays out and drinks all night."

So I think that we ought to be allowed in a multijurisdictional jurisdiction, which means where there is more than one judge on the bench hearing that type of case, that you should be able to strike that judge. In California, you have to do it first thing out. You can't have the judge hear something and then strike him. But if you file it and your trial judge is A, you ought to be able to say, "Okay, strike Judge A and draw me another one." I think that would make everybody happy.

Larry Rice, Memphis, January 7, 2004

5. "GRANDFATHER JUDGES"

Some of Tennessee's general sessions judges are still not trained lawyers. They are grandfather judges. They were already in office when the Tennessee legislature passed the statute that judges now have to be formally trained. Trousdale and Clay counties in Middle Tennessee are so small that they can't get an attorney to even qualify as a judge because that will remove them from legal practice. There is still a legal provision that states that if no lawyer qualifies, the judge can be a nonlawyer candidate.

David G. Hayes and Alan Highers, Jackson, August 8, 2001

6. "CHANGES IN THE PROFESSION"

I think things today are a lot better for women lawyers. First of all,

there are a lot more. There aren't any limitations on their areas of practice at all. A pregnant lawyer is perfectly acceptable now. When I was
pregnant in law school, I wasn't permitted in to participate in moot
court, because the professor didn't think it would look good. When I
started in practice, I was scheduled to try cases in front of juries when I
was very visibly pregnant. The judges didn't like it and didn't think it
looked good. The jurors didn't mind; they were very kind. But I don't
think it even raises a ripple now.

I think that's because of television. They now accept pregnancy
as natural. Nowadays, it's just acceptable for women to do what they
want to do. We've also freed men, by the way, because they can now
be stewardesses on airplanes, or stewards, as they call them. We've
opened it both ways! I think that's true in the law. I think the supreme
court has done a great deal in Tennessee toward bringing women equality under the law, but I question why it has taken so long for us to get
there.

I sometimes get disappointed by the fact that sometimes it doesn't
seem we've made much progress. We're still talking about a lot of the
same things we were talking about.

The Chattanooga Bar Association just spent hours on whether or
not to adopt an ethical code. Why do we need an ethical code? We all
know what we should or shouldn't do.

Selma Cash Paty, Chattanooga, July 16, 2002,
provided by the Tennessee Bar Foundation, Nashville

7. "LAWYER IDEALISM"

I've been practicing law for fifty-one years, and I've had an opportunity
to observe closely how lawyers practiced back when I began practicing,
and how the law is practiced today. When I first came to the bar, there
were only 200 to 250 lawyers in Nashville, and everybody knew everybody. There were always a few scoundrels, but you trusted most everybody. You didn't have any real concerns about them, and you were
friendly enemies. We've got approximately 3,700 lawyers in Davidson
County now, and there's no way that you can know everybody. So today
you get a more formal approach to things. When I started practicing,
and for many years, most lawyers took whoever came in the door that
would pay. You didn't have the sort of specialization that you have now.

One of my criteria for measuring costs was how much a good

cigar cost. Back then, you could buy a good cigar for a quarter, and a good cigar now would probably cost you five dollars.

What a lawyer has to offer clients is judgment, not time. What a lawyer has got, and what a lawyer has to offer, is his or her judgment. You can't measure that on a time basis. . . . Legal education has not been sufficiently akin to the way life is lived. We have to have the ability to work together, and the ability to support one another, if we are going to succeed.

William Val Sanford, Nashville, December 6, 2000,
provided by the Tennessee Bar Foundation, Nashville

8. "LAWYERS AND JUDGES, THEN AND NOW"

In criminal cases, the district attorney is usually the prosecutor. You have a state attorney general who is the state's lawyer and does a lot of work in civil cases as well as criminal cases, constitutional issues, and all kinds of questions. However, each district has its own district attorney, and his responsibility is primarily in criminal court, that is, a prosecutor in the criminal court.

Judge David Hayes was district attorney. He is from a rural background. Sometimes in the city, you just don't know as many lawyers, and don't have occasion to be as closely identified with them, but in the rural counties, everybody knows everybody. All their stories are known and circulated among all the people.

It's a little hard for me to say what the legal profession is like now, as I've been a judge for twenty-two to twenty-three years, and I'm not out in the courtrooms and in the practice of law the way that lawyers are.

Sitting on the appellate court as judge, we don't hear any trials. The cases come to us after they have been tried, and all we actually get are written records of the trial, and a breach from the lawyers as to why they think it was right or wrong. We review the written record, research the law, and issue a written opinion in every case about what transpired in the trial court.

When I was circuit judge, I sat in the trial courts and heard the cases. We had the juries, and we heard the witnesses. But being on the appellate court, you miss all of that. We do hear oral arguments from the lawyers, but we have no witnesses. We don't hear any proof in the case; we just review the proof that has already been presented in the lower court.

Alan Highers, Jackson, August 8, 2001

9. "COUNTRY LAWYERS"

I've noticed changes in the legal profession even since I started practicing in 1987. I think attorneys today are less civil with one another. They are not as human as they need to be. I don't know how to explain that except they don't deal with one another on a human basis. When I started going to court, I would go over and they would have a lot of cases set on the same day, or have docket callings. All the attorneys from the area would be there, and we would all sit together and laugh and talk and enjoy one another's company. But now, attorneys, and perhaps the general population, are so short-tempered and businesslike.

We have too many attorneys now, more than we need, and it's almost as if they're creating work for themselves. There are three law firms in Bledsoe County, and all three of these law firms have a much more laid-back type of attitude and way of practicing law. And I notice the difference even when I visit the Hamilton County court system, or when one of their attorneys comes here.

When I was trying to decide whether or not to come back to this small county, or whether to practice law in one of the urban areas, my partner, David Swafford, said to me, "I'll tell you what the difference is. In a big city, you're going to be a little fish in a big pond. But if you come back to Pikeville, you're going to be a big fish in a little pond."

I, and others like me, are considered to be country lawyers.

Lynne Swafford, Pikeville, December 4, 2003

10. "PUBLIC ATTENDANCE IN THE COURTROOM"

Back in the 1960s, when I first became a lawyer, there were a lot of people that would come into the courtroom off the street. I was told that they had fans and air-conditioning in the courtroom, and if it were hot outside, people would come in to keep cool. Then in the wintertime, they would come in off the streets to keep warm. Also, a lot of people came in because they didn't have television; thus being in the courtroom was their entertainment. But to my knowledge, people don't do this anymore.

Don Dino, Memphis, January 7, 2004

11. "COURT SESSIONS THEN AND NOW"

I think a big difference in the change in law practice was brought about by television. TV kindly opened up things in rural areas, and I guess in the metropolitan areas also. Back in the 1970s, when you tried a criminal case, you always brought character witnesses with you. But character witnesses mean nothing now. Jurors don't look upon particular individuals. You could bring Mr. So-and-so into court, and if he said, "That's a good boy there," the jury went a long way with that. But primarily, they don't do that anymore, as most of them that are being tried have criminal records. Nowadays, the nature of good character means little to nothing in court.

David G. Hayes, Jackson, August 8, 2001

12. "Changes in the Court Systems"

When I was an insurance adjustor, you would settle a case three times as specialist. For instance, if a person had $300 medical insurance, no matter what he had as far as injuries, unless it was a tooth or something like that, you would give him three times that, which would be $900. One-third would go to the lawyer, a third would go to pay the medicals, and he would get a third for his pain and suffering.

It blows my mind that these lawyers are advertising on television, because you couldn't do that back when I practiced. And from what I have been told, the settlements are astronomical. When these lawyers appear on television, they have clients on there who say, "I got a million dollars; I got $800,000." But all I think is that about one-third of that has gone to the lawyer! I don't think lawyers should advertise on television or in telephone directories on big-page ads.

Don Dino, Memphis, January 7, 2004

13. "Jury Service, Actions, Attitudes"

One of the big things that's happened in our judicial system within the last ten years or so has been mediation, which is a form of resolving a case without going to a jury trial. The argument for mediation from the standpoint of trying to determine why it is a good idea, why someone would want to mediate rather than go to trial to have his or her case decided by a jury is because of the uncertainty of a jury.

In mediation, the client has control. Either you take it or you don't. Yet, there will be a mediator there going between the two sides trying to find that happy median ground. So, that has changed a lot.

With respect to juries themselves, on the criminal side for the most part juries have become more conservative without question, easier to convict, and more likely to convict, less likely to forgive. In the small rural areas where I practice, you can actually profile a jury on an individual basis. I can say that person there belongs to the Church of Christ. She had a daughter who was raped in 1973. You just know so very much about each person as to whether or not that person's mind-set, or philosophical musings, will fit what I'm trying to get.

I still believe that one of the most important phases in both criminal and civil cases is talking to the jury. We're not limited in Tennessee about talking to the jurors. I can talk to them about their feelings on certain things. That's unlike the federal system, because there the judge just about takes over the questioning of the jurors, and I as a lawyer don't get that freedom to engage that juror in badinage, or dialogue, to get a feel for that person. But civil juries are more conservative.

What is called "tort reform" is a present-day movement to limit what a jury can give an injured individual. I think that's awful. In my opinion, the insurance companies in our country are lobbying away the rights of the individual. For example, most people don't know that the McDonald case could have been settled for $25,000, but corporate America in its arrogance wouldn't pay a dime.

I think that the jury most of the time is not right. They are easily influenced one way or another. Jurors are human beings, generally a cross section of your community.

Raymond Fraley, Fayetteville, September 20, 2001

14. "Mediation as a Tool for Settlement"

I think that lawyers have lost the ability to sit down together and talk. With our clients, we all used to sit down together and would try to work it out. We didn't need mediation. What difference does it make if there is some person sitting there neutral? The neutral person is going to work it out? What happens is that neutral person wants it to work it out because that looks good for their record. They can go back to the court and report that they settled in mediation.

So the strong party won't budge. What that mediator does is pull the weak one over there, and they are giving in. That's where lawyers used to come in and say, "Wait a minute, you're not going to do that to my client. I'm here because they are weak. I'm going to protect them."

I think that's where the fault is in mediation. Where the parties are willing to work it out, they don't need a mediator. When they're not willing to work it out, a mediator is not going to help in family law matters. But I think it does help in personal injury law. I think a lot of personal injury cases have been settled in mediation that would never otherwise have been settled without going to court, or never settled period. They'd have been litigated had it not been for mediation.

Sometimes it's hard for a plaintiff's lawyer to say to a client, "Your case really isn't worth as much as you think it is." You're in a position of negating a client's injury, and that's not a good position. A mediator can say, "Hey, I don't think a jury is going to pay much attention to your complaint of pain and suffering." The client will accept that from a mediator. I think that's where it helps.

Selma Cash Paty, Chattanooga, July 16, 2002,
provided by the Tennessee Bar Foundation, Nashville

15. "THE JURY SYSTEM VERSUS MEDIATION"

I haven't tried a lawsuit in six months, but I've prepared a lot of them, and they all go into mediation; they get settled. And that is what I see changing in the legal system. My question is, is mediation worthwhile? I'm not to say, but I have my own private opinion. Mediation is good up to a point. I will not agree in my mind with any process that takes away the party's rights to a trial by jury if they want it. I think that should be preserved, and I believe strongly in the jury system. Has anybody found a better one? More often than not, the jurors are right. So while I endorse mediation up to a point, I still say that more of these cases should be tried.

I had a competitor lawyer call me the other day and ask me, "Lacy, do you have any general sessions court cases that I could have my boys try for you?"

I said, "Hey, are you kidding?"

He said, "No, I'm trying to illustrate a point. Our younger lawyers are not getting any trial training."

And they're not. That's why I suggested early on, if you go to law school, come out and get yourself a job as a prosecutor or as a defense lawyer. Get in front of that jury and learn, because you are not going to get it in normal practice. I think our system is becoming more and more sterile, and with sterility comes weakness in effectiveness, which follows to where the real system that we started out with is absorbed in the name of "everybody get along and everybody be peaceful, and let's don't have any of these problems; just work it all out." In my opinion, when you do that, you are taking away the bite of the law. And the law has to have some bite. If it doesn't have any bite, it can't protect you.

Martin Lacy West, Kingsport, August 10, 2001,
provided by the Tennessee Bar Foundation, Nashville

16. "Divorce Cases, Then and Now"

Up until a few months ago, it had gotten pretty even as to whether it was men or women who won in court. Typically, women get custody of children, small children especially. Most men aren't equipped to look after small children. Their way of life is not suitable to that, although I have known some men who got custody of children.

A few months ago they passed what they call a parenting plan in this state, because now if you have small children and you are getting a divorce, both parties have to attend a parenting class that's offered out here at Columbia State Community College. It's about a four-hour class. Then each party has to file what is called a temporary parenting plan. It takes care of child support; it takes care of who gets custody of the children; visitation, which is now called residential time. What that's done, it has really cut down on the number of contested divorce cases. We still try divorce cases, but that has really cut down on the number of custody cases. It hasn't cut down on the number of divorces, but it has cut down on the number of custody cases. Now then, lawyers say to them, "Look, this is what the judge is going to tell you what to do, so you might as well save yourself some time, money, and heartache, so go ahead and settle this thing."

But years ago, I'd say that Joe Ingram, who swore me in as a judge, if you represented an attractive woman in his court, you were going to win. It was just as simple as that. Women used to come into court, and they were the weaker of the two. They weren't equipped to make a living as easily as men do. They wanted to look pitiful and typically could. Nowadays, they got to fooling with themselves and now they make about as much money as men do, and they want to portray themselves as equally as equipped as men, and they are.

Jim T. Hamilton, Columbia, December 10, 2001

17. "DANGEROUS DOMESTIC RELATIONS"

For the most part, if anything is going to happen to you in court, if you'll notice that every time you read about lawyers and judges getting shot in a courtroom situation, it is over domestic relations. These guys that we fool with in criminal court, they understand the game. They get telephone calls, and that's just a way of life with them.

Domestic relations is where the rawest emotions emerge, and people get bent out of shape when you get to taking people's children away from them, or making them pay some woman they hate. These are divorce cases, child custody cases, and things of that nature. If it's going to happen, that's where it's going to happen.

Knock on wood, we've never had any really serious problems in court. But we will in this district. We don't have adequate security at all, and someday we will know it when things begin to happen.

Jim T. Hamilton, Columbia,
December 10, 2001

18. "CHILD ABUSE"

Child abuse is a thing that has come to the fore in modern times. Child sexual abuse and family incest take place in all levels of society from the bottom of society to the top, like the cocaine and drug addiction problem that has overwhelmed the American and world population today. Back then, abuse was swept under the rug and not talked about. Now, it is more open, and children are aware of it. So, if some family member sexually abuses or molests a child, the child is more apt to report it and do something about it.

For every case that is real and legitimate, it is tragic to say that many times in divorce and domestic situations involving children, especially small children, one of the spouses will make false charges, which they may believe to be true in their own mind. That's a very tragic thing. The counselors in child services in Tennessee are aware that many of these charges are false charges brought by angered and embittered spouses in domestic relations cases.

This went on back in earlier times, because human nature is human nature, but people didn't report it back then.

Nathan Harsh, Gallatin,
May 8, 2001

19. "LEGAL CHANGES NEEDED RELEVANT TO FAMILY MATTERS"

Probably the greatest change in the legal system has been the breakdown of a family home. I'm a great believer in that if you train a child in the way they grow up, when they are old they will not depart from it. The dysfunctional families of today disturb me, and certainly when I came in in 1961, and even up until the early sixties, we had a lot of family continuity in which the family was pretty well together. Then there was seemingly a breakdown. Back then, people knew where their children were; they did things with them, but for some reason or another so many young people today are at home, and maybe their parents are somewhere else.

I think there's been a breakdown in that there are a lot of single mothers, no father in the home, never has been. So I think this breakdown in the home has made a real difference in the families I saw thirty-seven years ago compared to today.

Thirty-seven years ago, most of the children came from low-income, or middle-income families. I'm getting children in the court now who are coming from families whose income is maybe in the $300,000 to $400,000, or maybe a $1 million range. They are doing everything from counterfeiting twenty- and ten-dollar bills, plus doing many other things. Within the past couple of weeks, I'm getting more pressure from some of these so-called affluent society parents who call me maybe even at home, some of them with high positions in state government and elsewhere, trying to get you to change your opinion, particularly about a driver's license.

So I think this breakdown of continuity in the home has probably been the most disturbing feature. Then, at the same time, we have gotten to the point where we have, instead of strengthening the laws, we have made them weaker and weaker. I believe in probation, but I think there was a time thirty-seven years ago that our juvenile institutions kept them long enough to teach them a trade. I have in my office in Johnson City two nice benches that were made when we had the youth center at Joelton, Tennessee. Back then, we taught them a trade, but now they try to go a lot of other ways. We had a girls' school at Tullahoma that taught the girls how to do things—be a dietitian or beautician. A year or so ago, a lady beautician in Nashville called me and thanked me for having sent her to Tullahoma many, many years ago.

In trying to improve the juvenile justice system, we recently had a state meeting here in Nashville. We tried to look at the laws and tried to give our opinions. . . . Just yesterday I had a case in which a boy had been away to a state institution, and stayed there two and a half months, then they sent him back to what they call a step-down. . . . What we are going to have to do is build more juvenile institutions. Our population is increasing, and it has not being foresighted. When you just think it is all going away, it doesn't go away. I'm not in favor of a lot of the techniques in the laws they do. . . . We are going to have to have tougher laws, or lower the age limit to age sixteen. A juvenile isn't considered an adult until age eighteen right now. We've got to teach them the consequences of their conduct. Let them know if they go out here and steal a car, they're going to have to pay the consequences.

Shirley B. Underwood, Johnson City, September 25, 1998,
provided by the Tennessee Bar Foundation, Nashville

20. "Commercial Ads on Television"

Quite frankly, what I think has degenerated the bar more than anything else, and hurt the public more than anything else, is lawyer advertising. You had several U.S. Supreme Court decisions that have destroyed the bar as an association. Lawyer advertising may be "commercial speech," but it has destroyed the bar as a profession. It has made it a business.

They talk about "educate the public." It does not educate the public. There's not a lawyer anywhere that takes an ad to educate the public. That lawyer wants to get the client in his door. It has stirred up litigation. Back when I was in law school, anybody who solicited was frowned upon. Now, you can solicit anyway you want to, except in person. Nowadays, solicitations make people go out and bring lawsuits that should not be brought in court, and litigation has gotten so expensive that insurance companies are not giving a hoot about whether or not something is right or wrong. What they are interested in is whether or not they can get out of it economically.

My advice to someone is not to go to anyone that advertises. They encourage litigation. But this area right through here is not as bad as they are in a lot of places. If you want to get turned off, go to Florida or New York and see their commercials.

F. Evans Harvill, Clarksville, July 3, 2001

21. "ADVERTISING TO HELP OTHERS"

In the urban areas, I can see where there may be a need for lawyer advertisements, but in this area [small towns] it is just not necessary. The local attorneys in these small towns don't put advertisements in the paper, and they don't do television. My advertising consists of buying ads in the local school annuals, or sponsoring baseball teams where they have a firm's name on their T-shirts. That's advertising for us, but we view it as helping other people.

We do have some Chattanooga attorneys who place ads in local Bledsoe County telephone books. I also see television ads for Chattanooga attorneys occasionally.

In a small town, a good reputation is the only advertisement you need. But sometimes a good reputation can cause you to lose business. An old high school friend once apologized to me for going to the other attorney in town by explaining that his "ex-business partner was such a lying, cheating lowlife that he needed an attorney who better understood that kind of behavior."

Lynne Swafford, Pikeville, December 4, 2003

22. "LAWYERS' TELEVISION COMMERCIALS"

I don't think they've added anything to the profession, or to the service that the public gets. There's only one office that advertises that I have a lot of respect for, but there's a lot of lawyers out there that advertise and whose sole qualification is they've got a business plan that includes an advertising budget.

Larry Rice, Memphis, January 7, 2004

23. "NO INTENTION TO ADVERTISE ON TV"

I'm an old-school lawyer, so I despise these lawyer commercials on television. I loathe them. I never have advertised on TV and never will.

Raymond Fraley, Fayetteville, September 20, 2001

24. "THINGS THAT SHOULDN'T TAKE PLACE"

I started practicing law in late 1949, and at that time all advertising and solicitation for business was contrary to legal ethics and prohibited. At that point in time I felt that was an appropriate restriction on lawyers and supported it. I thought that it was nonprofessional to advertise for business. That is not to say that lawyers shouldn't be sure that the public is protected; however, open solicitation of business was carrying it too far. For example, I had a lady client, hurt rather seriously in an automobile accident, lying in the hospital hardly knowing where she was when another lawyer came in and gave her a long speech about how he could get a large sum of money for her. He persisted to the point where it was really adversely affecting her health, and they asked him to leave the hospital.

I had represented the lady previously on various matters, and she called me and wanted to sue the lawyer, which I refused to do, but did represent her, as I had done on prior occasions, in a manner that she thought was very satisfactory. I had then, in my early practice as I do now, disagreed with a substantial portion of the lawyers who I think puff their wares a little too much.

For several years I was chair of the Board of Professional Responsibility of the Supreme Court of the State of Tennessee and was amazed at complaints that were filed dealing with advertising, et cetera. Later, lawyer advertising was determined to be "business free speech." Lawyers now have the privilege and constitutional right to overstate their capabilities in some instances when they are puffing their wares a little too much. My hesitancy to approve all that is going on in that field is still present. However, all lawyers should be allowed to do that which is legal, proper, and fair, but as far as I'm concerned it has been carried too far, and there are too few restrictions. There is no doubt that contingent fee arrangements are in the public interest and a good thing. The rights of people, generally and in many instances, would be totally unprotected if it were not for the contingent fee arrangement, and if there is advertising by lawyers, I see no prohibition against that reference. Class action cases are perfect examples of another good concept, and I know that the rights of thousands of people would be unprotected without class action suits.

Cecil D. Branstetter Sr., Nashville, November 16, 1999,
provided by the Tennessee Bar Foundation, Nashville

25. "Lack of Comradeship These Days"

We used to have a tightly knit bar. We knew everybody; we'd have an annual bar party; we enjoyed being together. But we don't know each other anymore. The tornado that hit here January 22, 1999, caused some of this. We had so many lawyers back then in the downtown area, with offices closely adjacent to each other. We were clustered, so to speak.

The tornado that came through just wiped out Lawyer's Row to a large extent and scattered lawyers all over town. And now we've got our property section, registrar's office, trustee's office, and tax assessor's office out from downtown about ten blocks. The courts are here downtown, so it's all scattered instead of being in one central place.

We don't see each other as much, thus don't have the contacts like we once did.

F. Evans Harvill, Clarksville, July 3, 2001

26. "Busy Times"

There used to be times when we could sit around and swap yarns and tell stories, but we don't have time anymore to do that. Everybody is so busy now, there's just no time to do it. We all complain about that.

James H. Bradberry, Dresden, June 7, 2001

27. "Comradeship among Lawyers, Time Permitting"

In this law firm, starting about eight thirty in the mornings, we often hold court in the lounge. There are about ten or twelve lawyers that get together to talk about the issues of the day, many of which are not law related. I enjoy that time, as it helps us to know one another and to share.

William Val Sanford, Nashville, December 6, 2000,
provided by the Tennessee Bar Foundation, Nashville

28. "Humorous Storytellers"

Our former criminal judge here, Judge Ernest Pelligrin, was a humorist. He sat around and told stories a lot. He's a retired judge. And Alf McFarland, who practiced law for many years in Lebanon and is now retired, is also a humorist.

Nathan Harsh, Gallatin, May 8, 2001

29. "Coffee Time Storytelling"

Lawyers and judges still sit around and tell stories to each other like they used to. There's some places where the judges, lawyers, and deputies will still have coffee during a recess, and it's a good thing. They enjoy it. It is less prevalent these days, however.

Don Dino, Memphis, January 7, 2004

30. "Courtrooms as Centers of Entertainment"

It takes a very unusual case to entertain people today. When I first started practicing law in 1961, people who were retired, or were the loafers in town, would come and sit on the benches in the courtrooms and listen to the cases being tried. But now rarely ever do we have that because they are more interested in things for senior citizens to do, or involved in civic centers, and those types of things.

In former days, the courtroom was their entertainment, but nowadays there are so many more options for their entertainment. And they used to sit around and whittle and still do here in 2001 in Lafayette, in front of the courthouse.

Nathan Harsh, Gallatin, May 8, 2001

31. "Lawyer Get-Togethers"

We lawyers used to take time to talk to one another. Back then, we didn't beat ourselves to death. There was Red's Bakery, a café down on Third Street here in Clarksville. We'd all have coffee every morning, and coffee every afternoon. While we were together like that, a large portion of the lawsuits got settled right there.

Lawyers don't talk with each other anymore. Back then, we all knew each other; we talked. In those days when somebody filed a lawsuit, we called each other, talked about it, and often got it settled. But today, sometimes you don't hear from your opposing counsel until you get the pleadings filed. And sometimes you don't know who your opposing counsel is going to be until you walk into the courtroom. I guess this is the way it is now because it is just a sign of the times. People are so busy now.

I had a young female lawyer right out of the University of Tennessee five or six years ago, who told me that when she was a freshman at the UT Law School, they had a smoker [get-together], and the dean told them, said, "All you people enjoy tonight because this is the last time that you're going to be friends. Starting in the morning, you are going to be competitors, because the top 10 percent are going to be the ones who get the good-paying jobs, and sometimes the differential between the top 10 percent and the top 20 percent is just a fraction of a point."

I've also been told that students have been told in law school that the rules of civil procedure are designed to help you take advantage of your opposing counsel. I feel that any teacher who teaches that should be defrocked.

F. Evans Harvill, Clarksville, July 3, 2001

32. "Storytelling in the Office"

I've got two associates, my son and Laura Rogers. We sit around and talk and tell stories whenever the occasion arises. For example, when we come back from court, you'll hear us hooting and hollering and telling the stories when we come back! We'll stop what we are doing and we'll talk because that's the great part of the reward for having it done. One of the great reasons for going through the epic struggles is to recount the epic to your friends when you're finished.

Here in Shelby County at least, we don't otherwise take the time to sit around and talk with other lawyers and judges. But if you go up into the country, there's a lot of storytelling in terms of lawyers and judges sitting around talking and telling stories. But in the large urban areas, there is more of a separation between lawyers and judges. In the smaller areas, they are closer together.

Larry Rice, Memphis, January 7, 2004

33. "Significance of the Past Twenty Years"

The real change in lawyer billing practices, social gatherings, and other matters relative to the legal profession began to take place in the late 1970s and early '80s. I was president of the Tennessee Bar Association in 1979–80. I made the statement then at the bar association convention that we were "the last of the cottage industries," and it has accelerated since then.

F. Evans Harvill, Clarksville, July 3, 2001

2

COURTROOM BLUNDERS

Lawyers and judges are highly skilled and seldom make mistakes in the courtroom. On occasion, however, these legal professionals do make mistakes, some of which are indeed serious, while others are somewhat humorous, at least to those present in the courtroom when the described event occurs. Often, it is the judge who blunders by asking the wrong question, or by simply misunderstanding the nature of the case. Other stories in the blunders category include lawyers, judges, and police officers who do the wrong thing both inside and outside the courtroom.

34. "JUDGE MISTAKENLY CALLS IT BIGAMY"

The first case I tried dealt with this underage girl who came to see me, and she was about six to seven months pregnant. She had kept herself bound up to the point that nobody knew about her pregnancy. This boy that had gotten her pregnant was not willing to help her at all, so we got a warrant out for violation of age consent.

A JP [justice of the peace], who was not legally trained but was our general sessions judge, was hearing the case. I was going through all the legal steps very meticulously as a young lawyer would to prove that he [the defendant] was the father of this child. She was about eight months pregnant then, and she was only sixteen or seventeen years old. The old judge could care less. He was just letting the case go on. Then, in the evidence that came out, this boy, the defendant, was married. And when he said that he was married, the old judge just raised up and said, "You are married?"

The fellow said, "Yes sir."

The judge said, "Son, then you are in serious trouble. You are guilty of bigamy [marrying one person while still legally married to another]. You need a lawyer." Then he said to me, "What do you think, Mr. Harvill?"

I responded, "Your Honor, I don't know whether he's guilty of bigamy or not, but I agree with the court that it's serious."

He stopped the proceedings right then and said to this fellow, "You've got to have representation, because if a married man got this girl pregnant, you are guilty of bigamy."

That happened right here in Clarksville, either in 1949 or '50. That's one of the very first cases I ever tried.

F. Evans Harvill, Clarksville, July 3, 2001

35. "Jewish Lad Mistakenly Released"

I don't know why, but I think of a story that occurred while I was in a legal office in NAAS [Naval Air Auxiliary Station], Meridian, Mississippi. We had a Jewish boy who was always in trouble, and he had come to us to ask permission if he could go to the synagogue on one of the holy days, and the executive officer thought that was appropriate and gave him permission. What the officer didn't know, and I didn't know, was that the place he usually went to the synagogue was someplace in New Jersey. So that's what he did, and we felt foolish because we had told him that he could go to his synagogue for the Passover, or whatever it was, not realizing that he was talking about a place a thousand miles away.

John Acuff, Cookeville, November 7, 2001

36. "Elderly Man Admits Fathering Teenager's Baby"

I had another case that was also somewhat humorous. It was a paternity case. The young woman who was the mother of the child was in her late teens, perhaps eighteen years old. The more I questioned her about the existence of her child's biological father, the more puzzled I became as to the age of this person. So, finally, I asked the question in a general way, not specifically relating the question to the young mother or to someone else there in the courtroom. I asked, "Just how old is the biological father?"

And a squeaky, crackling voice of an old man there in the court-room said, "I'll be eighty-one my next birthday." [Hearty laughter]

The court's decision was that the paternity was established, and this eighty-one-year-old man had to begin paying child support on this child.

James H. Bradberry, Dresden, June 7, 2001

37. "Law School Errs in Student's Examination"

When I was in law school, 1946–49, we were next to the last class to take the bar exam after two years instead of having to wait until we graduated. So my whole class took the bar in 1948, and a large percent of my classmates passed the examination. We had one boy who didn't pass the bar, but he was as smart as the rest of us. Well, he was pretty well down. We were trying to console him. We told him, said, "Look, Judge Albert Williams is one of the bar examiners, and he is a delight-ful person. Call him to see if you can get an appointment to find out what you messed up on."

To make a long story short, he called Judge Williams, then he went down and Judge Williams had his papers. At that time, students took the exam in four sections, and they graded each section separately. All total, you had to have three hundred points, which would have been an average of seventy-five for each section. When this boy got there, Judge Williams picked up his papers, looked at them, then said, "Well, on the first section, you did very well. You passed that." The second section, "Well, you did well on that." The third section was also okay. When Judge Williams looked at the fourth section, he said, "Well, young man, we just failed to add in one of your four sections. I'll rectify that right away. Congratulations, you just passed the bar."

They'd added three of the four, but there was no way he could have passed the examination unless he had had one hundred on all of the first three sections.

The boy came in where all of us were, and he was on cloud nine. If we hadn't sat there and talked him into going down there, he would have had to go through all that agony of taking the examination again.

F. Evans Harvill, Clarksville, July 3, 2001

38. "Convict Runs Judge off the Road"

When I was general sessions judge here in Livingston, I put this guy in jail. He was James Ford, a habitual drunk driver. Well, that very night, he ran me off the road on the way home. And that made me mad, so I pulled off to a pay phone and called the sheriff, James Eldridge. I was just livid while talking to him. I yelled, "I want to know what in the hell James Ford's doing out. He just ran me off the road, and I put him in jail this morning."

The sheriff said, "Well, I had to let him go home to get some toothpaste." [Laughter]

I said to him, "Well, if you are going to turn them loose as fast as I can put them in, I'll just turn loose on the front end all the cases you and your department make, rather than wait and let you do it!" [Laughter]

That James Ford literally did run me off the road, but not on purpose. He just had blurry eyes and everything else.

John M. Roberts, Livingston, August 27, 2002

3

Legal Humor

Humorous stories are the Viagra of the legal profession and of the American populace as a whole. The following accounts describe humorous events that took place in courtrooms and elsewhere, primarily in urban settings. Some humor, both inside and outside the courtroom, portrays speech impediments; whispering lawyers; sexy persons; naked persons; animals in court; incorrect words (sometimes humorous, sometimes naughty) spoken in court; intentional pranks performed by lawyers, judges, or clients; political motivation; and misunderstandings.

39. "The Weak Liver Story"

My feeling about humor is that we always get picked on because we're the last safe group for everybody to pick on. Nobody seems to feel any sympathy for us, and I think it really undermines the respect for law, for society feels almost that they have a duty to pick on us. But in terms of us having a sense of humor about ourselves, what I tell all my people is that we take our work seriously but that we don't take ourselves seriously, and that we have to laugh. If we don't laugh to deal with the stress, we're in trouble because none of us have a strong enough liver to drink the stress away.

Larry Rice, Memphis, January 7, 2004

40. "Judge Gets Tickled at Woman on the Stand"

One of my law partners was trying a divorce case, a mean, mean divorce case. The husband and wife were both prominent local people. My law partner was representing this husband, who had really caught the wife in a hotel room in Nashville with this other man. She was an attractive woman, but haughty as she could be.

She had been on the witness stand for a long time. The judge poured himself a glass of water, and the lady on the witness stand asked if she, too, might have a glass of water. He poured her a glass.

Well, I'm sitting there in the jury box watching everything as it took place. An hour or hour and a half go by, and she's still on the witness stand. My law partner is bored, but she is getting more haughty by the minute. After another ninety minutes or so, the judge went to pour himself another glass of water, and this woman just thrust that glass under his nose! Well, I got tickled. The judge had his water in his hand, and he saw me laughing, and he also got tickled. He got up, and the water was spewing out of his mouth. He ran off of the bench and called for court recess.

He'd also gotten tickled about that woman's attitude, so he jokingly said to me, "I'm going to hold you in contempt of court." I said, "Don't worry about me. You've just got to keep that woman's water glass full. That's what you've got to do."

William J. Peeler, Waverly, June 14, 2001

41. "LAWYER WITH SPEECH IMPEDIMENT SPEAKS TO JURORS"

There's a trial lawyer in Nashville who is a very fine man but had a speech impediment. He was representing a streetcar conductor who had fallen and injured himself pretty seriously by cutting his head. The streetcar company had a doctor who testified that the man's injury was in the back of his head, when in actuality it was in the front of his head [top of the forehead]. The lawyer with the speech impediment was making his closing argument to the jury, and he said, "Now, gantilemen of the jury, what about old Dr. ———? Ain't he a dandy! He tastified that this man wuz injured in the back of his head, when in fact he was injured in the front of his head. And the dafandents have tried to make you balieve that that doesn't mean anythang. I just want to ask you gantilemen of the jury something, How would you like for old Dr. ——— to operate on you for hemorrhoids?"

Obviously, he got a plaintiff's verdict.

William J. Peeler, Waverly, June 14, 2001

42. "UGLY NUDE DANCING WOMEN"

I was district attorney in Weakley and other counties. One time I got a call from the sheriff over there on Saturday afternoon, and he said, "Dave, boy, you've got to help me. We've got a real mess in Weakley County."

I said, "What's the problem, sheriff?"

He said, "There's a sign out at Sammie Bradberry's bait shop that says, 'Nude Dancing Tonight.' We've got to stop that. We can't have that in this county."

Sammie had added nude dancers from Paducah, Kentucky, to his business that also dealt with several other things, such as sandwiches, cold beer, and videos. He had this big flashing sign up that said, "Women Tonight, Nude Dancing."

I said, "Sheriff, I can't do anything about nude dancing. It's Saturday afternoon. I'll be over in Weakley County Monday morning, so I'll get with you then, and we'll talk about it, but you've got to go through the county commission. They've got to pass some ordinances to regulate particular businesses. I'll be glad to talk with you about it, but you need to talk with the county attorney to draw up some of those county violations."

He called me back about ten o'clock that night and said, "Dave, you know I called you about that nude dancing out at Sammie's Bait Shop. Listen, just forget coming over on Monday to talk with me about it. I went out there and saw them women, and they're the ugliest-looking women I've ever seen in my entire life. There weren't but two people there when I left, and they were getting ready to leave!" [Laughter]

David G. Hayes, Jackson, August 8, 2001

43. "HUMOR IN THE COURTROOM"

We had one member of our bar to give up his profession to become a minister. I refer to Mr. A. J. Hathcock. He was a man of kindly expression and was always in a good humor. . . . Brother Hathcock, upon becoming the least excited, would likely mix his words. He spoke, for instance, of our court as a "circus" court, and talked of the "circuit show." Very often, when appearing in a case, he made the court a show. I will never forget Mr. Hathcock's last appearance in a case as attorney. He represented the defendant in a replevin [recovery of property] case. Mr. J. C. Boals represented the plaintiff, a farmer from district No. 5, who had sold a tenant some plows and other farming implements on credit.

The tenant had executed a title retained note, but Brother Hathcock contended that the landlord-plaintiff had breached his contract and that the defendant had suffered unliquidated damages to the degree that would more than pay and satisfy the note. The case was ably argued before Judge Flippin charged Hathcock's client out of court, giving him no room on which to stand. . . .

At the conclusion of the court's charge, Judge Flippin looked over his glasses upon the counsel and asked, "Anything further, Brother Hathcock?" The judge's face bore a real beaming smile. Brother arose with great dignity and replied as follows: "If your honor please, I would just like to say that your honor's charges were not in harmony with my speech." He bowed and sat down, but his remark brought a hearty laugh from the court and a roar from all the attorneys present.

Written by Judge W. A. Owen, Covington,
and published in the Covington Leader,
September 24, 1931; provided by Russell B. Bailey,
Covington mayor and Tipton County historian

44. "It Wasn't a Pocketbook on the Street"

There is an unpaved street story that was told to me by a pastor here in Bristol, who lived on Sixth Street. The way the pastor told it, it seems that a cow would sometimes be walking across or down Sixth Street, going down to the river or something. Well, one day, a frisky little ladies' man was walking down Sixth Street with a lady, when he thought that she had dropped her pocketbook on the ground.

He hurried to lean over to pick it up for her, but it turned out not to be a pocketbook but a pile of manure left by a cow.

Craig H. Caldwell, Bristol, January 5, 2002

45. "Woman's Skirt Flips Too High When She Falls"

At one time, pedestrians crossed State Street here in Bristol on stepping-stones at intersections. Well, this would cause problems when the rainwater had got it all wet, and even more problems if mud had gotten onto these stepping-stones there in the middle of the street. They were slippery, and at one time or another, people would experience splashing in mudholes. The twin cities had rocks shoveled onto loose earth there on the street.

An incident occurred on a slippery stepping-stone, which caused considerable conversation. Once, a lady was using these stepping-stones to be careful in getting across the street. In order to be careful, she raised up the bottom of her skirt, and before anything else had happened, she slipped on a rock, fell down with her dainty skirt sliding across her hips. This was caused because the rocks were slick and she had raised her skirt. She slipped and fell in the mud.

A male Bristolian whose reputation was that of a man who had a sharp and ready wit could not help laughing. The lady saw him laughing at her there in the mud, and shouted out, "I can see you are no gentleman."

He laughed back and said, "I can see that you are not either!"

Craig H. Caldwell, Bristol, January 5, 2002

46. "CATTLE WERE KNOWN INTIMATELY"

We formerly had a First National Bank here in Clarksville, and a gentleman by the name of William Bailey was president. He was a very dignified, articulate gentleman, who was former president of the American Bankers Association. He looked a lot like the banker in the *Mary Poppins* movie that came out about thirty-five to forty years ago.

The First National owned the Southern Trust Company that had a whole bunch of farms with a lot of cattle—several thousand head of cattle. On one occasion, they were bringing in a load of cattle, and as the truck was crossing the railroad track, the Tennessee Central train hit the truck. So Southern Trust Company was suing Tennessee Central for damages to the cattle. Well, Mr. Bailey in all of his dignity was testifying concerning the value of those cows. And the defense counsel, who was a good personal friend of mine as well as a professional friend, was cross-examining Mr. Bailey, and he got Mr. Bailey to extol the virtues of Southern Trust Company—what a tremendous operation it was, and how many cows they had, and how they spread out. And he got all that in the court record, then he said, "Now, Mr. Bailey, with all these vast holdings of Southern Trust Company, you are not really familiar with the particular cattle that were injured in this accident, are you?"

Bailey said, "Young man, I'll have you know, I've been intimate with each and every one of those heifers!" [Laughter]

F. Evans Harvill, Clarksville, July 3, 2001

47. "LAWYER'S WHISPER HEARD IN COURT"

A local lawyer was getting divorced many years ago, and his lawyer was John Roberts, who was later U.S. attorney. At some point, they were haggling there at the table with the other side and all trying to beat it out. In a whisper a little louder than he intended, or maybe not, John said, "Dammit, I'll buy you a coffee pot; let's get on with it."

John Acuff, Cookeville, November 7, 2001

48. "IT'S HARD TO TAKE ADVANTAGE OF A TENNESSEE WIDOW"

There was a case in which we were trying to get the oil well back. My company was Lucky Strike Oil Company, and the defendant was Susie Smith, or whatever. She was a widow woman from up in Clay or Jackson County. Bob Johnson, who was on the other side, has been known to be a country lawyer at times.

We were in the Tennessee Supreme Court. Judge Joe Henry was presiding. I said to Bob Johnson, "So help me, if you say 'widow woman' one time, I'm going to kill you."

Well, Bob got through his argument; never mentioned a widow woman, so I thought that maybe we had a chance to win. And I walked up to the podium, and Joe Henry, who was the light of the bench at that time, both for his vocabulary, which he would use freely, and just for keeping it lighter than it would have otherwise been at times, looked out over his half-glasses at me and said, "Mr. Acuff, what is it exactly that we're trying to do to this old widow woman?"

John Acuff, Cookeville, November 7, 2001

49. "LAWYER KNEW THE CORRECT WORD TO USE"

This local lawyer, Hughie Ragan, had to write a brief to the Sixth Circuit that he was appointed to in a case that dealt with some sort of sex offense crime about an indecent exposure. Ragan put in the brief that there's no proof that the defendant exhibited his private part, or something. He handed the brief to a lawyer and said, "Just read this. I want to see what you think about it."

So the lawyer read it and said, "Well, Hughie, I'm not sure that the Sixth Circuit Court will really use this. It's not real clear on what you mean here by this 'private part' thing."

Hughie spoke up and said, "Oh, yeah, you're right, let me have that." So he marked through the words "private part" and wrote in there the word "goober." [Laughter]

That really happened!

David G. Hayes, Jackson, August 8, 2001

50. "STATE TROOPER WITH A S-L-O-W VOICE"

One of the funnier stories that I know is from my uncle, Homer Bradberry, who was also an attorney. He was cross-examining this high-way patrol officer. My uncle's client had been charged with DUI or something like that. The arrest had occurred during the night, and the officer had seen this man operating his vehicle at a considerable distance away.

My uncle asked the officer this question, "Trooper Hood, just how far can you see at night anyway?"

Trooper Hood had a very s-l-o-w, d-r-a-w-l-y voice, and he said, "W-e-l-l, I can see the m-o-o-n. How far is that?" [Laughter]

That really happened, and that story is usually told at any gathering of lawyers in this area.

James H. Bradberry, Dresden, June 7, 2001

51. "SHORT WITNESS"

We had a case over in Memphis one day. It was getting about time for adjournment, and the judge was kindly looking at the clock, thinking about trying to wind the trial up for that day. They had a few minutes left, so he asked the defense lawyer who was putting on his proof at that time, said, "Well, it's getting late here. It's almost time to adjourn for the day, so do you have a short witness you could put on?"

So the lawyer stood up and said, "Your Honor, I think I've got one that's about five foot two." [Hearty laughter]

That did happen!

David Hayes, Jackson, August 8, 2001

52. "THE BITTEN-OFF EAR"

This is an old story that I'm sure everybody has heard. This fellow was being prosecuted for biting another man's ear off. The defense counsel asked this witness, "Did you actually see the defendant bite his ear?"

The witness responded, "No sir, I did not."

Instead of letting well enough alone, the defense counsel asked, "Well, how do you know he did it?"

"Because I saw him spit it out." [Laughter]

F. Evans Harvill, Clarksville, July 3, 2001

53. "WEE BIT UNWILLING TO TELL THE TRUTH"

I was swearing a witness in in a certain case, and the witness was from Samburg, Tennessee, which is an unusual town.

I said, "Raise your right hand. Do you solemnly swear to tell the truth, the whole truth, and nothing but the truth, so help you God?"

He looked at me, and responded, "Only if it is absolutely necessary."

Well, I realized then that "the truth" is a statement—only if it is absolutely necessary. So I said to him, "Well, let's go forward. Let's go."

He just laughed at what had been said.

David G. Hayes, Jackson, August 8, 2001

54. "UNINTENDED FLIRTATIOUS WORDS"

Billy Daniels, this lawyer I worked with for years, was like a big brother. He was very proper and very appropriate in all regards, a true southern gentleman. He was representing a widow in an estate case. She was a large, good-looking blonde, and she was in the office one day talking to Billy. It was a spitty, snowy bad day, and she had a cold. And she said, "Well, Billy, I think I'm going home and get a fifth of whiskey and go to bed."

Billy said, "I sure would like to go with you." [Laughter] Then he realized what he said, and he just started to blush, blush, blush.

Then she said, "Come ahead!" And that made it even worse for him.

F. Evans Harvill, Clarksville, July 3, 2001

55. "KILLING WOULD HAVE BEEN JUSTIFIED"

In a case I had in Lake County back in the midseventies I was representing some man for shooting at another man. It was an assault case.

He shot at the other man but didn't hit him. The judge gave him something like a thirty-days' sentence in jail, and that was more than you'd get even if you'd hit them when you shot.

I said, "Judge, it was an assault. He didn't even hit this other fellow when he shot at him. Yet, you've given my client thirty days in jail."

The judge said, "Dave, I'm not giving him thirty days for assault. I'm giving him thirty days because he missed him. I'd gone lighter if he'd hit him." [Laughter]

David G. Hayes, Jackson, August 8, 2001

56. "It Wasn't Like Beer"

I had an old friend who lived in Celina, and his name was James Reneau Sr. He had a drinking problem, and during Prohibition he drank a lot of rotgut moonshine. Some of his friends thought that was detrimental to his health, and they were trying to wean him off the heavy stuff.

About that same time, there was developed by some company a beverage called near beer. It was nonalcoholic, but it had the taste of beer. Tasted just like beer, and they sold it in drugstores. So one day Mr. Jim went into the drugstore there in Celina, and the druggist said, "I want you to try this new drink, Mr. Jim. It's nonalcoholic and tastes just like beer." So Mr. Jim uncapped a bottle and drank it down in one gulp and held it up and said, "Whoever named this *near* beer is a damn poor judge of distance."

James W. Chamberlain, Lafayette, November 5, 2003

57. "Feeding Cattle More Important Than Jury Duty"

This story is about a courtroom incident. When I first started practicing law, we had a judge, Paul Swafford, who was in his last years as a judge at that point in time. I think he retired in early 1990. He was a kind of gruff old character. He had a beautiful head of white hair, and enormous white eyebrows! He was a real character, and he could be extremely short-tempered. I don't know if that was in his later years, or if that was just an experience that I had with him. But he had this wonderful dry humor. He would say something funny but never crack a smile, just be hilarious.

Once when we were picking a jury for a case, I wasn't involved in this case, but I happened to be sitting in the courtroom. It was going to be a criminal trial, so the jury was going to be sequestered, possibly for more than one day. So Judge Swafford was explaining to the jury panel that they were going to be sequestered, which meant that they might not get to go home that night, that they might have to stay in a hotel and come back the next day. So, he had asked if there was anyone on the jury panel for whom that would cause an extreme hardship. Two or three different people raised their hands to tell why they just really had to go home that night.

The judge was patient through the first three of four people who raised their hands, but then he was beginning to get irritated because his jury panel was going down too low. It was making him cranky because he was excusing too many people.

Well, this one old farmer that was there in court in his overalls raised his hand and told the judge, "I'm a farmer and I've got about sixty head of cattle." This was in the wintertime, and he went on to say, "I've got to feed my cattle this afternoon. There's not anybody else that can do it."

By that time, Judge Swafford was irritated. He said, "You don't have to go home tonight. You can go one time without feeding those cows." He said, "Don't you think you can do this and come back here tomorrow? Your cattle are going to be fine. You can go feed them tomorrow afternoon."

The farmer said, "Well, judge, I don't know. How would *you* like to miss supper and breakfast?" [Hearty laughter]

Then, Judge Swafford in his tough manner, "Oh, okay you can go."

Lynne Swafford, Pikeville, December 4, 2003

58. "Jam on Boy's Face"

I was trying a case one time, and I had circumstantial evidence in the case. So in my circumstantial evidence to the jury, I was trying to explain to them what that kind of evidence was. I said, "For instance, if a little boy walks into the kitchen, and if there is a jelly jar or a jam jar setting on the table, as he gets ready to get into it his mother tells him, "Johnny, do not get into the jam."

She leaves and comes back in about five minutes, and he has jam all over his mouth and all over his hands. She asks him, "Johnny, did you get into the jam?"

He says, "No."

She didn't actually see him, but the evidence is circumstantial as it shows he went into the jam and had it all over his hands. So that was my way of explaining circumstantial evidence to the jury. The lawyer that was representing the defendant had his ten- or twelve-year-old son that had come up with him for the final argument. That boy was sitting in the courtroom. And so when we got through with the case, as they were walking down the street, the lawyer turned to his son and said, "Well, it's time to eat. What do you want?"

The son said, "Well, Daddy, I'd like some peanut butter and jelly. That guy was talking about jelly in the courtroom, and it made me hungry."

I threw that explanation out, and at least the kid was listening to me, but he was really looking at it from a totally different standpoint.

Don Dino, Memphis, January 7, 2004

59. "ALL VISITORS IN THE COURTROOM STOOD UP"

One time I went into the courtroom that had about 150 people there. Before the judge got on the bench, I had a witness named Paul Stang. I wanted to find out if he was in the courtroom, so I walked in through the side door up to the front where everybody is looking at me. I spoke up and asked, "Is Paul Stang in the courtroom?"

When I asked that, everybody there in the courtroom stood up because they thought I said, "All stand in the courtroom." Well, I was looking at all these people standing up, and I didn't know what to do, so I looked over at the door I came in through, where the judge usually comes out. I said, "Well, he's not ready yet. You all have a seat, and when he comes out, I'll tell you." I didn't know what else to do.

Anyway, I went in and told the deputy what happened, because I was laughing up a storm. So, he goes out, and he calls for Paul Stang, and everybody stood up again! [Laughter]

Don Dino, Memphis, January 7, 2004

60. "WITNESS REFUSES TO IDENTIFY DEFENDANT"

One time when I was trying two defendants, I asked one of the witnesses to identify two people in the courtroom who had committed this offense, probably an armed robbery. He looked around the courtroom and then said, "I can identify this one fellow right there," and he pointed to one of the defendants. I asked him, "Well, what about the other fellow next to him, can you identify him?"

He said, "No, I cannot identify him. But I can identify this one."

At that time, the defendant that was not identified said so loud at his codefendant and everybody in the courtroom, "Anthony, you are in serious trouble."

I'll always remember that case.

Don Dino, Memphis, January 7, 2004

61. "RUN OVER BY STATUE OF LIBERTY"

I had a fellow whom I was asking about his past record when I was practicing law, and I was asking him if he had any prior offenses. He said, "Well, I've had some in the past, but they were so long ago that the Statue of Liberty has run on those offenses."

Of course, he was thinking of the statute of limitations, but he said, "The Statue of Liberty has run on those!"

Don Dino, Memphis, January 7, 2004

62. "GOD LOVES A NEWSMAN"

A newspaper man named Clay Bailey used to cover the courts. He was sitting there one day in the courtroom at the counsel table, and he just looked kinda bad, kinda down. I walked over to him and said, "Clay, are you all right?"

He said, "I've just got problems, you know."

So I walked away, and as I would be in the courtroom, I'd look over at him and could see that he wasn't all right. So I walked over to him and leaned down and said, "Clay, I want you to smile, because God loves you and I want you to think of that."

Well, he smiled. I turned around and walked out of the court-room. When I came back into the courtroom, he was sitting there, and he had a smile on his face. It had kinda perked him up. I walked over to him and said, "Clay, I'm glad you're smiling."

We had a lawyer named Walter Bailey, but this fellow's name was Clay Bailey. I said, "I see you smiling, but I meant to tell you when I walked out of the courtroom, God told me that he didn't mean you! It was Walter Bailey that he meant, and that he made a mistake!" Of course, I was just trying to perk him up with that.

That's probably been twenty years ago. I see Clay Bailey every now and then, and when he sees me, he says, "God loves you."

Don Dino, Memphis, January 7, 2004

63. "Wrapped in Toilet Paper"

This is a little off the beam, but I want to tell it. I didn't always report timely to my clients. The Fireman's Fund was so glad to get a letter from me, they said. They wrote back immediately and said, "While your pen is still hot, send us a bill."

So I did, and it came back from Homer Ayers, who is a good friend of mine and is a lawyer now. His note said, "I can't get but about $2,500 out of this bill, I think you're a little bit too high. Resubmit it."

I wrote back and said that I wasn't too high, that I had spent a lot of potty time on his bill.

Well, back came the check wrapped in toilet paper!

Martin Lacy West, Kingsport, August 10, 2001,
provided by the Tennessee Bar Foundation, Nashville

64. "A Smart Judge"

I had to run for popular election as general sessions judge. Back then, when I married a couple, I felt like I should not receive a fee for marrying them. But I would not let them know that. The groom would ask, "How much do I owe you, judge?"

I would respond to his question something like, "I don't receive a fee. You just pay me whatever you think she is worth." That would put him on the spot. So when the groom gave me, say, five dollars, I would give it to his wife, saying, "This is your first wedding present."

And they would say, "Isn't he a fine fellow?"

One day we had a dressed-up man. He had a bow tie on; his wife was dressed in white, and they were just fine. I put my robe on and went through the long ceremony. When I got through, he said, "How much do I owe you, judge?"

I said, "Fifteen dollars."

"Fine."

He paid me, and I gave it to his wife. As I was walking out, taking my robe off, an old gentleman came up to me and said, "Judge Summers, you are a smart man."

I said, "Why do you think I'm so smart?"

He said, "You're not doing anything but buying these folks' vote with their own money." [Laughter]

Well, I did have to run for popular election as judge.

Paul R. Summers, Somerville, July 9, 1999,
provided by the Tennessee Bar Foundation, Nashville

4

DIVORCE AND ADULTERY

"Diverse" is a key word for describing the contents of these typically unpleasant stories about divorce, even if humor, off-color words, or curse words are involved at unexpected times. Most divorce cases are settled by nonjury decisions. Critical matters include verbal and physical spouse abuse, disagreements involving bigamy, affairs with another single or married person, and total lack of child support or inadequate child support. In a more unusual vein, one story herein describes an argument between a husband and wife regarding ownership of a pet hen, and two accounts tell about couples seeking divorce after having been married for three weeks or less.

While various married couples eventually seek divorce for whatever reason, this lawyer story category is not a favorite one with these and other attorneys. A hesitancy to relate stories of this type may be due to the truly unpleasant matters that provoke divorce cases.

The final three stories in this chapter deal with adultery, another story category that is not widely shared among legal professionals. Of course, one reason for this is that adultery, or fornication, is no longer settled in court. Most area residents agree that a penalty should not be assigned to a married man or married woman not wed to each other who are caught in the act of sexual intercourse in a public area such as a city park or parking lot, restaurant parking lot, or even a hotel or motel. The three stories focus not so much on adultery but on different issues, such as divorce, that brought the clients into court procedures.

65. "Husband Offers His Wife to Her Lawyer"

One of the stories which I like to tell is probably about the worst divorce case in which I was ever involved. I represented the wife, and this man was really, really out of it. Nobody could control him, not even his own lawyer. We got ready to serve him, and he was running from the deputy, a great big fellow who served the hard ones. We got inside the house, and this man ran and went into the bathroom and locked the bathroom door, took off all his clothes, and got into the bathtub.

I told the deputy, "Since you are in the house, you've got the right on civil process to break down interior doors." So the deputy pushed the door open, and this man was sitting there in the bathtub just buck naked. Jim, the deputy, started reading the summons to him in the papers, and this fellow stuck his fingers in his ears. The deputy looked at me and said, "What do I do now?"

I said, "Just give him the papers."

So he handed him the papers by just dropping them there in the water and said, "Well, here they are." He said that was the only time he ever served a man in a bathtub, buck naked.

In that same case, when we finally got around to trying it, I was cross-examining the husband, and all of a sudden he stopped. He said, "Okay, I give up. You can have her."

I said, "I can do what, sir?"

He says, "You can have her. You told me when this case got started, you were going to do all you could do in your power to get my wife a divorce from me. I know why now. You want her for yourself. Well, YOU CAN HAVE HER!"

Then I turned to the chancellor, who was a wonderful jurist, and said, "Your Honor, I admit my client is a lovely lady, but Your Honor, I've got more than I can say grace over at home." [Laughter]

He proceeded to chastise this fellow quite heavily for pulling something like that.

That was a nonjury case, but a jury would have gotten a real kick out of it. Most all of our divorce cases back then were nonjury, and most of them still are nonjury. It is a rare case if they ask for a jury.

F. Evans Harvill, Clarksville,
July 3, 2001

66. "Distraught Man Tries to Kill Himself"

One day, my secretary called me in my old office here in Fayetteville and said, "There's a man here to see you. He seems somewhat distraught."

I said, "Go on and send him back to my office." I didn't know the man, but he started telling that his wife had left him and divorced him, and asked me if I could represent him. I couldn't understand it, but about that time he pulled a pistol out. I thought, "Oh, my lord, I'm trapped. I can't go anywhere. He's going to shoot me deader than a doornail." I was just frozen in time. About that time, he turned his head and shot himself in the stomach there in my office. My secretary heard the shot, and she peeped in and said, "What is it?" He was just sprawled on the floor.

I had just got my red convertible, and she said, "We've got to get him to the hospital."

I said, "Yeah, we've got to get him to the hospital. Where's his vehicle?"

She said, "He's driving a truck, but your car is closer."

I said, "I'm not going to let him bleed in my car." So we put him in a truck. As it turned out, the bullet didn't hit anything that would cause him any serious harm. He was kept in the hospital two to three days and then released. I learned later who he was and what he wanted. He just wanted somebody to talk to, and I guess to witness the shooting to let his wife know that he still loved her and was willing to kill himself for her. He was just one of these tragic characters in life.

Raymond Fraley, Fayetteville, September 20, 2001

67. "Divorced after Seventeen Days of Marriage"

The quickest legal thing with which I was ever connected dealt with this lady who came into my office and said, "I want a divorce."

I asked her how many years she had been married. She told me, "Seventeen days."

I said, "Wait a minute. You mean seventeen years, don't you?"

She said, "No, no, seventeen days." Then she said, "Oh, by the way, Ms. Cripps, I've got to get a divorce before December 25 because that's my next wedding day."

I said, "All righty." [Laughter]

We got her divorce based on irreconcilable differences. They were married seventeen days but just couldn't work things out. She had tried to make a go of it but just couldn't stick it out. I thought that was funny. I told the judge that this marriage had existed for seventeen days. Then he asked, "Is there any hope for reconciliation?"

Of course, she got the divorce because he hadn't filed or contested anything. They had nothing to divide, so it was a real simple case. I was shocked over the seventeen-day marriage.

She got married again on the twenty-second or twenty-third of December. We barely avoided bigamy!

Sarah Cripps, Smithville, May 8, 2001

68. "HIS ONLY WIFE"

We had a judge in Memphis who was truly a fine judge. He's deceased now. He was trying a divorce case one day, and the man was suing the wife for divorce. He didn't have very strong grounds. He was just talking about his wife nagging him. The judge, seeing that this man didn't have much in the way of strong grounds, very seriously looked over at him and said to him, "Sir, you said your wife nagged you. All wives do that, don't they?"

The man looked at the judge and uttered sincerely, "I don't know, Your Honor. This is the only wife I've ever had."

Well, that really embarrassed the judge! [Laughter]

Alan Highers, Jackson, August 8, 2001

69. "ELDERLY WOMAN DESCRIBES TWO PERSONS HAVING SEX"

I don't remember the full context of this case, but it was a divorce case here in Waverly. A dear old lady was a witness, and they had her on the witness stand. Supposedly, she had either seen a husband having sex with another woman, or the wife having sex with another man.

The lawyer that was examining her was trying to get her to tell just what she had seen. I can almost see her now, sitting there. She had on a long, print, calico-type dress and an apron. She just sort of kept resisting the questions. Finally, the judge said to her, "Well, just go ahead and describe what you saw."

The old lady thought for a minute, then said, "Well, he was dicking her." As soon as she said that, she reached down and took hold of her apron and slid it over her head. [Laughter]

William J. Peeler, Waverly, June 14, 2001

70. "Man Quickly Assigned to Jail"

I remember the case in which this man was cited for contempt of court for not paying child support. We were taking it up right after lunch. He was there without counsel [a lawyer]. The judge came in and hadn't even got seated, and was telling the sheriff to reconvene court. This man jumped up and said, "I'll tell you one thing, judge. If you've got one of them cells down there, you might as well dust it off, 'cause I ain't going to pay her a dime."

The judge's eyes got as big as his glasses, and he said, "Take him, take him, Mr. Bailiff, take him. Lock him up. Lock him up right now. Get him out of my sight. I'll give you the mittimus [jail admission] papers later."

The defendant called right after he heard the steel door shut and agreed to all back child support.

F. Evans Harvill, Clarksville, July 3, 2001

71. "Elderly Couple Involved in a Divorce Case"

There was an elderly lady who lived on the lake right over near Paris, Tennessee. She came here one day to hire me in a divorce case. Her husband was suing her for a divorce. It was the second or third marriage for each of them. Her husband was in a nursing home. He wanted the divorce, but she didn't.

I went over there to Paris to see her. I asked her why she wanted to hire me. I said, "There are many, many fine lawyers in Paris. I'll have to charge you a lot more money than they do because of the fact that I've got to come over here and talk to witnesses. I've got to go try the case, and a lot of travel is involved."

"Well, I want you," she told me.

I don't know how she got my name, but I finally spent a great deal of time with her, and she would pay me. I went over to her neighbors. They all had a nice home there on the lake. They knew she'd been a very fine wife.

Well, I went to try the case. And I would ask her, "Why are you objecting so much to this divorce?"

And she would say, in this type of voice, "I l-o-o-v-e him."

She was about seventy years old, and he was about eighty-five.

Well, the chancellor's courtroom was a very small room, and the bench from the counselor's table was about eight feet away. So the old man's two children by a previous marriage rolled him into the court-room in a wheelchair. He was white as a ghost. He got on the witness stand and testified. He said that he didn't really have any grounds for divorce either, but the main thing was that she had eight or nine thousand dollars of his money in the bank, and he wanted it back. He said something to the effect that she cursed him a lot, and when he said that, she said, "Well, I'll be goddamn!"

Well, obviously the judge could hear what she said. But, anyway, the judge said, "All right, Mrs. ———, calm down. Now Mr. Peeler, I want to hear what your client has to say."

He then put her on the witness stand, and I asked her a few questions as to why she objected to this divorce. "Well, I love him."

Then I said, "Now, Mrs. ———, you've heard your husband testify that you cursed him. Is that true?"

"I don't curse," she said.

Well, just two minutes before she said that, the judge heard her use some curse words. So, anyway, when she testified, the judge said to her, "Well, I don't know what I'm going to do about this case. But if I don't grant this divorce, and I don't think I will, you are going to have to pay for his nursing home bills."

So then we go outside, and I asked her, "Do you know what he is saying?"

She said, "Well, I don't know."

I said, "What he is saying is that his children are not going to have to pay for his nursing home bills. *You* are going to have to pay his nursing home bills as long as he lives."

She said, "Pay it out of my money?"

I said, "Yes, you are."

Then she said, "Then let's divorce the old son of a bitch."

We went back in and said to the judge, "You explained it perfectly. Just go ahead and grant the divorce."

A lot of funny things happen in the courtroom.

William J. Peeler, Waverly, June 14, 2001

72. "Elderly Couple Argue over Ownership of a Hen"

In the late 1960s we had a divorce case between two elderly people, and they had no property at all. They were in their late seventies. The lady's grounds for divorce was that the husband was too demanding for sexual attention, and she just couldn't tolerate it anymore. So she wanted a divorce.

They got a divorce, and the only property they had to divide was a setting hen. She wanted the setting hen, and he also wanted the setting hen. They were renters on a back street here in Gallatin, but the big dispute was which one was going to get the big setting hen. They were both on welfare, and that hen was the only property they had.

The court gave the hen to the lady. When these matters come about, you are amazed about the human conditions.

Nathan Harsh, Gallatin, May 8, 2001

73. "Married for Three Weeks"

I had this case once in which this lady took her deadbeat fiancé, as she called him, over to get married at the courthouse under the canopy over there. Come to find out, she couldn't marry him because he wasn't divorced. And she came back into my office holding him by the nape of the neck and said, "Get him divorced."

I said, "William, are you not divorced?"

He said, "No, I don't guess so, but I filed."

I called the courthouse, and sure enough he had filed but hadn't followed through with it. I asked him, "Where's your wife?"

"Well, I don't know. The last time I saw her, she was drunk over in Taft, here in Lincoln County."

I said, "Well, that's not too far from here. Where does her mother live?"

He gave me a number, and I called her mother and got her on the phone. She said, "Oh, yeah, she's down at some roadhouse."

Well, we sent a car out there, found her, and brought her here and got her in the court that was in session. We got a divorce, and then took the old gal that was sitting there in cowboy boots, cowboy hat, and a white wedding gown with a little bouquet of flowers and went across the street, and they got married.

He got a divorce and got married the same day. In about six weeks she came in and she said, like the country folks say, "I want to be shut of him."

So she got shut of the new husband. Their marriage didn't last but three weeks. I tried to explain to her, "Mary Lee, he's just a derelict."

"No, he's the love of my life." And he was, for three weeks!

Raymond Fraley, Fayetteville, September 20, 2001

74. "LAWYER AND HIS OPPOSITION BECOME FRIENDS"

I had a bizarre divorce case twenty-three years ago in which there were allegations of bestiality and attempted murder and just all kinds of things. I subpoenaed a fellow, and he told the deputy sheriff what he, the deputy, could do with this subpoena [ugly words]. So I pulled out a writ of attachment and had his body attached and held in the common jail until it was time for him to testify.

Well, I thought after that the guy would hate me as long as he lived. It turned out the first time he needed a lawyer after that, he came to see me. Since then, we have become friends.

John Acuff, Cookeville, November 7, 2001

75. "WOMAN GOES BERSERK IN COURTROOM"

I've had some confrontations in the courtroom, one in particular where this woman went berserk one day, turned over the counsel table, cussed me out. This was in a divorce case in which this woman was just a blithering idiot. She just went crazy in the courtroom. We finally got her calmed down and all went to lunch, and I came back after lunch. Well, she was sitting in my office reading a Bible. When I walked in and before I could say a word, buddy, she was right up in my face giving me all kinds of verbal cussing. My bailiff came running in there, and he was an elderly guy, and she grabbed him, broke one of his fingers. Finally, the sheriff and a deputy had to come in there and literally bodily carry her out of the courthouse.

Jim T. Hamilton, Columbia, December 10, 2001

76. "WEIRD SEX CASE"

Many years ago I tried a divorce case in Cookeville. A man who was fairly wealthy had been divorced for a while, and he fell in lust with a doctor's assistant. There were also allegations of their beastliness and all kinds of things. The lady happened to be the mistress of both the doctor and the doctor's wife. The chancellor simply would not accept that this kind of thing went on in our world.

Several years passed, and the doctor and his wife were living in Nashville. There were allegations of their beastliness and all kinds of things. His wife had sued him for divorce, and he and his son were taking target practice in the basement. They were planning to put a rare poison on the bullet and shoot the wife's lawyer. Somebody from the *Nashville Tennessean* called me and said, "I understand you had some involvement with him years ago," so I basically told him that story, plus a couple of others. I told him, "He at one point was heard to say that she was guilty of alcoholism, Romanism, and lesbianism."

They ran this in the paper, and somebody high up at the paper went ape over that kind of quote and called the paper's general counsel, which was Bob Walker in Nashville, and Bob said, "Oh, my God! Who said that?"

When he was told that I did, Bob said, "John Acuff, but don't worry about it."

John Acuff, Cookeville, November 7, 2001

77. "Husband Unwilling to Tell the Truth"

Several years ago I was representing a gentleman in a divorce case. He was probably in his mid- to late forties and had a teenage daughter and a son who was an adult. He'd been married to the same woman for twenty-some years, and they were going through divorce. When he first came to see me, he was just really despondent about the situation. His wife had had an affair, and he still loved his wife and wanted things to work out. We went through this for two to three months over a period of time. I'd make suggestions about marriage counseling, and he tried different things to put their marriage back together, but eventually he realized it wasn't going to happen.

He worked in the construction business and had a fairly good income, and their family had had a fairly nice home and were financially stable until the divorce. But a divorce leaves very few people financially stable once it's over with. There were a lot of expenses related to divorce, and normal type of expenses when you try to suddenly support two households on the same amount of income. You can't live as well, so this family was going into debt.

Their divorce case went on for a year and a half. Over time he started seeing someone else and got involved with a girlfriend, and he told me about that; told me about the situation. Well, we went down to take depositions one day, and that's where the other attorney gets to ask my client questions about the case in what we call "discovery." During this man's deposition, the other attorney was asking him questions about whether or not he had any sexual relations with anyone else before the separation. Of course, he hadn't, but then he told the other attorney about developing a relationship with a new girlfriend since the separation, and described what that situation was all about.

So then the other attorney began asking him, "Has there been anyone else?"

My client began to squirm in his seat and acted really strange, then he suddenly started crying, I mean just *sobbing* in the middle of his deposition, and asked if he could speak to me in private. So, we go into a private conference room, and I sit down with him and ask him, "What's wrong?"

He proceeded to tell me the story about how he was in a bar one night and he was approached by a woman who told him that she ran an escort service. He was in dire financial need, and she evidently made a financial offer to him. He explained to me that he was under the impression that he was to dress in nice clothing and take women out on dates to parties and social events where they didn't have dates. He explained how the woman had bought him clothing that was appropriate, and that he'd actually taken some ladies in Chattanooga—maybe older ladies—out to public events, and that it was very private. He was an escort but in situations where ladies felt like they wanted a date and didn't have one otherwise.

Then he starts to tell me about how that situation developed into something completely different, that he started being paid by women to have sex. He was so upset, and I felt so sorry for him because he suddenly realized that he was under oath in the deposition, so he either had to commit perjury, or he had to let these people know what he had done. And his main concern was his teenage daughter. He was so upset and concerned that she was going to find out what he had done. In talking with him, he told me, said, "I'm not going to tell it. I don't care what the consequences are; I realize it's a crime to commit perjury, but I am not going to tell the truth. I can't because of my daughter."

At that point as an attorney, I can't participate in allowing a client to lie under oath, but I know that's what he is going to do. So I had to go back in and basically tell the other attorney that we were not able to continue that day. I stopped the deposition and had to withdraw from representing him. He had to go out and get another attorney. I think he probably figured out when I did that, since I wouldn't let him lie under oath, that the next attorney didn't hear the full story.

Lynne Swafford, Pikeville, December 4, 2003

78. "Dividing Up the Goblets"

This story is the one I end all my lectures with. It sounds like one of those made-up stories, but I've had lawyers come up and tell me they knew the lawyers that were involved, and it is a true story. It took place back in the early 1960s.

This couple goes to get divorced. But back in those days you had to have grounds to get a divorce, and the judge denied it. He found the doctrine of recrimination applied. That is when both parties are guilty and neither party could get a divorce. So the only thing you could do if you couldn't prevail on grounds is you had to work everything out and get an uncontested divorce.

The parties divided up their property, their bank account, custody of their children, child support, alimony. They were down to dividing up personal property in the big house, and they were at last in the dining room, a big and wonderful room with a fireplace at one end.

It had been a long day, but given the case's history it had gone pretty well for the partners and their lawyers. Finally, the butler brought in a crystal tray with seven crystal goblets on it. The wife looked at them and said, "I need four. You can have three."

The husband looked over and said, "Why do you need four?"

The wife said, "So our two children and my mother can have dinner, and we can talk about how you have ruined this family."

The husband said, "No, I think you've got that wrong. I need four; you only need three. I need four so I can have my two children over for dinner, and my girlfriend, and they can see how a man and woman who love each other behave, not how some dried-up hag ran off the best thing that ever happened to her."

And they began to yell, to fuss, and they began to scream. Finally, one of the old lawyers sitting at the table looked over at those goblets, picked up one of them, threw it in the fireplace, and it shattered.

He said, "Now you can each have three, and you can bill me for one." And that settled the case.

Larry Rice, Memphis, January 7, 2004

79. "Too Much Child Support"

This is true, and I was there. This was back early in my law practice, and this woman was married to a biker.

This woman got on the stand back in the 1970s, and the judge was proceeding on with an uncontested divorce case. They had a marital dissolution agreement. It set out what everybody got, and she got basically everything they had. She got the kid, and $50 a month child support.

Even back in those preinflation days, $50 wasn't much. The judge looked over and he said, "Fifty dollars a month? That's not very much child support. Ma'am, would you like me to raise that to $100 per month?"

Probably the most insightful moment this woman ever had, she looked over at the judge and said, "No, I'd just as soon you not, because I'm not going to get it anyway, and it will only hurt half as bad not to get $50 a month as it would not to get $100 a month."

Larry Rice, Memphis, January 7, 2004

80. "OPPOSITION LAWYERS HAVE LUNCH WITH CLIENT"

John Turnbull, who is now circuit judge here, and I were practicing law together when he took a divorce case over in Jamestown. The client was having problems with her husband, and in the course of interviewing her, we found out that she and her "husband" were not really married. Nevertheless, we planned on suing him for divorce anyway, because they had some property and whatever. We did some research and found out they had lived in one or two common-law states, so we were ready to prove a common-law marriage. So the way it turned out, we had to prove that and get the divorce. So he hired the best lawyers in Jamestown, Neal and Cravens.

During the trial, this guy threatened Turnbull with physical violence. Turnbull is a much better lawyer than I am, but he said he would feel more comfortable if I'd sit with him during the trial to keep this guy from slipping up behind him. I said, "Well, I'll do the screaming and you can do the fighting!"

It ended up with us winning the case, but they appealed it. We then had to go to Nashville to argue the appeal. Hollis Neal and Bill Cravens both came to Nashville to represent their client, and quite out of the ordinary they brought their client with them. So this guy was sitting there in the court of appeals, and we were arguing the issue about a common-law marriage. When the court was over, Turnbull and I invited the other lawyers to go to lunch with us.

They said, "Well, we can't, since our client rode down here with us."

Then Turnbull said, "Well, bring the old so-and-so with you. I don't care. We'll take him to lunch, too."

So, we went to St. Clair's Restaurant at Hundred Oaks Shopping Center, a really nice place to go eat. We went, got seated, and were eating. Everybody there ordered a shrimp cocktail, and also ordered a steak, but their client didn't know what a shrimp cocktail was. Turnbull told him, "Well, you'll need one of them, too. You'll like it."

So he ordered one, and they served it with the horse radish and red sauce by the side in little containers. Of course, this guy didn't know how to eat the shrimp cocktail, and his lawyers wouldn't tell him how. They should have been disbarred for letting Turnbull do their client this way!

Well, Turnbull taught him how to peel the shrimp and had him dip it in the red sauce. Turnbull would say to him, "Well, get you a spoonful of this white stuff, too."

That guy put that in his mouth, and tears were in his eyes. Well, Turnbull made him eat every bite of it. This poor fellow sat there, and all the lawyers began giggling. I was sitting there thinking that he ought to whip Turnbull.

Just the other day, somebody asked him about that. I'd told them about it. He said, "Ah, John Roberts is a big mouth again!"

John M. Roberts, Livingston, August 27, 2002

81. "JUDGE DISMISSES DIVORCE CASE"

The first case that I vividly remember was when I had been introduced to the bar in Bristol. Chancellor Joe Worley, a very outstanding jurist in our area, was a prince—a prince of a person as much as he was a judge. He was so gracious when he gave a little talk after I was introduced.

I had a divorce case before him, and I was representing a young man that was in the military. He was suing his wife for divorce, claiming she had been unfaithful and so forth. So, Judge Worley, being the law scholar he really was, asked the young man if he had been true to his marriage vows and so forth.

He asked the judge, "What do you mean?"

Judge Worley said, "What I want to know is, you are charging her with running around on you, as we say in East Tennessee, and stepping out on you. Have you been true and faithful and have not gone out?"

He looked up at Judge Worley, and I can see the judge up there now with his glasses on, and the young man said, "Well, Your Honor, I figure if she can run around on me, I can run around on her."

The judge just cracked his gavel and said, "Case dismissed."

That made a real impression on me, because no lawyer likes to lose a case, and certainly not just being a young woman attorney, but he is one of the best friends I ever had, even in late years. He's now deceased.

Shirley B. Underwood, Johnson City, September 28, 1998,
provided by Tennessee Bar Foundation, Nashville

82. "IN NEED OF CHILD SUPPORT"

My first case involved a black man who had only one leg. He walked around on a crutch. I don't know how he came to my office, nor how he got there. It was a divorce case, and he was very outspoken. He and his wife had several children. He wanted me to file a petition to require the wife to help support the children, which I did.

I filed a petition requesting that the judge issue an order requiring her to help support the children, which I thought the statute permitted. The judge just practically laughed me out of court. He said, "There is no such thing as a woman being required to support the children. That's a husband's responsibility."

This black fellow would come back and see me from time to time, and we had pushed it as far as we could. The judge denied the request, and no order was ever entered requiring his wife to help support the children, although the father had only one leg and could not get a job.

Cecil D. Branstetter Sr., Nashville, November 16, 1999,
provided by the Tennessee Bar Foundation, Nashville

83. "WIFE LEARNS ABOUT ADULTERY IN COURT"

There was a lawyer here in Clarksville, who is now deceased. In uncontested divorce cases, he always had his litany that he went through. He was representing this wife, and he said, "So your husband stays out late at night?"

"Yes, he does," she responded.

"And your husband is not supporting you?"

"No, he is not."

"And your husband drinks a lot?"

"Yes, he does."

"And he is running around with other women?"

Surprised, the woman raised her voice and said, "Well, WHO IS SHE? I didn't know about that." [Laughter]

F. Evans Harvill, Clarksville, July 3, 2001

84. "SOLDIER CATCHES HIS WIFE IN BED WITH ANOTHER MAN"

This lawyer here in Waverly was representing this young man, who was a soldier in Vietnam. This story is about this soldier who got a furlough to come home to check on his wife, who was having an affair with another man. He got a compassionate furlough to come home to check on what was taking place. His wife viewed him as being fifteen thousand miles on the other side of the world. Well, he got home one night about sundown and walked in the front door. And the man that she was having an affair with was there in bed with her. Well, he obviously took flight out the back door, with this young soldier right after him. As I recall, a dog got after the fellow he was chasing and bit him. And then, as it was about dark, he ran into this clothesline and knocked himself down. This soldier just beat him every way he could.

There was an old abandoned cistern there—a well, covered with some rotten planks, and this man fell in the damn cistern, which wasn't very deep. He finally got out of the cistern and was running on around the house. He thought he was getting away, but he ran out right in front of a car. The car hit him.

Obviously, the young soldier got a divorce. There is much more to the story than that, but that is basically it.

William J. Peeler, Waverly, June 14, 2001

85. "BEST TWO WHORES"

A well-known Memphis lawyer was representing this man of somewhat dubious moral character. Not only had he committed adultery, he had committed adultery thoroughly and enthusiastically with members of the oldest profession. Both lawyers were trying to get the case to trial, but there was always something else already on trial.

Well, they had this definite "drop-dead you're going to go to trial this day" setting. When they showed up for it, another trial was under way. The judge called them back in chambers and talked to them, and the wife's attorney wanted to go to trial and had subpoenaed her husband's covey of prostitutes, and had them out in the hallway. The bailiff had told Judge McPherson about them.

So they are back there talking about how he wants to go to trial, and the judge is talking about how he's got a matter on trial but that he's going to get it finished this morning, and they are going to go to trial this afternoon. The question about how many witnesses everybody is going to have came up. The judge lights into the wife's lawyer about its not going to be a long, drawn-out trial. He said, "You just need to put on what you need to prove your case; I'm not going to listen to a bunch of who shot John, and I don't want those women out in the hall."

About that time, they started to leave chambers' conference room. The door was open, and the courtroom was full of people. The only thing people in the courtroom heard was the judge's final instruction, "Be back at two o'clock with your two best whores, and that's it."

Larry Rice, Memphis, January 7, 2004

5

HOMICIDES

Persons across the nation commit atrocious deeds for which they typically go to court, but the truly gross offense is homicide, or "killings," which is the term used by many locals in the Upper South. Regrettably, verbal accounts of these episodes are plentiful, but they are also insightful and interesting from beginning to end. The stories in this section describe spousal killings due to physical abuse; sexual misconduct; killings of persons, both male and female, guilty of sexual activity with another person's spouse; a son guilty of killing a parent; or gang killings, even by college and high school students, fueled by alcohol and/or drugs that were consumed or being sold. These stories typically indicate that judges do their very best to see to it that justice is done, whether the final verdict is "guilty," "not guilty," or "forgiven." In a few instances, killing was justifiable in the opinion of the judge and members of the local populace.

86. "HELPFUL DECISION"

There was an old supreme court justice from here in Tennessee back about the turn of the century [early 1900s]. He said, "The first question that you should decide in any homicide case is, should the deceased have went?"

William J. Peeler, Waverly, June 14, 2001

87. "NONGUILTY PERSON THOUGHT HE DID IT"

This is a true story I was involved in that had to do with a murder in

Red Boiling Springs, here in Macon County. A few years ago, in the early 1960s, there were two rival gangs nearby. One gang was from Celina, and the other gang was from Monroe County, [Kentucky]. There were eight to twelve single young men in each group. They worked five days a week, pretty hard, thus looked for a little R & R on Friday nights. They would customarily meet on Friday night in Red Boiling Springs at a place called the Wagon Wheel. There, they would drink beer, square-dance, and fight.

On this particular night, there was a murder—a boy had his throat cut. His jugular vein was cut, and on his way to the doctor, he died.

My client was a small, scrawny fellow from Tompkinsville by the name of Boyles. He was about five feet four inches and probably weighed no more than 120 pounds soaking wet. He worked for a pipeline, and what he did was scrape out deposits that would build up in gas lines, or liquid lines. He had a pocket knife that he used to do this that would not cut hot butter. It simply would not cut anything. He was a member of the Kentucky gang, and he went to this gathering at the Wagon Wheel and drank a beer or two. And he was the one that usually started the fight, and usually the first one to hit the ground because he was so small. Well, he sure enough started the fight that night and spent the rest of the night on the ground looking up at his assailant, because he was small.

A boy was cut, and he was cut within four inches of a complete loop around his neck. They took him to Dr. Tim Lee Carter in Tompkinsville, and he testified at the trial that this was almost a 360-degree cut, lacking only four inches. Of course, obviously the cutting could not have been done by this boy's knife. We figured and speculated that the only way it could have been cut was with a sharp hawk bill knife, a knife that has a peculiar shape to it and a hook on the end.

After this boy was killed, they arrested Boyles, and that was in the days before *Miranda*. Well, Boyles confessed to doing it, and thought even through the trial that he was the one who did it. There was no coercion, because he was fighting on the ground with his knife out with a boy whose name was Smith. It turned out that the Smith boy who was killed was not the same Smith boy with whom Boyles was fighting; it was his brother. Thus, Boyles was not even fighting with the same Smith boy who was killed. All of this came out in the trial, of course. The point that we had as defense council, and by the way, one of the defense lawyers was Jared Maddux, who later on, or maybe before, was lieutenant governor of Tennessee and a lawyer from Cookeville.

The point of the story is that this was a case in which we had to convince our client that he was not guilty. We observed from the physical facts that this boy could not have done the killing, but he had confessed to it and had thought he had done it. He was never convinced otherwise until the trial of the case was held, and he was found not guilty.

After the trial, the attorney general came to us and said that the state didn't think he was guilty either. They later determined who did it, and the culprit was later found by Jim Jernigan, who was a lawyer at Tompkinsville at the time, as a result of some federal investigation. Well, the twist was that we had a prosecution of a fellow who could have gone to prison by an attorney general who didn't think he was guilty, and didn't tell us that until after the case. But later on it was determined who did it, and the culprit was actually in the same group [gang] from Tompkinsville. He was cut by his own friend. Boyles didn't know it. The man who killed him probably didn't know it. There was a lot of testimony about the severity of it. But it was dark, and nobody knew who was fighting.

Of course, the victim didn't live long. They got him in a car and tried to get him to Tompkinsville. They put pressure on him to try to keep the blood from coming out, but by the time Dr. Carter saw him he was dead. So, there are two things strange about that case. Story number one is that we had to convince our client, Boyles, he was not guilty. And number two, the attorney general knew he was not guilty but put his freedom in jeopardy, and that was an unusual twist of the case. I didn't think the attorney general should have done that, but he did anyway. It's history.

There's a possibility that the Boyles boy is still living. It's been at least forty years since that took place, and that's the strangest murder story I can think of.

James W. Chamberlain, Lafayette, November 5, 2003

88. "Woman Killed Her Husband"

We had a criminal case tried here several years ago. I was talking to one of the fellows who was on the jury, and there was no question but that this woman had killed her husband. However, the jury turned her loose. The juror said, "Sure she killed him, but he was so mean he deserved killing. We just figured that we weren't going to punish her for doing it."

I don't do any criminal practice. The last criminal case I tried was actually before Earl Warren took the federal bench. I didn't like it; I didn't get into it; didn't want to try it.

F. Evans Harvill, Clarksville, July 3, 2001

89. "LEGAL CHATTER IN THE HALLWAY"

I was in federal district court, and John Maddux, now a circuit judge, was there. He was defending a criminal client in the United States District Court before the Honorable L. Clure Morton, who was a very tough judge. We had taken a break, and all the lawyers were gone out into the hallway, and the judge was out there smoking. We were all talking, and the judge said, "Mr. Maddux, I think you've got a real good chance of getting your client off."

John Maddux, who was young at that time, began to talk about when he first took the case how he thought it was a really, really bad case, as this guy he was defending was obviously guilty. But he said, "The more investigation I did, and the more work I put into it, the more I really became convinced that he didn't do it."

Judge Morton said, "Wait a minute, Mr. Maddux, I said I thought you had a chance of getting your client off. I didn't say he didn't do it."

John Acuff, Cookeville, November 7, 2001

90. "MURDER OF A WAITRESS"

The most famous, notorious murder case in Gallatin happened when I was in Vanderbilt Law School. I came up here and sat in on it and heard some of it. That was the time when a lady was a waitress in the Cordell Hull Hotel dining room. All the businesspeople would gather there for coffee in the mornings and eat lunch. She was a very beloved lady who was living in a small house on South Westland Street, writing an Easter card to a grandchild when she was murdered, bludgeoned to death. It was apparently a sex-related murder, and there was purely circumstantial evidence that this African American man had done this to her. He was convicted and sent to the penitentiary and served a long sentence. Many of the residents in the African American community here never thought he did it, but others thought he did.

Back then, there were many attacks on middle-aged to elderly white women in the vicinity of this lady's house, which had happened previous to this. Once this fellow was sentenced to the pen for killing Mrs. Gregory, all that ceased.

That happened back in the 1960s, and it produced a lot of local talk and a lot of local headlines in the newspapers.

Nathan Harsh, Gallatin, May 8, 2001

91. "STUDENT KILLED FELLOW STUDENT"

The most tragic case in my legal career was when I represented this young fellow in high school for killing another student. This young man was an honor student, a top graduate, going to Mississippi State on an academic scholarship. He worked a full-time job in a theater while he was in school. Well, in his senior year he met a girl and fell in love for the first time. And this girl was also involved with another young man, who was a good boy, an athlete here. Both boys were from good families.

This girl kinda played in between the two of them. The story goes that the senior year evolved into a real tragedy in that he began to lose interest in school. He began to not sleep. At one point the little girl said that she thought she was pregnant and went to get a pregnancy test, and said that she'd already had one of these with the other fellow.

It was just killing him. And on the days of the exams when school was to be over, within two days of graduation he had written a letter. Anyway, he went on home and got this gun and came back into the parking lot and shot this other boy to death. Shot him three or four times. That case was tried nationally on TV because it was one of those cases that was of national interest because it involved student shootings. Not a lot of those students were tried, but I tried mine because it was that my client suffered from diminished capacity to form the requisite intent to commit first-degree murder. We couldn't get a jury here because families and students were so interconnected. I had to go to Dickson County to get a jury. They brought the jury here to Fayetteville. We tried that case for a week. It was sad, and hard for me because I knew all persons involved. I knew the kid who was killed, and I knew all the families, but I had to do my job. Jacob Davis was my client, and I was convinced that Jacob did not have a reckless intent to commit first-degree murder. But everything went against him. He had a note that talked about pumping this fellow's blood, listening to a Smashing Pumpkins song. He had other telltale signs about getting the gun and, of course, the way he had shot him. He shot him by moving closer and closer in to him. The district attorney really played that up. He shot this other boy four or five times, then he just put the gun down and sat down. Never made an attempt to escape; never did anything other than that.

The first thing I had to overcome was the capital murder charge. Then the next thing was first-degree murder without the possibility of parole. In Tennessee we have to bifurcate those trials and try the first to seek guilt or innocence. They found him guilty of murder; then the jury had to come back and decide if there's to be another hearing to determine whether or not he should have the possibility of parole from the state penitentiary. So we won that, and he's got a possibility of parole. What that amounts to is that I'm going to have to find some humane governor at some point. I think I'll run my young son, Gus, for governor someday so we can get this sentence commuted. Presently, this young fellow is in the state penitentiary, but with a chance of parole.

Raymond Fraley, Fayetteville, September 20, 2001

92. "HUSBAND SHOOTS AND KILLS THE OTHER MAN"

When he was a lawyer, Judge Turnbull represented a man in Jamestown who found out that his wife had slept with another man. The client just walked in and shot the other man. That man didn't serve a single day of jail time. The jury acquitted him, as they viewed what he did as a case of temporary insanity, that he killed the other fellow in defense of personal property. Prior to that event, the husband had never had any violent behavior, had no violent predisposition. The guy is doing fine now. Has done nothing wrong since that happened.

Judge Turnbull was a good defense lawyer, and he's a good judge.

Sarah Cripps, Smithville, May 8, 2001

93. "HUSBAND KILLS WIFE'S LOVER"

Many years ago, when I was practicing criminal law here in Sumner County, I defended a man who killed his wife's lover. My client was a man who had some mental handicaps, and this other fellow had been openly going with his wife for some time and boasted of it. Well, the husband finally killed this other man. I represented him. We tried the case twice, and we had hung juries both times. The third time the case was to be tried, it just dissipated. The district attorney never prosecuted it the third time.

That was one of those situations in which some members of the jury felt that the deceased needed to be killed; therefore, it was a hung jury.

Nathan Harsh, Gallatin, May 8, 2001

94. "Young Man Tried for Burning Father"

Probably the most serious case I ever had in juvenile court was this young man that had set fire to the trailer in which his father lost his life. The attorney general had filed a transfer hearing on this young man, whom I remember as being about sixteen years old. So this young man had to come into court.

As to the background details, his father was sleeping in the trailer. The boy was in the trailer, too. He is the one that started the fire. I think he started it with some kerosene and some rags in the front of the trailer. He claimed in the transfer hearing that he was trying to start a fire to warm up the trailer, but the facts did not support his position.

That was his father's trailer. The two of them had had a lot of problems in times past. The father was sleeping. Anyway, when the flames really caught fire in a big way, the boy was up the street. He had left the trailer. Then he came back, so he claimed, to help his father. However, there was no corroborating witness that the father had received any assistance from his son, because the father woke up and came out of the trailer but was on fire when he came out. He was trying to beat out the flames. He was transported to the hospital down in Memphis but subsequently expired as a result of the burns.

It was likely the sheriff's office that brought the charges against the son. And it was the attorney general that prosecuted the case. The young man was transferred to the circuit court as an adult. He was tried there as an adult, but I really don't remember what the outcome was.

James H. Bradberry, Dresden, June 7, 2001

95. "Wife Kills Husband in the Courthouse"

We've had one killing here up on the third floor of the courthouse. This lady's husband was very abusive to her, and he had beaten her up pretty badly, and she had him arrested for assault. On the morning that

they were to go to the general sessions court, that's the small misdemeanor court, he came and burned her car in the driveway of her
house. I think they were already divorced. She told the policeman,
and a fireman came. Of course, the car was burned. She told the policeman that came out there with the fire trucks, said, "I'll kill him
before noon today."

Well, that was the morning that they had to appear up here in
general sessions court, up on the third floor. He was sitting on a bench
up there out in the lobby area, waiting for the court to open. She got
there about a quarter 'til nine, and she walked up to him and pulled this
pistol. He said something like, "My god, what's this?" Well, she shot at
him but missed him. And he ran and ran through a door that he thought
was an exit out of the building. But it was an air-conditioning room,
and he was trapped. He got down on his knees and begged her not to
kill him, but she shot him twice in the heart.

I was the prosecutor, and I drew that case. Well, I'm here to tell
you, if she'd killed him anywhere else except the third floor of the Maury
County courthouse, she would have walked out. He was that much of a
no-count person. He needed killing. I tried the case, and the jury gave
her ten years, and I know they had as hard a time doing that as I did
prosecuting her. She went to the penitentiary. She had two or three
children, and they were living with her mother. And when her mother
got cancer, they let her out of the pen early. She served maybe a couple
of years, if that long.

Jim T. Hamilton, Columbia, December 10, 2001

96. "Death of Migrant Hispanic"

I think the most horrendous murder here in Sumner County is probably one of the more recent murders, and that was the killing of the
Mexican man in Portland, Tennessee, who was working for this white
man on his farm by cutting tobacco. The tractor overturned, and it
made headlines and is still making headlines in the Nashville paper and
all over the world, for that matter. The tractor pinned him underneath
it. His Mexican friends went and got help and reported to the law. When
they came back, the tractor had been taken off the man, and he had
been dragged and drowned in a hog pond. The autopsy verified that he
was drowned in that hog pond.

It was a horrendous thing, so that farmer has been charged with
his death. It excited the indignation of the whole county here. People

took up money to send the body back home, et cetera. It's still a very ongoing thing. Some $40,000 has been raised here in the middle Tennessee area for the widow who doesn't even speak Spanish. She lives in the state of Chiapas in south Mexico and speaks an indigenous Indian language. Sumner County in modern times has been a very tolerant county, and by and large the majority of citizens here will not allow any form of extreme discrimination against any minority. That makes Gallatin and Sumner County a very pleasant place to live.

It went to court, and the farmer, who owned the tractor and dragged the Mexican and drowned him, was convicted of the death of the Hispanic fellow. I don't know what the exact sentence was. I think they worked out some sort of plea bargain arrangement where he pled guilty to some lesser crime and got a lesser amount of time in prison.

Nathan Harsh, Gallatin, May 8, 2001

97. "Lawyer's First Murder Trial"

During my private practice years, I did a lot of trial work. The first murder trial I ever had took place while I was in Selmer. I'd been practicing law for about a year when I got a call one day from Judge Walker, who was a circuit judge. He said, "Would you come over here to the courthouse? The grand jury is going to report, and they are going to indict Billy Wayne Tate for first-degree murder." Back then we didn't have many indictments except for stealing a hog, or burglary, or something, but this was a murder case. He had killed Fairlee Surratt; shot him in the left eye.

So I went over to the courthouse, and sure enough the grand jury indicted Bill Wayne Tate, and Judge Walker said, "I'm going to appoint Mr. Hamilton here to represent you, Mr. Tate." That was on Monday. He then turns over here to the district attorney, who was General Will Terry Abernathy, an old grizzled trial lawyer. Judge Walker said, "General, I'd like to get away from here Friday, so can we try this case Thursday?"

Well, I didn't know what to say. I was just standing there. General said, "Why, sure we can."

General Abernathy and my daddy had grown up together, and they were very close—fished together, hunted together, played golf together. He said, "I'll take Jim T. in and tell what kind of case I've got."

So come Thursday, we were picking a jury. And they weren't asking for the death penalty. I didn't know how to pick a jury. They didn't teach us that in law school—no real training about how to try a lawsuit, how to protect your client's rights. They teach some theories about criminal law, and they teach criminal law, but as far as basic things go, they don't teach it. Or they didn't when I was in law school.

Anyway, we had a jury seated by noon, and General Abernathy always put the mother of the deceased as his first witness on the witness stand. He'd ask her how many children she had, how many of them are still living and how many are dead, and which child is dead as a result of this case. Well, she had big crocodile tears in her eyes. "When did you last see Fairlee?" he asked her.

"At the hospital."

"Were he living, or were he dead?"

"He was dead."

"Thank you ma'am." Then he'd walk over there and say that you could cross-examine her.

Well, hell, you didn't want to cross-examine her. You'd want her off the witness stand and out of your life.

We tried that case and got it to the jury by about four thirty or five o'clock that afternoon. I didn't have but two witnesses. The jury stayed out about an hour or so and came back in and found my client guilty of murder in the second degree. So I'd dropped it a degree. They sentenced him to about fifteen years and took him on to the penitentiary that afternoon.

I went home that night and was sitting there at my house drinking a beer, wondering what had happened all day, and the phone rang. It was the general, who asked me, "Jim T., what are you doing?"

"Well, nothing. I'm just sitting here."

He said, "I'm down at your daddy's house, and we've run out of whiskey."

They didn't have whiskey in Selmer then. It was dry and still is. Now he was the district attorney, and he said, "Run by the bootlegger's down there and get us a pint of whiskey. When you get here, I'll tell you what you did wrong in that case today."

I went and got some moonshine and went down there. My mother was cooking fish, and there Daddy and General Abernathy sat at the kitchen table, and I set down with them. Well, for about an hour, I got a lecture on the proper way to try a murder trial.

See, that had been my first murder trial. Since then, I've probably tried one hundred murder cases as a prosecutor before I got on the bench as a judge.

Jim T. Hamilton, Columbia, December 10, 2001

98. "The Boundrant Brothers' Murders"

The worst murder case I ever tried dealt with the Boundrant guys, Pat and Pete. They were identical twins, weighed about 450 pounds each, and were from Pulaski, Tennessee. They killed a bunch of people—I say a bunch, for the DA's theory is that they probably killed eight or ten people, but they were only able to indict them on three or four. And I tried every one of them. They got a lot of publicity because of their size and because they are identical twins. They were drug dealers, and they killed this woman, and that was the first murder I tried them on. Her name was Gwinn Dugger, who disappeared one afternoon, never to be seen again.

These twins lived down in Giles County in an old antebellum home, located almost to the Alabama line. Pete and Pat and Pat's wife, Denise, all lived there, and they had a retarded child that has since died. They all lived in that old house, and they dealt drugs out there. This Dugger girl came up there one day to get some drugs, and they killed her. They beat her to death with an ax handle, then took her body and shot her. Then they dumped her body in a fifty-five-gallon drum.

Pete and Pat worked at the Pulaski Rubber Company. They had all these pieces of rubber scraps. They burned her body for about a day and a half till it was just nothing and then dumped it in the Elk River. That was in 1986.

Denise, the wife of Pat, came forward in 1990 and went to the DA's office and told the story of what really happened. She was granted immunity. There was some talk that she might have been involved in it, but she told the story, and it resulted in a trial in Giles County that lasted about two weeks. It was the type case that screamed for the death penalty, but they didn't get it. They don't give the death penalty in Giles County.

One thing about that case that I'll never forget is that one of the state's witnesses was a lady who danced in this club that was located right near the Boundrant house, maybe 150 yards from it. It was called the Booby Bungalow Club, and her stage name or dancing name was

Snoby. Her whole family had a streak of white hair that ran down the center of their head. The rest was dark hair.

Well, Snoby testified for the state and said that this Dugger girl came by the club that afternoon and was very depressed because the state had taken her children away from her because of her drug addiction. Snoby testified that the Dugger girl told her, said, "I'm going to get some drugs. I just can't stand it." Well, Snoby noticed that she had on a pair of black, high-top tennis shoes, and one had a diaper pin in it. She told Miss Snoby, "The reason why I wear those like that is that it reminds me of my baby."

Then the Dugger girl left, never to be seen again. Well, Denise testified that after they killed her in this room that had a carpet and a couch, there was a lot of blood. So they took the couch and the carpet and her clothing, including that tennis shoe that had the diaper pin in it. They took these things outside and put them in this pit and burned them. That was in 1986. Well, in 1990 when this case was tried, that farm where they lived had been sold to a doctor that bought it. And he had done a lot of grading and changed the topography of the land, et cetera. Well, Denise went out there and said, "Right here is where that pit was." So the state gets a backhoe, and they go out there and they dig. Well, she [Denise] said, "Guess what they found?"

They found a charred piece of black tennis shoe with a diaper pin in it! And when that TBI agent got on the witness stand and introduced that into evidence, you could just see the jury; I mean their ears even perked up. See, what that did was to add instant credibility to everything that Denise said. She stayed on the witness stand about two to three days and underwent intense cross-examination from the defense. But she stuck to her guns. That little piece of tennis shoe beat any damn thing I ever saw in my life. It was like something out of a movie!! That plastic diaper pin was still stuck in that shoe.

At that time, the most prison time I could give them was twenty-five years, and that's what I gave them.

Jim T. Hamilton, Columbia, December 10, 2001

99. "ANOTHER KILLING BY A BOUNDRANT"

Denise Boundrant told about another murder her husband and his brother committed that same year that they killed the Dugger girl. The man they killed was a guy named Gaines. Denise and her husband, Pat, had a child that had frequent seizures, so they kept a lot of phenobarbital there at the house to help with those seizures. Pat and Pete would drink that stuff.

This kid that was retarded was on SSI; got a check from the government for his disability. Well, that check didn't show up one month in the mailbox, and somebody told Pat Boundrant that this Gaines guy had stolen it and had bragged about stealing it and had used it to buy drugs. So later that day, at Gaines's house in Giles County, he confronted Gaines about that. And Gaines denied it. When he did that, Pat Boundrant beat him to death with a chair. And after he did, he called Pete, said, "We've got to get rid of Gaines; I've killed him. Come on over here and help me get rid of him." So they put him in the bathtub and cut him up and put him in a plastic bag, took him out behind the house, and burned him.

Well, Denise was telling this. She said she came over there later that day and noticed what she called a "gray heap" that was smoldering. She asked Pat, said, "What is that?"

He said, "That's what's left of Ronnie Gaines. If you ever say anything about this, that might be you out there."

In the house where they had killed Gaines, they had set it on fire. Of course, they put it out.

But Denise told that story, and they moved that case, since they were asking for the death penalty. They had a real good lawyer defending Pat, and he wanted to change the venue, so we moved it up here to Columbia to try it and thus to get it out of Giles County. So Pat got the death penalty. That's the only person I ever sentenced to death, but the supreme court reversed the decision because of the manner in which we selected the jury.

So I've got to try Pat again some time during the spring 2002.

Back in 1990 when we tried that case, we found some bone fragments out there where Denise said she saw this burning heap.

So, in 1990, what the DNA said was just thought, really. They hadn't perfected the DNA analysis like they do now. Of course, now the DNA is used every day. So the lawyer that's representing Pat in this second trial wanted these bone fragments tested to see if indeed they were human bones. So, this Ronnie Gaines, who was killed, has a sister, and they can take a sample from her and can thus narrow it down to the point to where they can say, "Well, it could be," or "It absolutely is not human bones." We're waiting on that analysis to be completed before we set this case for trial.

Jim T. Hamilton, Columbia, December 10, 2001

100. "THE NATION'S FIRST SCHOOL SHOOTING CASE"

I tried the first school shooting case in the United States. It happened down here at Richland High School, a school in Giles County out here in a rural area. That happened in 1995. A student there named Jamie Rouse, who was seventeen years old, did it. There is some evidence that he was into devil worship and this type of thing. And one day he and this other student named Abbott planned to kill teachers there at Richland High School. Well, actually Rouse is the one who was going to do the killing, but Abbott was going to help him out by driving the truck and that type of thing.

On the day the killings happened, Rouse slipped a .22 rifle out of his house, along with four hundred rounds of ammunition. This rifle held a clip that held twelve shots. Their original plan was that Jamie had gotten into it with a sheriff's deputy that was traffic director there at the school. They planned to kill him first, then go up to the school and kill as many teachers as he could shoot.

Well, the morning this was to happen, the deputy sheriff who was to be the first victim wasn't there that morning for whatever reason. So they just drove on up to the high school. Jamie Rouse walked in with the gun kinda down to his side. Abbott stayed out in the truck. Rouse walked into the high school building, and the first two people he saw were two female teachers standing in the doorway of one of their class-rooms. They were talking about a recipe for Thanksgiving, a recipe for turkey and dressing. He just very calmly raises his rifle and shoots one of them in the head and killed her. He shot the other lady in the head, but she survived. But after he shot them, he left them both lying there and walked on down the hallway. He turned the corner, and there stood the football coach down the hallway a little ways. He meant to kill him. He shot at him, and this little fourteen-year-old girl just happened to walk in front of the coach. The bullet hit her in the neck, and she died later that day at Vanderbilt Hospital.

A male teacher and a couple of students subdued Rouse, jumped him, and got the gun away from him.

They charged him with two counts of first-degree murder and one count of attempted first-degree murder. It took three years to get him to trial. He suffered from depression. This guy that treated him up at the Middle Tennessee Health Institute said that he wasn't able, be-cause of his depression, to assist counsel in his defense. Finally, we tried him in 1998. The jury found him guilty of two counts of first-degree murder. The state couldn't ask for the death penalty because of his age. He was seventeen when it happened. But he was convicted of two counts of first-degree murder and one count of attempted first-degree murder.

I gave him two consecutive life sentences without possibility of parole and fifty years on attempted first-degree murder. He is now housed in an adult penitentiary in Clifton, Tennessee, and will be there the rest of his life, I'd think.

That was a case that drew national attention. The courtroom TV stayed with me the whole time during that trial. The psychiatrist that testified for the defense said that Jamie Rouse suffered from a lot of pressure. Said he was trying to work in a convenient mart and go to school; that he had broken up with his girlfriend; his car motor had blown up; he'd gotten a speeding ticket; some teachers at school had gotten onto him about his grades. He wore black to school every day; he carved an inverted cross on his forehead. His father testified that he, the father, was a recovered drug addict and an alcoholic. They lived in a very tiny house, and there were holes in the walls all over that house where his daddy had hit him with his fist. It was just a very dysfunctional-type situation. Jamie's mother was a computer data processor. He had aunts and uncles who were teachers, one of whom was even superintendent of schools.

Jamie himself never testified. I never heard him utter a sound, and I lived with that case for three years. He sat with his head down almost between his legs the whole trial. Never said a word, not even after the sentence was issued.

I think that was the first school shooting case in the entire nation.

Jim T. Hamilton, Columbia, December 10, 2001

101. "Mother Killed by Her Son"

I just finished a trial case in Giles County that lasted for eight days. A boy killed his mother in her sleep. She was guidance counselor for Giles County High School in Pulaski. She and her husband were divorced. She had a daughter in her twenties, and a son who was in his late twenties. He's the one that did the killing. Her ex-husband lived around there, but he wasn't in the picture. Her father was a very prominent physician there for about forty years. He was in a nursing home at the time his daughter was killed. She lived in an old antebellum home there on the same street where they have the Sam Davis Confederate memorial.

The one who did the killing went to University of the South, Sewanee, on a soccer scholarship. He played up there for two years, then transferred to Middle Tennessee State University and got his degree there. He never did testify, so we didn't hear it from him, but the theory of the state was that his grandfather, who was a physician, had set up some trust funds for those children—this fellow and his sister. And the grandfather wanted one of them to cash out. The one who later killed his mother had already reached a certain age, but his mother wouldn't give it to him. She went to bed every night about nine o'clock. He was working as security guard for some company in Nashville. He knew that she never locked the door to that house. Everybody in the neighborhood also knew it. He left work in Nashville and drove to Pulaski, went in the house, up the steps. She was asleep in her bed. He shot her with a .25-caliber pistol; contact wound to the right temple. That's where they press the weapon against the person. He then doused her with gasoline and set the house on fire. It burned her so bad that the fireman who testified in that trial said that she almost literally melted into the bed clothing. That was terrible.

Well, the state didn't have any witnesses. They did not have a weapon, although they did get the slug out of Mrs. Vaughn's—her name was Vaughn—brain. The ballistics showed it to be a .25-caliber slug. So they questioned this guy:

"Did you ever own a .25-caliber pistol?"

"Yeah, I did."

"Where is it?"

"Well, I lost it fishing."

"Where did you buy it?"

"Well, I bought it at a pawn shop in Lewisburg."

So they went over to the pawn shop, and they keep records. "Oh, yeah," they said, "we sold it to him four days before this murder."

"Well, do you have paperwork here as to who pawned that pistol?"

He said, "Sure I do. It was some old boy from over at Cormishville, Tennessee."

So they go over to his house and asked him about it. He said, "Oh, yeah, I remember the gun." Then he testified at the trial, "I never did like that pistol. I needed some money, so I pawned it. Never needed to pick it up."

"Well, did you ever shoot it out in the backyard?"

He said, "Yeah, I did. Come out here, and I'll show you."

There was a piece of tin laying there that had three bullet holes in it. So they got a metal detector to dig the slugs out of the ground. They took those three slugs from that target shooting, and that slug from Mrs. Vaughn's brain, sent all of them to the TBI ballistics lab. The TBI agent came down and testified. The district attorney asked him, "Do you have an opinion as to whether or not those four slugs were all fired from the same .25-caliber weapon?"

"Yes, I do."

"What is your opinion?"

The fellow said, "To the exclusion of every other .25-caliber weapon in the United States of America, these four came from the same one."

Now, that was pretty stout. The jury stayed out about two to three hours and came back and found him guilty. I sentenced him to life in prison. They didn't ask for the death penalty, because the family didn't really believe that he did it. They told the DA that they didn't want him to ask for the death penalty. So he didn't.

There'll be a new trial set within the next few weeks.

Jim T. Hamilton, Columbia, December 10, 2001

102. "The Purple Monkey Killing"

There was a murder down in Lawrenceburg. This woman had been living with this guy for several months. They weren't married. Lived in her trailer. She worked, but he was kinda trifling; didn't half work. Well, she came home one day, and he was piled up in there, and she just told him, "You are out of here. I want you out of here. I'm tired of fooling with you and don't want to fool with you anymore, so get out." He did.

She came home a day or two later. On the way home, she stopped at a little market and got her some cigarettes and told the clerk, "Well, I'm going home to can some green beans. I've got my mother's recipe. I'm going to use it and can some green beans."

Well, she went home, went in; had a pressure cooker. Put her beans in the jars like you do, and put them down in the pressure cooker. Then she goes over and sits down on the sofa reading a book. Well, when her sisters found her the next day, she was still sitting on the sofa. The book was laying there on the sofa beside her. She had a bullet hole right between her eyes, and there was a stuffed purple monkey sitting on her shoulder with "I love you" written across its chest. I've got a picture of her sitting there dead.

Well, they don't have any witnesses, don't have any gun, but they did take a slug out of her skull. It was .22-caliber. Of course, this man became an immediate suspect because her sister knew about her throwing him out and all that stuff. And his parents lived, as the crow flies, about a thirty-minute walk from where he had been staying with this woman. If you cut across the woods, you could walk from her trailer to where he had been staying in about thirty to forty minutes.

The state gets a search warrant and went over to search his parents' home. They find a half-empty box of .22-caliber federal cartridges—long ones. And those shells were old. They'd been there just forever. Well, they confiscated them, and they got the FBI involved in it. They took that slug out of this lady's head, and they gave the FBI agents those cartridges from the house.

This guy from the FBI lab in Washington came down and testified about the bullets. He says that most of the bullets in this country are made from melted-down car batteries, that when a company decides to produce a batch of cartridges, they just dump all these batteries in a cauldron and melt them down. And every batch of batteries will have a different batch of components in them. In other words, this batch of batteries might have zinc and lead, while the next batch that they produce, say a year from now, will probably have something else in it.

What he did, he took those cartridges that were in that box, and the cartridge that came from her head, and melted them down. He compared the metallic units that were in each. He then testified that, in his opinion, with no question whatsoever, that the slug taken from this lady's head came from that box of cartridges.

Well, I'm sitting there, and I couldn't believe what I was hearing, but they convicted him, and I gave him a life sentence.

This old boy was right pitiful and ignorant. He wasn't incompetent, but he was mentally slow. During his testimony, he denied any knowledge of it, said he loved her, blah, blah, blah.

Well, the defense calls his mother to the stand as a witness. The courtroom in Lawrenceburg is rather large. It is quite a distance down the aisle up to the bench, and the witness chair is seated right close to where I was sitting.

They called this lady, and she started down the aisle from the doorway that leads out to the hallway. And I got to looking at her, thinking, where have I seen her before? She finally got up there in the witness box, and I swore her in. And when I was swearing her in, it dawned on me who she was. She had another son who had committed a murder in Lawrence County. He cut a woman's throat on this farm where he was working. This guy had hired him out of the goodness of his heart. Well, this guy that hired him left to go somewhere, and while he was gone, this woman's other son cut this farmer's wife's throat and killed her.

I'd sentenced him to life in prison about four or five years ago, and when I was giving her the oath it dawned on me who she was. Of course, she said what you think a mother would say about her child, that he was really a good boy, and blah, blah, blah. But I sentenced this guy in the purple monkey killing to life.

I've thought about that a lot of times, what it would be like to have two sons and both of them in the penitentiary doing life for hideous, heinous murders.

Jim T. Hamilton, Columbia, December 10, 2001

103. "A Justifiable Killing"

Here in Bledsoe County, we still have a distinction between a killing and a murder case. A killing is basically when somebody dies who needed to die. My husband swears that still goes on today. A few years ago, he had a murder case that caused some trouble at home.

We have a community in Bledsoe County that's called the Luminary Community. It's out on the mountain between here and Dayton. There are a lot of people who have moved in. We've had a developer that has subdivided some really rough, rough areas out there and sold tracts of land for what they call affordable prices. Folks who couldn't afford to buy real estate have been able to move into Bledsoe County and buy these tracts of land out there. But they live in some rather difficult situations. There are no restrictions on anything out there. A lot of people there just live in lean-tos and buses, or shacks, just whatever they can put up if they own the real estate.

There was a family that lived in the Luminary Community—a husband and wife had initially moved there. And as my husband described their house, it had three walls, but was open to one side. They hadn't finished building the house yet. There was either plastic or tar paper or something that would keep the elements out of that fourth side. Then the man's brother and his wife moved into the area. This latter couple wasn't quite as fortunate as the family with the three-wall house. They had a tent out back and were actually living in the tent.

The weather here in the wintertime can be very harsh. And evidently this husband that had his wife living in a tent wasn't described as a real go-getter. He didn't really care for work. They'd been there for about six months living in a tent before he ever found a job or started working. He went out when he had his first job, and he worked for the first week. Evidently, after that first week of work, he got a paycheck, but he didn't come home promptly after work. And when he did come home, he was drunk, and he had bought quite a bit of beer.

His wife went inside, got a shotgun, came outside, and just started blowing away at the man. Killed him, just killed him.

So my husband comes home, and he's got photographs of the housing, if you could call it that, and the situation they were in. He went over all that with me. Of course, the other couple living there witnessed the shooting. She just went off the deep end and went inside and got a gun and just started shooting at him. Thus, she killed him. When my husband laid all this stuff out in front of me, I said, "David, you'll never get a conviction in Bledsoe County against that woman."

He said, "What are you talking about? I've got two eyewitnesses. He didn't threaten her in any way; she just blew him up."

I said, "I don't care. It's a killing. That man deserved to be shot, and that's what happened."

We argued about it for a month, but her defense attorney got a psychologist to say that she'd suffered from a mental illness. I think the district attorney realized that what I was saying was correct. They weren't going to get a conviction against this woman. They settled the case. I think they gave her a manslaughter six-year conviction and put her on probation. She served some time before she was able to make bail, but that was all the time she served. So, that's a "killing."

She finally moved back to where other family members were located. She didn't stay in Bledsoe County.

Lynne Swafford, Pikeville, December 4, 2003

104. "No Questions Due to Inadequate Payment"

I had a murder case one time in which the defense attorney, who was trying it by himself, told me that he had hired another defense attorney, who used to be a prosecutor. And I knew he was very good. The defense attorney said he was bringing him in to cross-examine a Dr. Francisco, the medical examiner. And I had just a run-of-the-mill homicide case, and I couldn't figure why he would bring in this other lawyer just to examine Dr. Francisco. They must have known something, but in reading the file I couldn't find nothing. So I explained to Dr. Francisco that they were going to bring in this lawyer that was going to cross-examine him.

Dr. Francisco said, "I've looked at the file, and there's nothing that's outside the ordinary homicide, so don't worry."

So I put the doctor on the stand, and I was very particular as to the questions I asked him, and I kept watching out of the corner of my eye this defense attorney to see if he would object. Because he was brought in especially to cross-examine, and he never objected. And when I got through I checked everything to make sure, and I said, "That's all I have of this witness. You may cross-examine him."

I was ready to see this great defense attorney cross-examine the doctor. Well, he stood up and said, "I have no questions." When he said that, I was just shocked. He sat down, and the regular defense attorney turned to him and said so loud that everybody in the courtroom could hear him, "What do you mean, no questions of the doctor? I brought you in just to cross-examine the doctor."

The lawyer turned to him and said, "For the thirty-five dollars that you paid me this is all you get; it's no questions." [Laughter]

I always remembered that case!

Don Dino, Memphis, January 7, 2004

105. "ATTORNEY'S CROSS-EXAMINATION QUESTION MISUNDERSTOOD"

I tried a murder case in Celina when I had just been appointed district attorney. I believe the defendant's name was Cherry, I believe. The sheriff, Hugh Davis, had lost the murder weapon. The defense attorney was from Glasgow, Kentucky, Jim Gillenwater. He was one of the most colorful lawyers you'll ever meet. A really great guy, too.

The facts of the case were just really simple. The victim was an old man who had a tenant farmer and his wife or girlfriend living on his property right on the state line. They both saw this shooting at a tavern right up on the Kentucky line at Moss, Tennessee. The victim had gone by and picked them up that morning and took them with him to Tompkinsville, probably to the grocery store. On their way back they stopped at a tavern here in Tennessee, and the old man ran into somebody that he'd had a quarrel with, and they had a shootout. Well, this other guy killed the old man.

The woman that lived in the tenant house with her husband, or friend, was the best witness by far. I mean, she saw it all. On the morning of the trial, she saw me in the courtyard and said, "I can't testify. I can't testify."

I said, "What do you mean, you can't testify? You saw a man killed, so you are going to testify."

Then she said, "No, I can't testify. Everybody knows that Mr. Gillenwater is the best lawyer anywhere around here, and he'll make me look bad."

Then I asked her, "Well, how can he make you look bad for just seeing some man killed?"

She sort of whispered, "Mr. Roberts, I haven't told you this, but Jim and I are not married. We are living together in sin."

I said, "I don't care if you are. That doesn't have anything to do with this. I'll just bring that out right quick that you and this fellow live together but are not married, so whatever he wants to make out of it, let him make it. But you have to testify."

Jimmy Reneau was sitting right behind me, and of course it is distracting to have him whispering to you during a trial. The facts are so simple. They were both at home when the old man pulled up there to get them. Her boyfriend was out in the front yard working on a lawn mower, and that's the key part of the story. He was outside working on the lawn mower when the old man pulled up. She was in the house washing dishes. The victim says, "Do you want to go up to Kentucky with me to get some groceries?" Well, they left to go get groceries.

When she testified, I said, "I'll introduce you and say that you and Mr. So and So are not married, but that you live on Mr. Marshall's farm."

She said, "That's right."

"Mr. Marshall came out to see you all that morning, and your boyfriend was out in the yard. What was he doing?"

She says, "He was working on a lawn mower."

"What were you doing?" I asked her.

"I was washing dishes, and he said, 'Do you want to go to Kentucky?' I got in the car with him and rode to Kentucky, bought our groceries, stopped at the tavern, the shooting took place, and Mr. Marshall got killed."

Well, then Gillenwater gets up to cross-examine her. And he doesn't talk. His voice sounds loud and growly, like "gr-r-r-r." He just blows everybody out. Nobody ever notices another lawyer after they hear him. He had on a royal blue suit with a vest, gold chain, small glasses on his nose. His hair was flipping up and down. He charges across the courtroom, then says in a slow, bass voice, "Now, Miss Jones, on this fateful day, you and your paramour went to Kentucky."

Thinking he said "power mower," she came right back with the words, "No, we left the lawn mower there in the yard." [Laughter]

That just took the whiz out of his cross-examination. Finally, Gillenwater, who was my good friend, looks at me and says with his growling-like voice, "Now-w-w, General-1-1-1, you have laughed enough."

The final verdict in that murder case was second degree.

John M. Roberts, Livingston, August 27, 2002

106. "PRELAWYER INPUT"

I was still in law school when I got associated with my first real case. The episode in which I was involved took place here in Knoxville. My father, who was an attorney, gave me a call and asked me to do some research on this case.

There was a murder in which a husband was charged with throwing his wife off the bridge in Jefferson County into the French Broad River. Of course, it killed her. This man was represented by a firm of lawyers, Kilgore and Easterly, out of Greeneville, which was his home county. That firm employed my father as a local attorney to join them.

It was a case that created quite a bit of discussion by people up and down the road and over the byways. The judge, George Shepherd, would not allow bail. So a habeas corpus petition was filed by their attorneys, seeking bail. They filed it, and knowing what Judge Shepherd would do with it, they filed it before Judge Hamilton Burnett, who was the circuit bench in Knoxville. He later became chief justice of the Tennessee Supreme Court.

I was in law school at the time, and my father called me. He told me about this situation. I knew what was going on anyway. He asked me to do some research on the matter of when a person under those circumstances was entitled to bail. And I did; I researched it pretty thoroughly. . . .

So, they were having a hearing that was set on Saturday morning by Judge Burnett. The hearing was in the old courthouse, and I attended. I had already presented to the Greeneville lawyers and my father what I had found, and they were impressed with the law that I gave to them. And somehow Judge Burnett had found out that I had done the research. When one of the Greeneville lawyers got up, he said he believed this had been worked on by a law student. He said if this law student was there in the courtroom, and he knew I was, and wanted to present it, and if it was all right with the lawyer, he'd like to hear from me.

I argued the issue of bail, then did a petition for habeas corpus. As a result, we got a bond of $10,000 and got him out on bond. We argued the criteria that the proof was evident and the presumption great. They couldn't meet it.

That was my first day in court.

Chester S. Rainwater Jr., Knoxville, July 24, 2000,
provided by the Tennessee Bar Foundation, Nashville

107. "GUILTY OR NOT?"

In 1974, I was appointed to a high-profile case, the case of the *State v. Richard Nunnally*. It involved Hancock County. There was a young man by the name of Richard Nunnally, who lived in Knoxville and was starting out in the contracting–home building business. He had contracted to build a home for a couple from Georgia, who had bought some acreage in a rural area of Hancock County, and was in the process of building a home for them.

Apparently some difficulty arose between the contractor and the owners, this man and his wife. On this particular day, the owners had gone to the courthouse and taken a criminal warrant for the contractor for misappropriation of funds that they claimed they had paid, and that he hadn't done the work, et cetera.

A few days after that occurrence, the sheriff of Hancock County went out for some purpose to the site where the home was being built. When he drove up, he found a van belonging to the Georgia couple sitting in the driveway beside the home under construction. The husband was sitting in under the steering wheel, and the wife was in the passenger seat, dead. They had been shot in the back, sitting in the vehicle. As a result of that, charges were later brought against this contractor, charging him with first-degree murder.

Ordinarily the case was going to be tried in Hancock County, but they decided to change it to Jefferson County and have the trial there. Judge Porter had appointed Clyde Dunn, a lawyer in Newport, to represent Nunnally in Hancock County. But when they moved it to Jefferson County, he wanted a local attorney. So Judge Porter called me and we had a not-too-friendly conversation, but he wouldn't relent and I had no choice. So Dunn and I represented Nunnally.

It was a bitter-fought case but a totally circumstantial case. They never could find a gun, a weapon; had no motive other than the fact that the couple had taken out a warrant for him. But it hadn't been served on him. Whether he knew about it or not was an issue. Thus it was a tough case to be tried from the standpoint of the prosecution.

So we went to trial, and there was a lot of feeling over it. Those people in Hancock County just were not in sympathy with the defendant in any way. So we tried the case, and it took several days. One of the things that occurred during the trial was the defense tried to get in the evidence that the defendant was an informant for the FBI. We were trying to establish his credibility as a witness, and we started asking about him. The attorney general objected, and the court sustained the objection.

So, on cross-examination after some period of time being examined by the attorney general, they closed his examination and walked back over to the table. He turned around and said, "Mr. Nunnally, is there anything about this case that you know that you haven't told us?"

He said, "Yes, sir, I know a lot about this case."

The attorney stood there and finally said, "Well, why didn't you?"

He shot right back and said, "Well, my attorney tried to bring it out, and you made an objection, and the judge sustained it. We couldn't talk about it."

So that was the end of the cross-examination, and from the defense standpoint we just sat down. So the jury came in about 11:00 P.M., and they were hung nine to three for acquittal. When their hung jury announcement was made to the judge, he was not very happy about it. He had a habit of using the gavel and coming down real hard. He adjourned court right quick and went down off the bench and out into the hallway. I don't know why, but I just followed him, just right on his heels.

He got out in the hallway, and nobody else was out there. He said, "We'll get that so and so the next trial." He was never one to hold his opinions back, and he was a good judge. But he couldn't keep from taking sides at times.

When the second trial came out, the accused was declared not guilty, and the state did not appeal.

Chester S. Rainwater Jr., Knoxville, July 24, 2000,
provided by the Tennessee Bar Foundation, Nashville

108. "THE PERSUASIVE PHOTOGRAPH"

I was defending a man in a murder case. On the Fourth of July he had a carload of kids. He'd went to this house and had an argument with this man, and they had been celebrating the Fourth of July. The man pulled a gun on him, and he reached down to the floorboard of his car, pulled up a rifle, and shot this man and killed him.

I represented and defended him. I thought I had a real good case, and I did as it turned out. But the question was whether my client had pulled his gun out first, or whether the one that was killed had pulled his pistol first.

This was a dilapidated old house out in the country, and this group had gotten together on the Fourth of July, as they liked to do, to have a party. They had all been drinking, I'm sure. And this woman standing on the porch was the prime witness of the attorney general that my man had gotten his rifle out because she saw him with the rifle before the other man pulled his pistol.

I went out and looked and found that she couldn't have because the other man was halfway back in the yard by the side of the house. And if she was on the front porch, she could not have seen him. So I took a picture of the house, a great big photograph that I had a professional to come out and take the picture and put it in a great big frame. So when she got on the witness stand, I said, "Where were you standing?"

"I was standing right in the doorway."

"Well, could you see my client?"

She said, "Yes, I saw him get that rifle."

"Well, how do you know whether or not the guy that was killed pulled the pistol?"

"Well, I saw him pull it. He didn't pull the pistol until after that rifle was out."

Then I got the picture up and said, "Now, show me where you were standing."

She said, "Right there."

Well, obviously she couldn't see it, and as a result of that my client was acquitted.

I kept that picture—a great big framed picture—and hung it on the wall. It was a great thrill to me to have people come into my office, look at the picture, and say, "John, what's that a picture of?"

"That's my old home place."

John Richardson Rucker Sr., Murfreesboro, March 31, 2000,
provided by the Tennessee Bar Foundation, Nashville

109. "The DuBois Case"

One day a young man came into the office to Mr. Jewell, the attorney general, and said, "I'm the twin brother of the man that was killed by Banham DuBois."

Mr. Jewell and I shared offices and the reception room. I could hear what was going on. The twin brother said, "I want somebody to represent me in that."

Mr. Jewell said, "Well, I'll take care of the prosecution. You don't have to have a lawyer."

He said, "Yeah, but I want a lawyer representing me, to be sure."

Mr. Jewell said, "Well, why don't you go talk to that lawyer across the hall?"

So he came over into my office and sat down and started talking with me; told me who he was, and what he wanted. He said, "I just want to make sure I've got somebody I can talk to and see that DuBois is prosecuted."

I said, "Do you want me to do it? I'll be happy to do it."

He said, "Well, I haven't got but $100 dollars."

I said, "Okay, I'll take it for a hundred dollars." And I did represent him.

Banham DuBois had already killed one person in the penitentiary. He was really a bad character here. He had fought with the man that he killed, but he thought that fellow had reported him one time that resulted in him getting caught being drunk and put in jail. And then he had said something about his wife. So, he sat in the barbershop and had his hair cut with two other friends, and one of them said, "Okay, DuBois, let's go get him. If you want to get him, let's go get him."

He said, "All right," and the proof showed that the three of them walked out to this taxicab stand and pulled out a knife, stabbed this fellow and killed him. So we were trying the DuBois case, which resulted in a first-degree murder conviction and sentenced him to the electric chair. And he did eventually die in the electric chair after a couple of years. But it didn't take but a couple of years of appeals until he was electrocuted. That was the last person from Rutherford County to be electrocuted. I don't think there's been anybody else that's received the electric chair as a punishment since then.

I thought I had really gotten into a real case for a hundred dollars! And it gave me some publicity, because the courthouse was filled every day. I got a lot of good exposure in that case.

John Richardson Rucker Sr., Murfreesboro, March 31, 2000,
provided by the Tennessee Bar Foundation, Nashville

6

MORE STORIES ABOUT LAWYERS AND JUDGES IN THE COURTROOM

Most of the numerous accounts in this story category are first-person narratives. However, the focus of each story is not the storyteller but another lawyer or judge. These stories describe incidents involving lawyers and judges both in and out of the courtroom, primarily the latter. They deal with various issues, including frequent appropriate or inappropriate confrontations with other lawyers and judges, and judges trying to influence the jurors. Other accounts in this broad category are stories about judges who try to favor certain clients, public visitors and courtroom incidents in earlier times, settlements involving lawyer fees, lawyers' first cases in the courtroom, lawyers who lack business money, women in court, and a dozen or so stories about events that are somewhat humorous.

These bench and bar stories constitute the most popular category in the entire book. They also provide insight into the legal system that is so very important in helping the reader understand what it was like across the years down to present times.

110. "GOING TO COURT WAS ONCE A FORM OF ENTERTAINMENT"

It is absolutely true that in the 1950s and 1960s, the general public was far more inclined to come in and sit in the courtroom to listen to and observe what took place during a trial. I think it is true that in the old days, even before I began practicing law, that there were three forms of entertainment that people in rural areas had. (1) They'd go to church, to revivals; (2) if they lived on a river, usually a showboat would come down the river and people wanted to see it; and (3) they would go to court. Going to court was a form of entertainment, and in the old days, in addition to being very fine lawyers, many of the lawyers were actors. They were very damn good actors, too, I might say! They were representing their client, and their primary concern was what the jury was going to do. So these lawyers played with that jury, and the audience got the benefit of seeing and hearing it. So a court session was a real form of entertainment.

About two weeks after I was admitted to the bar in August 1952, I started a murder case. My law partner at that time did not like to try lawsuits, and this other law partner from Alabama didn't want to take the lead because he thought that these local people would not look with favor on that, so they asked me to take the lead, and I didn't have any more damn sense than to do it.

Our client was an escaped convict from Alabama. His name was Henry Benefield. He had a paramour from Mayfield, Kentucky, whose name was Lucille. They'd been on a sort of Bonnie and Clyde spree for six weeks to two months. They had been here in Humphrey County for a week to ten days. There was an old fellow who lived out in the south part of the county whose name was Dick Mayberry. Dick sold whiskey, and he was a brute of a man. Allegedly by the state, and of course there was a good deal of proof to support this charge, Henry and Lucille were attempting to rob Dick. Well, in the course of the robbery, they shot and killed him, or at least one of them did. They were each trying to blame it on the other. They had ceased to be lovers and became adversaries.

There was an old former attorney general, Bill Howell, from Dover, Tennessee. He was a tremendous lawyer. He had long, flowing white hair, and that was before long, flowing white hair was in vogue.

My law firm had accepted to prove that Lucille had committed the murder, and the other side was obviously saying that Benefield had committed the murder. In an effort to attack the credibility of Lucille, we had found an old photograph that really stretched your imagination. It might have been pornographic, and then we proved that she was the mother of an illegitimate child. Now, in those days, a mother with an illegitimate child was not viewed as they are today.

We had the jury set up, and I remember that there was an old man on the jury named Coleman Hooper, a great big fat man, sitting on the front row. I took him as a juror because his mother and father lived near my mother and father at McEwen.

I remember when General Howell was making his closing argument—I shall never forget it, he said, "Gentlemen of the jury, what have they proven on little Lucille to indicate that she's a mother? She's the sweetest, most precious word in the English tongue. And the most precious memories that I have was seeing my mother sitting in a rocking chair singing those sweet old hymns that we loved so well. So, gentlemen of the jury, I submit to you that when my time shall come to meet my Maker, that the Streets of Gold, nor the Gates of Jasmine, shall hold no attraction to me. But to see once again that little old lady with a shawl wrapped around her shoulders and to hear her singing 'With a Charge to Keep Have I.'" That's an old hymn.

Well, when he said that, Coleman Hooper didn't just have tears in his eyes. He absolutely exploded! And I thought, "Oh, hell, they're going to send us all to the penitentiary." Obviously, Benefield was convicted, and little Lucille was acquitted.

William J. Peeler, Waverly, June 14, 2001

111. "Lawyer Writes Unofficial Driver's License"

I had a client one time, back when I had to work on Saturdays, and on Saturdays we didn't have a secretary. My partner would just come into the office and see people who had to work through the week. One Saturday morning I thought I had locked the door, but I looked up, and there were about six black men standing in my office. I could tell that they were drinking, and one of them was my client whom I had represented in the past. That startled me when I looked up, but I said, "What can I do for you?"

He said that he had come there because he wants to drive his car, but they took his driver's license away. And they were all moving around the office and picking up stuff, and I didn't know what to do, so I called for my partner, but he was gone. Evidently, he had gone out the door and left it open, so that's how they got in. I tried to explain to my client that he would not have a driver's license for two years. Well, he stood right in front of my desk, and he was a pretty good-sized fellow.

He said that he and his friends were not leaving my office until he could get something to drive his car with.

At that time, I immediately said, "Well, if all you want is something to permit you to drive your car, I can help you." Then, I took a scratch pad and on it I put the date, his name, and wrote "This is to authorize ——— to drive his vehicle," then signed my name, including the words "Attorney at Law," and I handed him that piece of paper. He then read it, then showed it to all of his friends, then smiled and said, "That's my lawyer, and that's why I got him." Well, they all were happy and then left my office. I assume, as I told somebody, that he is still driving with that piece of paper in his pocket that's got my signature on it!

Don Dino, Memphis, January 4, 2004

112. "Prostitute Offers Services to Lawyer"

I once had a prostitute I was getting ready to take to court. I told her what my fee was, and she said, "Is there something we can work out in regards to the fee so that I won't have to pay you any money?"

I thanked her, but told her, "No, I had rather have my money," and that we were to forget all about this other thing she was offering. So, we go down to the court, and while I am presenting her case to the court, they have a blood test they do on them. Well, the man for the county came up and addressed the court and told them that she had VD.

When I heard that, I looked at her and said, "Now you know why I don't want to work that out; I'd rather have cash than VD."

She responded to me, but I don't remember what she said. But she was good-looking!

Don Dino, Memphis, January 2004

113. "The Scottsboro Rape Case"

Hal Smith was a catcher for the Pittsburgh Pirates when they beat the Yankees, when Bill Mazeroski hit that great home run. After he got out of baseball, he wrote some country songs. To this day, I love the lyrics of one that he wrote. "I've got a stomach full of chitlins and a belly full of you."

I had a case that shows that you have to be lucky in life. I was still playing baseball when I was thirty-three years old in 1976. After pitching a shutout one day, I went to the commissioner's office of this particular league, and we started talking about the tournament coming up. And on TV was a show that NBC put on called *Judge Horton's Scottsboro Case*. It was the story of a very courageous judge in Decatur,

Alabama, who had set aside a jury verdict in the thirties that had condemned seven black boys to death by hanging. The case came out of accusations made by two white women about what happened on a train from Chattanooga to Huntsville, Alabama. The train stopped in Scottsboro.

Dan Carter, who is now professor of history at Emory University, wrote as the topic of his dissertation, "Scottsboro: The Tragedy of the American South." He researched it well and did a wonderful job in writing it. LSU Press published it as a book. He mentioned in the book that these two white women were dead. And when the movie came out in the mid-1970s, they thought they were dead, so the producers and directors took the liberty to paint the judge in a better light, and painted the women in a less favorable light. Well, these women were very much alive, and I was hired by Victoria Price, who has since died. After the movie was shown, she came to my office the next day and asked me if I had ever heard of Victoria Price. After thinking a minute, I told her, "Yes, I saw you on TV last night. I thought you were dead."

"I'm very much alive," she said to me.

I took that case without any knowledge that it was going to be such a big case. Everybody in the country was interested in that case. It was just incredible. The *Washington Post* came down here and did a story about it. Well, I took that case and sued NBC. But the judge that heard that case took it away from me. It had to go to a jury. I appealed to the Sixth Circuit Court of Appeals on the invasion of privacy and defamation of character. The judge found that these women were public figures but obviously had been unheard of for forty years, living out here in the country. They literally lived in a country home. Finally, I asked for certiorari [referral of records] with the Supreme Court of the United States, and it was granted. They gave it to me, and NBC settled before we got into court.

That may have been Justice Sandra Day O'Connor's first case. I don't know that for sure, but it seems to me that she'd just gone on the bench.

When I settled the case before we got to argue in front of the Supreme Court, somebody asked me what this lady and I had in common. She was a feisty country woman, but very bright. I said, "We chew the same kind of tobacco." She was truly a country woman, and a good woman. At that time, she was living in a little area called Temple, right here in Lincoln County, Tennessee.

After the case was settled, Carter did an addendum to his book and included my picture in that book. So I'm now in a history book. He didn't like me during the trial because I had berated him so badly for saying the women were dead, but afterward he and I would speak from time to time or be involved in some of the Judge Horton things in the South. They'd invite him over and invite me down there, so we became friends. When he wrote the definitive work on Governor George Wallace, I wrote and told him how much I appreciated how much he was doing.

The first trial in reference to this case was tried in Scottsboro, Jackson County, Alabama. After that case was tried and those boys had a drunken counselor representing them, the Communist Party, which was just forming, and the NAACP, which was also just forming, were vying for the right to defend these boys. Samuel S. Leibowitz, famous trial lawyer in New York, came down to Alabama and defended those boys. He later became a wonderful jurist in New York. He defended them and appealed every decision that was made, and as a result of those appeals, some of the great laws we have in effective systems of counsel and rights of the accused are part of our law today. Judge Horton, of course, was an absolutely courageous judge for setting aside the verdict that condemned these boys to death again after they moved the case from Scottsboro over to Decatur, Alabama.

Raymond Fraley, Fayetteville, September 20, 2001

114. "A Personable Juror"

One time I had a case in Moore County, Tennessee. I was a marine [at one time], and when I profiled the jury, I noticed that one of them had been a former marine. So I got a marine emblem and put it on my notebook that day. And every chance I had, I flashed that marine corps emblem.

You really can't speak to jurors. Instead of saying "How are you?" you can say, "Good morning," and that sort of thing. Finally, he saw that emblem and once when he was passing through the courtyard, he looked at me and said, "Semper fidelis." [Laughter]

I thought to myself, "That man is going to be my jury person," and sure enough he was.

Raymond Fraley, Fayetteville, September 20, 2001

115. "Lawyer without a Secretary"

There's a famous lawyer in this part of Tennessee who is still practicing law. His name is Hughie Ragan, a lawyer noted primarily as a criminal defense lawyer in these parts. He has represented a lot of people in the criminal court, but he's tried cases in other courts as well. He's a legendary figure in this part of the country. As far as I know, he never had a secretary. He types all his own briefs and does all that work himself.

We got a brief from him here in the court of appeals office one time, and we got tickled at him. He had a typewritten heading in the brief that simply read, "SOME LAW," and he went on to cite some of the principles of the law he relied on in that case. Down a little farther on the page was another heading, "SOME MORE LAW."

As I said, he didn't have a secretary. He typed all his own briefs. Generally, a brief is made up of several parts. One of them is a statement of the facts in the case on which you, the attorney, is relying; also included is the law that you think is applicable in those facts. Typically, there is a section of the brief known as the "Statement of the Facts," and another identified as "Argument from the Law."

Well, in typing his own briefs, he just put headings in there to distinguish his brief. That was simply his style.

Alan Highers, Jackson, August 8, 2001

116. "Lawyers Settle Financial Matters in a Basketball Game"

I took depositions against the Ford Motor Company in Dearborn, Michigan, back in the 1970s when gasoline tanks were exploding. One of the great stories that came out of that Ford case was when I associated with a fellow named Bob Peters over here in Winchester. He is one of the most intellectual readers and intellects I have ever known. He is a great storyteller and a great fellow. I asked him to get involved in this case with me, and we went to Dearborn to take depositions against engineers that particular day. When we came out of the deposition room, I ran into another lawyer who was also taking depositions in other cases—Mark Robinson from Newport Beach, California, near Los Angeles. I knew about Mark because he had tried this case in California and got one of the largest verdicts in the history of trial work.

I spoke with him about the case, and at dinner with him that night I asked him about joining me in my case because I was within six to eight weeks of trial, and that I needed him to maybe get the corporate council. He said that he would, but that his firm would insist that he get

12 percent of the settlement. Well, I'd already spent two years in this case, and I thought that 12 percent would be a lot of money; then again, 12 percent of nothing is nothing. So I looked at Bob, and the next morning at breakfast, I talked with Mark again. I said, "Look, I'll tell what we'll do. We'll finish the depositions, and then this afternoon we'll go to the YMCA and play basketball. You've got your brother here, who was a football player at the University of Mississippi." Mark played football at Stanford, I was a basketball player in North Carolina, and my buddy Bob Peters was a high school dropout basketball player.

But Bob was a big fellow, so I figured he could set some picks. So I said to Mark, "We'll play, and if we win, we get you for 8 percent, but if we lose, we'll pay you 15 percent of this case."

Well, they accepted the challenge, being as competitive as they were. And we played that night in a two-on-two basketball game, and it was a bloodbath. In the deciding game, Bob Peters threw up a twenty-foot hook shot. I said, "Bob, God dang it, give me that basketball. Just set the picks, and I'll take care of us." Well, we got him for 8 percent!!

Later, Mark invited me out to speak to the Trial Lawyers Association in California, which was meeting at the Disneyland Hotel, and my topic was "Tips from a Country Lawyer." Of course, I shared that story with all the lawyers out there about how their great trial lawyer Mark Robinson lost in basketball.

Mark and I became friends and have stayed friends across the years.

Raymond Fraley, Fayetteville, September 20, 2001

117. "Intended Duel Didn't Take Place"

Do you remember Holmes Cummins, one of the most brilliant members of the Covington bar?... A soldier during his teens, he came out of the army with his best years for study having been given to the hardships of war. . . . Upon reaching his majority, he asked to be sent to the Legislature. His wish was granted. He made an enviable record his first term and the people returned him. . . . He became a great corporation lawyer, being chief counsel for C. P. Huntingdon, operator and controller of the Chesapeake and Ohio railroad and the Southern Pacific. . . .

The amusing thing I recall connected with Mr. Cummins's life occurred about 1893. Hon. E. W. Carmack and Col. W. A. Collier became estranged over a newspaper fight between the *Avalanche* and the *Appeal*. Col. Collier and Mike Connoly were editors and managers of the *Avalanche*, in which Mr. Cummins owned a big interest. Maj. Crawford was president of the *Appeal*. . . . A challenge to a duel was passed and accepted between Col. Collier and Mr. Carmack. Crawford was the latter's second and Mr. Cummins was Collier's second. It was to take place in Mississippi.

On the day the duel was to take place, a number of gentlemen were seated on the north porch of the courthouse. Among these were Esq. R. R. Shelton, W. H. Feezor, Col. William Sanford, Capt. Charles B. Simonton, John R. Sloan, Peyton J. Smith, and others. The forthcoming duel was being discussed, when in his usual terse way, Mr. Feezor said, "Boys, they won't fight. Holmes Cummins is managing this thing and he is too smart to even let them see each other, let alone fight one another. Mind what I say, nobody is going to be hurt and Holmes will make each man think he won the victory."

What Mr. Feezor said the crowd agreed to, and it turned out just as predicted. Col. Collier and Mr. Carmack became fast friends and the colonel supported him in every one of his campaigns thereafter.

Written by Judge W. A. Owen, Covington,
and published in the Covington Leader,
September 15, 1931; provided by Russell B. Bailey,
Covington mayor and Tipton County historian

118. "YOUNG BUCKS IN COURT"

Colonel Tom Elam from Union City was known to have a booming voice and command of the office. When he walked into a room, he just kindly took over, took control. That was the last word you'd get to say when the colonel was there. He was a colonel in the army, and he just commanded the audience. He was also athletic director at the University of Tennessee, Knoxville. He was truly an excellent orator, and he was in what is called the Sixth Circuit Club, or something like that. It is a club of the elite lawyers that meet in Cincinnati—the Sixth Circuit of Appeals.

He had the tendency to call people "young bucks." He would say, "Young buck, how are you doing today?" and he'd slap you on the back. He went into the Sixth Circuit during some of his older years, taking those liberties you can do when you get that age. He walked into court on a conversation from what I've been told, and kindly interrupted it. Then he started his story about something, and then introduced himself to a few people he didn't know. When he got through, he turned around to one of these people in the room and said to him, "I'm afraid, young buck, that I didn't get your name. My name's Colonel Elam."

This fellow said, "Mine is Anton Scalia," and he shook Elam's hand.

Well, Elam didn't know it, but Scalia was the U.S. Supreme Court justice. They said that was the only time that Tom sort of squatted down, for he had called Scalia a "young man, young buck." [Laughter]

David G. Hayes, Jackson, August 8, 2001

119. "AN UNDERSTANDING JUDGE"

There was a case that we tried in which I was involved. I had been successful in my defense, and the plaintiff's lawyer had filed a motion to reconsider. In his petition, he had basically accused me of subordination of perjury because two witnesses had testified differently from what he had anticipated. Well, I had talked to the witnesses, and I knew what they were going to say. I got them back in, and they said, "We didn't tell them anything different from what we told you. You just asked us different questions."

So I took an affidavit from them, and we were over there arguing the motion to reconsider. I was pretty well upset, being accused of something like that. We were there before a very wonderful jurist, Bill Leach, who was a real down-to-earth judge. I was on the floor, and this man got up and made some movement like he was going to come toward me. I said, "Your Honor, please ask Mr. So-and-so to stay away from me, for there is nothing but the utmost respect I have for this court, that keeps me from knocking the goddamn hell out of him right here in the courtroom." Then I thought to myself, "Oh, my God, what am I saying?" [Laughter]

The judge looked at him and said, "Mr. So-and-so I believe Mr. Harvill means it. If I was you, I'd stay away from him."

I thought sure that I was going to be laid out!

F. Evans Harvill, Clarksville, July 3, 2001

120. "LAWYERS AWARDED HALF INTEREST IN JACK DANIEL'S DISTILLERY"

John Hooper, U.S. attorney in Nashville, had a brother-in-law named Seth Walker, who was also a very young lawyer in Nashville. This would have been probably in the very early 1930s, as Prohibition was still in effect.

Mr. Lem Motlow, who was Mr. Jack Daniel's nephew, was going to St. Louis. On the train, he got mad at the porter, shot at him, but missed him. It killed another fellow. Of course, they indicted Motlow. He didn't have any money. The distillery was closed and with no particular prospects of it reopening anytime soon. So he came and saw Mr. Hooper and Mr. Walker and said to them, "If you boys will represent me, I'll give you one-half of Jack Daniel's Distillery."

They represented him, and he was acquitted. True to his word, Motlow gave them half of Jack Daniel's. Of course, you can imagine what that stock was worth when Jack Daniel's was finally sold to Brown-Foreman in Louisville. Not much.

Hooper had this enormous capacity for friendship. He was as kind to the most senior member of the bar in New York City, and he would have been equally as kind to a fledgling young lawyer in the most rural areas of Tennessee and Kentucky. He was truly one of Tennessee's outstanding lawyers of all time.

William J. Peeler, Waverly, June 14, 2001

121. "Hunting Injuries Cause Uncle and Nephew to Become Lawyers"

My uncle, Homer W. Bradberry, as a young man of about twenty-two was injured in a hunting accident and lost his left hand. After he did that, he went to law school. And when I lost my eyesight during a hunting accident, I, too, went to law school! That's an irony.

One of the other ironies of our accidental experiences is that when I came back to Tennessee from Michigan, circumstances arose during the spring of 1980, and they needed a juvenile court judge. I had only been practicing about five months. The other attorney said to me, "Well, you're not too busy. You take the job." So I took over the juvenile court in Weakley County at that time.

I've been on the bench since that time, but my uncle who had retired during the early 1990s, well, when Chancellor Lanier was removed from the bench in Dyersburg, my uncle went down to replace him. He went into court there one day and looked out over the crowd that was assembled there and saw a number of young faces that were present that day. He asked the clerk why all those kids were present in the courtroom. The clerk said, "Well, this is juvenile court day."

The chancellor there in Dyersburg was also the juvenile court judge. My uncle said to the clerk, "I'm not a juvenile judge." They were able to work out the problem.

The irony of all this is that my uncle was serving as a juvenile court judge in Dyer County, and I was juvenile court judge here in Weakley County. He was in his late seventies or early eighties at that time.

James H. Bradberry, Dresden, June 7, 2001

122. "Judge's Decision as the Thirteenth Juror"

Here in Tennessee, the trial judge serves as what is called the "thirteenth juror." What it means is that in a civil case, if the jury comes in with a verdict, even though all twelve of them agree, if the trial judge does not agree with the verdict, he's like a thirteenth juror. He can set all that aside.

The lawyer has a certain number of challenges. He can challenge jurors. He has so many challenges "for cause," that is to say, he has to state a reason. And he has other challenges that are called peremptory challenges because he doesn't have to state a reason. He can just say, "I don't want this juror."

Hughie Ragan tried a case one time before Judge Tip Taylor, who ran for governor of Tennessee against Buford Ellington many years ago. . . . Judge Taylor was a pretty well known judge, who presided here in Jackson at the Madison County Courthouse. One day, Hughie got a verdict in a civil case. He was awarded money damages, but Judge Taylor said that he was not satisfied with the verdict because of something he considered amiss in the trial. He stated that he was going to exercise his prerogative and set aside the verdict.

Hughie was just steaming about the judge's statement, so he went over to see his friend Carmack Murchison and asked Carmack, "Can he do that?"

Carmack said, "Why, yes, he's the thirteenth juror."

Hughie said, "Well, I'm glad to know that. The next time, I'll save one of my challenges for him!"

Some of these stories are funny to me because I know the people, or the characters involved.

Alan Highers, Jackson, August 8, 2001

123. "Potential Contempt of Court Charge"

This is a story that I heard before I got out of law school, but it was told to me as true. We had a new criminal judge to take the bench, a fellow by the name of Jack Broadbent. He died the second year I was practicing law, so I never knew him very well, but I knew him by reputation.

He had a small bar. Had this fellow by the name of Horace Stout who was an excellent lawyer but was very much an individualist. The story is that when Judge Broadbent took the bench for the first time, Mr. Stout was sitting down with his feet propped up on the table. So he didn't get up. Judge Broadbent looked at him and said, "Horace, you'd better stand up when I take the bench, or I'll find you in contempt of court."

He said, "Go ahead, Jack, for I ain't got nothing but contempt for your damned old court anyway." [Laughter]

Today, it would have been horrible for that to be said. In those days, they laughed it off as a joke; they were friends. But I thought I would never have enough nerve to say that to any judge, whether I had a lot of respect or no respect at all for such persons.

F. Evans Harvill, Clarksville, July 3, 2001

124. "Judge Distracts Lawyer with Odd Question"

I remember one time trying a lawsuit in Nashville for Judge Langford. It was a personal injury case. I was making my closing argument to the jury, and I felt like I was doing a pretty good job. All of a sudden, right in the middle of my argument, Judge Langford said, "Peeler, are you any kin to that fellow down in Dickson that hunts doves all the time?"

I was the one! When he asked me that, I knew I wasn't making near the impression that I thought I was.

William J. Peeler, Waverly, June 14, 2001

125. "Case Dismissed for Want of Prosecution"

A number of years ago, I tried a county case where two men were building houses on shares. They were to split the profit. It was the dullest case that you can imagine. And the judge sat there and actually went to sleep during the case. The lawyer on the other side looked at me, and I said, "Wake him up."

We got through, and the judge said, "I'll take it under advisement, and you'll hear from me."

About six or eight weeks later I got a notice in the mail that the court was dismissing the case for want of prosecution. And I called the lawyer on the other side and said to him, "Roger, you know this *Haines v. Hogue* that we tried about six or seven weeks ago. I hate to tell you, but I thought you did try a pretty sorry lawsuit."

"What in the hell do you mean, sorry?"

I said, "No, no. I'm on your side Roger. I don't think it was bad enough that it ought to be dismissed for want of prosecution. You did try."

He sort of yelled, said, "What are you talking about?"

I said, "The court just dismissed your case for want of prosecution."

He said, "The hell you say!"

So he filed a motion that it had been heard and requested the court to rule the decision. And to this day, the case has never been decided.

I could care less, as I was defending in this case.

F. Evans Harvill, Clarksville, July 3, 2001

126. "Uncontested Divorce Case"

I remember the story about this one attorney that walked into my uncle's court, who was judge. The docket was never specifically set, so just as it came your turn, you just got up. This fellow got up and said, "Your Honor, I'm here this morning on an uncontested, no-fault divorce."

Because it's kind of a redundancy to say, "Uncontested, no-fault divorce," my uncle looked at him and said, "Well, Bill, do you think you'll win?"

I don't think the fellow had anything to say in response to that question. My uncle could be quite humorous at times.

James H. Bradberry, Dresden, June 7, 2001

127. "First Employment as a Lawyer"

I went on the GI Bill to law school, then when I got out of school I didn't have anything, but I didn't owe any money either. That made a big difference. Well, I was trying to find a place to start practicing law. I interviewed around, but nobody hired lawyers in those days. But I talked with a man whose name was Billy Daniel, who was ten years my senior. His father, grandfather, and his uncle had all been lawyers. The Daniels were a legacy of lawyers in Montgomery County.

Billy called me one day and said, "Evans, come back up. I want to talk with you again."

I walked in, said, "Yessir, Mr. Daniel."

He said, "Now, that office right there is vacant. I'll let you have it, and I won't charge you any rent. Whoever comes in the office and calls for a lawyer, or calls for me is mine. If they come in and call for you, it can be yours. My secretary will help you when she's not busy on my stuff, but that's not going to be very often. I will expect you to help me on anything I want help on without compensation if you are not busy on your own things. And you're not going to be busy. And I want you to understand one thing. Those steps you came up, and that hall you came down, runs both ways, and if either one of us gets the least bit dissatisfied, my advice is, don't let that door hit you in the butt as you go out."

I reached over and shook his hands. I said, "Mr. Daniels, that sure sounds like a good deal to me." Well, thirty-two years later, he retired. The second year, we became partners, and we had three or four other lawyers in the firm before we ever reduced anything to writing. It was all done on a handshake. You could do things like that in those days.

F. Evans Harvill, Clarksville, July 3, 2001

128. "Lawyer's First Appearance in Court"

My first case that I remember in front of the general sessions judge— that's the small court, a misdemeanor court basically, or bind-over court. They had a substitute judge that day. He's dead now but was a wonderful man. His name was Jimmy Thompson. He was city judge. He practiced next to my office with an old curmudgeon-type judge named Templeton. We all called him Temp.

Temp was out that day, so I had this first case in general sessions court. It was a nonjury hearing. I was fresh out of law school. My client was charged with some little small crime. I stood up and made this compassionate argument, and the judge said, "Mr. Fraley, approach the bench." When I approached it, he said, "You are doing a wonderful job arguing your case, but this is a criminal case. You are arguing the civil…

I said, "Yeah, Judge, you've got to really help me because this is my first case and you know what they say, 'You've got to win your first one, or it's bad luck for the rest of your career.'"

He said, "If you'll just shut up, I'll take care of the rest."

I said, "Yes sir," and I stepped back, then he dismissed the case for me. So I won my first case, thanks to a compassionate judge.

Raymond Fraley, Fayetteville, September 20, 2001

129. "GENERAL COURT SESSIONS BACK THEN"

TLH

A judge in Lake County that I once practiced before in court didn't use a gavel. He literally used a fly swatter with which to rule. He would slap the fly swatter down on the bench, and he'd say, "Now, Dave, or, John," and you knew that the first name he called out would usually be the winner, because he would go back and forth, and you knew who'd won the case.

It wouldn't be uncommon when you were making this brilliant argument to the judge that all of a sudden the phone on his desk would ring, and he'd pick it up and say, "Yeah, I need those tires rotated by noon. Do you think you can get me those tires fixed by then?" That was the kind of general sessions court like it used to be. It was the kind of court that was closest to the people.

That same judge also had a small dog that set next to him. And I set down in the seat one time, and the dog tried to bite me. So you've got to watch where you set in the general session courtroom sometimes, because the seat may sometimes be occupied by the judge's best friend—his dog.

David G. Hayes, Jackson, August 8, 2001

130. "SERVING REGULAR PEOPLE"

One of the first big cases that I ever got was the result of a horrible personal injury case in Alabama, at a place called Bobo Section Road. My client and her retarded son were hit by a bus of senior citizens. I sued the senior citizens because they almost killed her poor son. The case was settled for a lot of money, and after the case was over, I asked my client how in the world she ever found me from the Bobo Section of Alabama.

She said, "Mr. Fraley, you know that DUI case you had that dealt with Billy Bob Price?"

I said, "My Lord, that was a couple of years ago, and I lost that case."

She said, "You did?"

I said, "Yeah."

She said, "My God, you were wonderful in that court. You screamed at that judge, and that judge screamed at·you. And I said to myself, if I ever need a lawyer, I'm going to get that man right there because he is really mean."

I learned a great lesson from that. I learned that people equate lawyering not so much with skills but with being loud and abrasive sometimes, but even more importantly taking on a cause for a client. She didn't know if I won or not. She just knew that I was a zealot. So I learned from that, and to this very day, I still go to general sessions court twice a week, and I have the biggest docket. If you went to the courthouse right now and asked, "Who has the biggest docket in the general sessions court?" they would tell you me. I just take them on as clients because that's where the little guy is. And I've never forgotten that story when she told me that's why she chose me. So I thought that I'll just take that to heart, and I've always been here for regular people.

Raymond Fraley, Fayetteville, September 20, 2001

131. "OLD ENGLISH 'TETHERED ASS' STORY"

We had a general sessions judge here in Clarksville whose name was Billy Beach. He was coming off the bench but had one more case to try. He later went back and was our criminal judge and county executive and had a very distinguished career here.

We were trying an automobile accident in front of Billy. My client was from the southern part of the county; came over a roly-poly hill, and this car had been backed out of the drive and was trying to get started, and my client hit him.

The lawyer on the other side was a gentleman named Sam Boaz, who was a very dignified lawyer and a very good lawyer and went on to be a judge. He is now retired. Sam was trying to put on a little bit of show for Billy, because we were taking advantage of this being his last case. In his summation, he says to the judge, "Now, Your Honor, I'd like to point out to the court the old English case of so-and-so. The facts of that case were that the plaintiff had his tethered ass in the highway, and this defendant driving his wagon and team in a reckless fashion came upon, into, and injured the Englishman's tethered ass and was held liable."

The judge was sort of snickering at him but was trying to keep a straight face. I got up and was making my response, and when I got ready to close it up, I said, "Now, Your Honor, Mr. Boaz has cited to the court this case about the Englishman's tethered ass on the highway. I have no problem with the decision as rendered at that point in time. But I can point out to the court that was in the days of animal power and low-speed vehicles and the like. I'm certain had this tethered ass case come up in court today, in a time when we've got high-speed automobiles and blind curves and blind hills, that same old English court would have held that Mr. Boaz's Englishman should have got his ass out of the road!" [Hearty laughter]

I hushed, then turned my back on the court and went back to my table and looked at the lawyer that was there with me. I said, "What did he do?"

He says, "He's halfway over the bench after you!"

After the case was over with, Judge Billy Beach says, "You'd have never done that if you hadn't known that was the last case I was going to hear. You just shouldn't have done that."

I said, "What did I say wrong, judge?" And to this day, Sam Boaz still says, "That was the darndest thing that ever happened to me in a courtroom."

F. Evans Harvill, Clarksville, July 3, 2001

132. "The Governor, Not Insane"

I've heard John Patterson, who at one time was governor of Alabama and attorney general, among other important positions, tell this three or four times. When he was governor of Alabama and was up in Cullman campaigning for reelection, he missed his caravan going back home. So, as governor, they put him on a train. He didn't realize it, but he got on the train of the insane asylum going back there. He was on the train with his deputy. They were sitting there in a seat, and the workers were checking off the names, "This is Haines, this Hodges, this is Hayes, this is Hires." They got to Patterson and said, "And you are who?"

He said, "I'm the governor of Alabama."

The fellow came right back at him in a joking way, "Sure you are!! You bet you are!!"

John tells that story that really happened. It's a jim-dandy.

David G. Hayes, Jackson, August 8, 2001

133. "When Lawyers Ask the Wrong Question"

One of the great lawyers in Tennessee who is still living in Memphis is   7L4
Frank Glankler. He had a law partner named John Heiskell, who is
now deceased. They were representing a very wealthy grocery owner
there in Memphis who was accused of murdering his wife. John Heiskell
was questioning a witness, and Frank Glankler objected. The judge
spoke up and said, "Mr. Glankler, that's your partner that you're objecting to."

Glankler said, "I still object."

Now, that's a little unusual. You usually object when it is an adver-
sary case.

Alan Highers, Jackson, August 8, 2001

134. "Two Look-Alike Lawyers"

Many years ago, two young lawyers moved to the Upper Cumberland,   TL4
and each now has a very successful career. These were John Atman,
who moved to Jamestown, and John Roberts, who moved to Livingston.
At that time, they were both sharp young men. Since they both had
very black hair and whatever, some people confused them. John Roberts was going to court in Jamestown one morning when he picked a
farmer up on the side of the road. The farmer said, "Well, John, how
do you like Jamestown?"

John said, "Well, I really like it. It's really nice."

So they talked, and it was obvious that the guy thought he was riding
with John Atman. Well, they got to the end of the destination that Roberts was going to, so he let the farmer out. Well, the farmer sort of patted
his overalls and said, "Well, what do I owe you for the ride?"

So Roberts looked at him and said, "You owe me three dollars,
and if you don't have it down to my office by nine o'clock in the morning, I'm going to sue you."

I don't know what happened the next morning, but it must have
been interesting.

John Acuff, Cookeville, November 7, 2001

135. "Judge Corrects a Lawyer"

I remember a dressing-down that Judge Morton gave to a lawyer/politician/fund-raiser. It was one of Gary Hart's people, when Gary was running for president. Every time the local lawyer, John Camp, asked the lawyer/politician a question, he got another question, or whatever. Judge Morton finally stopped it and said, "Mr. Colorado lawyer, I don't know exactly how you all do it out there, but here the lawyers ask the questions, and the witnesses answer them. Now, if you could get on with it, [go right ahead]."

John Acuff, Cookeville, November 7, 2001

136. "A Lawyer's Memory and/or His File"

We had a lawsuit where two carloads of people, both drinking, had merged at a local highway intersection. There were a whole lot of people injured, and some were killed, I think. We ultimately tried it to a verdict in circuit court. Subsequent to that, there was a bankruptcy filed, and then litigation in federal court that I was not involved in.

Each lawyer had asked me if he could look at my file, and I said, "Yes." They proceeded to look at it. It was about a four- or five-inch file. So they called me as a witness in the federal case, and I walked up there with my file, and a young lawyer from Nashville said, "Mr. Acuff, in 1973," which was about five to six years ago at that time, "did you write a letter to Mr. So-and-so, saying so-and-so?"

I said, "Counsel, I don't have a clue what letters I wrote yesterday. Both you and he have both been through my files."

Judge Morton turned to the young man, said, "Mr. Lawyer, if you have a copy of the letter, show it to Mr. Acuff." The young lawyer took the letter that was in his hand and allowed me to read it.

John Acuff, Cookeville, November 7, 2001

137. "Can We Get John Jones to Lower the Tab?"

I was in a settlement negotiation once with John Jones. A lot of lawyers were involved from a lot of different cities. A lot of money on the table. They asked me if I would make one last pitch and see if I could lower the amount [of the settlement]. John had already told them in pretty short, plain sentences that was the amount. Well, I called him, and we exchanged pleasantries for a few minutes, then I said, "John, I've talked with the defendants, and I think we could come up with X amount of dollars."

He said, "John, I don't want to be short with you, but would you please ask them what part of my demand don't they understand, because if they have somebody to call me again, it will go up."

Well, we settled the lawsuit.

John Acuff, Cookeville, November 7, 2001

138. "Judge Scares Plaintiff into Dismissing"

Recently, I was in Nashville with some younger lawyers, and we were in Judge Thomas A. Higgins's federal district court. He was always the hardest-working lawyer I knew when he was practicing. The lawsuit in front of us was a bit unusual, somebody might say not terribly serious. And the judge absolutely ate them alive!

When the case in which I was involved was called—I was defending—the plaintiff stood up and told the court he was entering a nonsuit. I've always felt that was because the judge had rattled him so bad that he just didn't want to go through that.

John Acuff, Cookeville, November 7, 2001

139. "Judge Protects Lawyer"

We've all seen cases in which a judge seems to be protecting a lawyer for one reason or another. I had one years ago where I was defending, and the plaintiff's lawyer was still suffering from the aftereffects of the fruit of the vine. At the end of the plaintiff's proof, which proved nothing, the judge said, "I am entering a mistrial. There's no way this jury could understand this case."

Well, I kindly took umbrage [offense] at having a lawsuit dismissed because the other side couldn't prove its case. But then I thought, "Well, maybe sometime it just might be my tail that is caught in the crack."

John Acuff, Cookeville, November 7, 2001

140. "Judge Favored Beautifully Dressed Women"

Judge Ingram was a great judge, serving in that capacity from 1942 to 1982. Those of us lawyers that practiced in his court really enjoyed practicing in his court. Judge Ingram had one fault, and that is if one of the parties to a lawsuit was an attractive woman, all she had to do was show up in court and she'd walk away with a farm.

I remember one personal experience I had in reference to the way he viewed these women. A lady came to see me, whose son and his girlfriend had lived together for many years without benefit of clergy, that is, they had never married. They had never had children. They just lived openly as man and wife, in a home they had built.

The boy's mother came to see me. She had given them $3,000 toward the construction of the home. They'd mortgaged the rest of it at the bank. So when they split up, although they were never married you'd have to treat that almost as if they were married insofar as the division of their assets were concerned. So the boy's mother said to me, "Look, all I want is my $3,000. I don't want any interest. I gave them the money in cash. I don't have a note; I didn't want a note. I just thought this would never happen."

And I said, "I don't think there will be any problem with that. It's in Judge Ingram's court. He's a fair man."

So I typed up a little petition to intervene, and got her in court. So we went up there the morning of the hearing. Judge Ingram was going to divvy up the assets. And for the first time, I saw this woman that her son had been living with. And one of my good friends here in town who has been practicing law for about fifty years was representing her. Buddy, he had her dressed fit to kill! When I saw her, I called my client out in the hall and said to her, "Marie, sweetheart, we've got real problems in this case."

She said, "What do you mean?"

I said, "Well, why didn't you tell me what this woman looked like?"

"Well, I didn't think it made any difference," she said.

I said, "Well, it shouldn't, but it does. But I'll tell you what I'll do, I'll do the best I can, but we've got real problems."

Well, we went into the courtroom, and Judge Ingram let us yack for about an hour, then he tapped on the desk, then said, "I've heard enough. This is marriage by estoppel—holding yourself out as husband and wife. I'm going to let this lady have this house and whatever furniture she wants in it." Then he turned to this man and said, "You can have that truck you bought, but you've got to pay for it."

I stood up and said, "Your Honor, what about my client's $3,000?"

He said, "You should have had a note Mr. Hamilton; you should have had a note."

That was the end of that case.

But Judge Ingram was a fair man, and he loved to try lawsuits. He really respected the lawyers that appeared in his court. Except for what

I've just described, you always left his court with the feeling that you've had a fair hearing, win, lose, or draw.

Jim T. Hamilton, Columbia, December 10, 2001

141. "Lawyer Visits Lawyer Friend Too Much?"

This is a story about one of our beloved legends that is no longer with us—Aaron Thompson. John Atman used to leave Jamestown on Sunday morning and go to Nashville, and he would always stop at Aaron's house in Cookeville and have a cup of coffee and read the paper. I think that Aaron thought at one point that this was a little more fellowship than he knew what to do with. He probably began acting accordingly. Supposedly, John Atman was talking to some friends of Aaron Thompson and said, "I don't know what's going on with Aaron. You know, he used to be really, really friendly, but he just doesn't seem as friendly any more. I wonder if he no longer wants me to stop and visit?"

They told him, "Don't you worry about it, he's going through some tough stuff, so he needs you to stop and visit now more than you ever did."

John Acuff, Cookeville, November 7, 2001

142. "Religious References in the Courtroom"

I remember being in the Supreme Court of Tennessee. Val Sanford, a giant of the bar in Tennessee, who died just this past year, was up arguing. The case was the issue of whether or not Tennessee could raise interest costs above what the law said, which I believe was 6 percent. Joe Henry was on the supreme court bench, and he had on his little reading glasses, and he leaned his head back and said, "Mr. Sanford, as King Agrippa said to St. Paul, 'ALMOST thou persuaded me.'"

And Val, who also had a pair of those little glasses on, turned around to the audience and said, "If we could have one more verse of 'Just as I Am,' please."

You've got to be around awhile to get by with that type humor in the courtroom.

John Acuff, Cookeville, November 7, 2001

143. "Dogs and Lawyers in Court"

There was a hospital discipline case that was appealed to the U.S. Sixth

TLH

Circuit Court years ago. I was representing the executive committee, and Jerry Jared from Cookeville was representing the city of Cookeville, or the hospital. Jerry said, "I haven't been up here, so would you lead off?"

Well, having clerked there and been there many times, I said, "Sure."

So when the case was called, I walked up to the podium, and Judge Martin said, "Mr. Acuff, isn't this really Mr. Jared's problem?"

So I kinda reluctantly said, "Well, yes, sir, I guess it is." So Jerry walked up there and just delivered a stem-winding jury speech, and they ate it up. When he got through, I stood up, and Judge Martin said, "Mr. Acuff, what do you have to add to that?"

I said, "Your Honor, not a lot, but I'd hate to come all the way to Cincinnati and not say something."

Judge Martin looked right at me and said, "Mr. Acuff, I understand, dogs and lawyers have to mark their passing. So go right ahead."

Rather meekly I made some inane remarks, then sat down.

John Acuff, Cookeville, November 7, 2001

144. "LAWYER AND CONVICT HAVE IDENTICAL NAMES"

I never will forget the first time I met Judge Frank Wilson, who was a highly respected federal district judge from Chattanooga, my home town. There was a John E. Acuff, same first name, middle initial, and last name as mine. He lived in Jasper, Tennessee, near Chattanooga, and had had interaction with law enforcement authorities on occasion. I remember once after one particular thing happened to him, there was an article about me in the Chattanooga paper, and right next to it was an article about him being convicted of counterfeiting. I then wrote a letter to the editor, which they published, saying to this man, "I'm trying to raise my children to be gentlemen. I'm trying to show them what it means to be a Christian lawyer, and they see your name and it's confusing to them. I would appreciate it if you would either clean up your act or change your name."

I didn't get a response, but the first time I met Judge Wilson, I was clerking for Judge Harry Phillips, who was chief judge of the circuit. And as I went down to welcome Judge Wilson, who was up to sit on the Sixth Circuit for a short period of time, I met his clerk, and he took me back to meet Judge Wilson. He said, "Judge Wilson, this is John Acuff."

Judge Wilson had a big smile on his face, and he said, "Oh, I know John. I sentenced him a couple of weeks ago."

John Acuff, Cookeville, November 7, 2001

145. "THE JUDGE HAS TO LISTEN"

One time as an assistant district attorney, I was in charge of cases of the court. I was settling all of my cases, and the judge in one instance said, "General, I haven't tried any cases in about two weeks. You've settled every case, and I want to go to trial."

Well, I looked at him, and I said kindly out of the corner of my eye, "Judge, you've got to pardon me, but you don't try cases. I try cases. As the judge, all you have to do is just sit there and listen. I'm the one that prepares all these cases. I put no witnesses on, and I try them."

As a result, the judge kindly chewed me out a little!

Don Dino, Memphis, January 7, 2004

146. "FRIENDLY LAWYER AND JUDGE PLAYED GAMES IN COURT"

I had a judge I was just crazy about. He was a great judge in my opinion. As a prosecutor, you become real friends with a judge, and he used to play a lot with me in the courtroom. When they would arraign an individual, he would turn to me and say, "General, what do you recommend as a bond?"

I would respond, for example, "Twenty-five thousand dollars."

He'd say, "General, $25,000 is a lot of money. Don't you realize that the bond is not punitive in nature, and that it is only to show that the defendant will show up in court? So, I think you are just too high." Then he would go ahead and set the bond for something like $1,000.

Well, in the process of arraigning other people, he'd turn to me and say, "General, what do you recommend on the bond?"

Well, I'd recommended $25,000, and he'd put it at $1,000. So this time I said, "I would recommend $1,000."

And he said, "Now, General, you know that $1,000 is not very much money for the offense this man caused. Your amount is too low in your bond recommendation, so I will set it at a higher amount."

So, no matter which way I went, he would always have sport with me, that I was either too high or too low. So, finally in the same day he turned to me and said, "General, what amount do you recommend that I should make the bond?"

I looked at him, and I had a little stool that a shorter prosecutor used to stand on because she was so short at the counsel table. So I stood up on the little stool and leaned over and said to the judge, "You're making the big bucks. You make a decision."

Well, when I said that, he thought that was very funny. Of course, we played that same game all the time!

That same judge, whenever he'd get tired in a hearing, he'd kick the bench. And every time he kicked the bench, no matter where we were and what was going on, I would holler, "Objection!"

Then he would say, "Sustained," which meant for us to move on. He was getting tired of the defense attorney dragging it out. In those days, you could play and get away with it. You can't do that now.

Don Dino, Memphis, January 7, 2004

147. "Everyday Court Sessions Back Then"

I used to have a judge that I dearly loved, and I will not mention his name. When we used to have petitions for suspended sentences, the probation report would come in, and it would tell all about the background and facts of the case. The judge got a copy, the prosecutor got a copy, and the defense got a copy. We always got those two or three days before, and we would set petitions like five, six, or seven in one day, and everybody would come in, and we would have the petitions and the judge would sustain them, or deny them, let them out, or what.

I once had this judge, and I used to go up to him and he would say, "General, what do we have this morning?" He always asked me, "What do we have?"

I'd say, "Judge, all we have is about four or five petitions for suspended sentence."

He'd say, "Yes, I am going to deny every one of those."

I'd say, "Yes, sir, I know you are, Your Honor. But let's do this. For the benefit of the defendant, and the defendant's attorney, let them put the defendant on, and his witnesses. Let the defense attorney ask him questions. I'll ask him a few questions, and after we've had a hearing, then you can deny him."

He said to me, "All right." And that's the way the judge pretty much worked. But now then, a lot of people never knew that.

Don Dino, Memphis, January 7, 2004

148. "Eating Mints in the Courtroom"

I used to have a female general sessions judge. She was a schoolteacher before she became an attorney, and she ran her courtroom kinda like a schoolteacher. She wouldn't allow anybody to chew gum or anything. You couldn't stand up; you had to sit down. So what I used to do when I was assigned to her, I always carried mints. And all the lawyers would be lined up before the judge came on the bench. So I used to go around and give each lawyer a mint. And when she came out on the bench and looked around the courtroom, they would all be sitting there smacking their lips. And she would look down, and she would say, "You know better than that." And she would chew them out and have them take their mint out of their mouth.

One time, I had a lawyer stand up and say, "General Dino gave me the mint."

I said, "Yes, Your Honor."

Then he said, "General Dino eats mints all the time. In fact, he's got one in his mouth!"

Well, I turned to the judge and said, "Yes, Your Honor, I do."

The only way I could get her without jumping on me is that I told her in these words, "Your Honor, I said I have bad breath, and I smoke. I use a mint as a medicinal purpose because I am in close proximity to these attorneys when I whisper to them, and I don't want to offend them."

When she heard what I said, she smiled and she said, "Very good." So I could use mints in her courtroom where nobody else could. She was a sweet lady.

Don Dino, Memphis, January 7, 2004

149. "Just Teasing the Judge"

Every now and then, I used to blow smoke up at judges. You have to. So with this female judge, I would purposely say, "We will reset this case to a certain date," knowing that the date I gave her would be wrong. So she could correct me and say, "No, General, the date is such and such and not when you said." She loved to do that. And I would purposely give her wrong dates so she could come back at me, and it would make her feel good.

Don Dino, Memphis, January 7, 2004

150. "Doing the Right Thing in Court"

Back a long time ago, when I used to do criminal cases, I had a guy who violated probation. He was in criminal court, and he had pretty thoroughly violated his probation. He'd quit meeting his probation officer; quit paying his probation costs; got into trouble again; got arrested for two more things.

By the time he came to me, he'd gotten his notice for violation of probation, and he straightened up his act and started going to church. We got one of the arrests cleared up, but we still had his violation of probation downtown in criminal court in front of one of the meanest judges in criminal court. This judge used to yell at people, and he was good at it. The deal was, if he were going to send you to jail, he wouldn't yell much. If he were going to put you on probation, he'd yell at you big time. He yelled at one guy so bad, the man turned around to his lawyer and said, "Could I just go to jail instead?"

That judge would just get mean and chew the heck out of folks. Well, we were in front of him, and the night before the hearing I was trying to figure out what to do. It was a tough case. My son, Nick, who now practices with me, had just been born and was still a little bitty baby. He woke up one night, and I was in charge of him. I turned on the TV, and on came Henry Fonda doing Clarence Darrow. That was a great one-man show. Clarence Darrow was the trial lawyer in the United States at the turn of the century. So, Henry Fonda was portraying Clarence Darrow as he talked about his life and his cases.

I was sitting there watching this show with my infant son on my lap. Darrow got to talking about this case in which these miners went on strike and another miner was killed during the strike. The leaders of the strike were being prosecuted under a felony murder rule for that man's death. As a result of the strike, this man died. The prosecutor was trying to convict them of the murder because they started the strike.

The final argument was, "Ladies and gentlemen, the easy thing to do is to hold these men's strange last names against them. The easy thing to do is to hold their origins from a far country against them. The easy thing to do is to be overcome by pity over the death of that miner and take it out on these men. But ladies and gentlemen, you didn't sign up to do the easy things; you signed up to do the right thing."

About that time, my baby Nick started crying, so I had to get up, take care of him. I finally got my son to bed, but by then the show was over. I didn't care because I knew what I was going to do the next day.

I got up in front of the mean judge and said, "Your Honor, the easy thing to do is to see that this man didn't pay his probation fee. This man has turned himself in. He's found Jesus, and he's been a good family man since then. Your Honor, you're not here to do the easy thing; you're here to do the right thing. So that's what we have to do, not the easy thing but the right thing."

You couldn't hear a sound in court. And as I turned around, I found out why. Veins were bulging out of the judge's forehead—just about to leap right out of his forehead. His face was crimson, and he shook so hard he could not speak. When he finally recovered his voice, he said, "The easy thing is sending your client to jail, Mr. Rice. The hard thing I'm trying to figure out right now is whether I can send you to jail with your client."

Well, I was upset for years and years about that, and I used to tell that story when I did my seminar about how just because something works for one lawyer doesn't mean it would work for another lawyer. One day, a seminar attendee came up to me after the program and said, "You didn't see the end of that program, did you?"

I said, "No, why?"

She said, "Clarence Darrow lost with that argument, too."

Larry Rice, Memphis, January 7, 2004

151. "Some Men Need Killing"

I've heard this story many times, but the first time I heard it was about a judge up in the country here in Tennessee. But as I have gone around the country lecturing, I have heard it over and over about "a judge up in the country" in several different states. The story is told about this judge who is out riding his circuit, which means he holds court in one place, and may not be back in that place for a month or two.

So this up-in-the-country judge comes into court and starts calling his docket. A man is charged with being a horse thief, and he stands up in front of the judge, and the judge says, "Mister, you can either hire you a lawyer, or you can plead guilty or innocent today. What do you want to do?"

The man says, "Well, I want to hire me a lawyer."

The judge says, "Wise choice. I'll be back in sixty days. You're set on March 7. I'll see you then."

The man says, "Okay," and sits down in the courtroom.

Then this other man stands up in front of the judge with his lawyer. The lawyer announces, "Your Honor, the district attorney and I worked out an agreement in this case where Sam Jones was killed and, according to the agreement subject to Your Honor's approval, my client is going to be placed on probation for the next five years."

The judge says, "Fine, I approve that. Guilty plea accepted, so you all can go on now."

Well, at that point, the horse thief in the back of the courtroom is thinking, "Oh, here's this man, and he's killed somebody. He gets probation, and all I did was steal a horse."

So he raises his hand and says, "Your Honor, I want to change my plea."

He strolls up in front of the judge. The judge says, "Are you sure you want to change your plea? You don't have a lawyer."

The man says, "I'm sure, judge. I submit myself to you for sentencing."

The judge looks at him and says, "All right. You're guilty of stealing that horse?"   .

"Yes, sir, I am."

The judge says, "Bailiff, take this man away to the penitentiary. He's going to serve two years."

The man looks at the judge awestruck and says, "Judge, how can you do that? That man killed somebody, and he got probation. All I did was steal a horse, and you're going to give me two years in prison."

Judge looks at him and says, "Sir, there's some men in this county that need killing; there's absolutely no horses that need stealing."

Larry Rice, Memphis, January 4, 2004

152. "GOOD TO THE LAST HILLDROP"

Before I was a lawyer, I was a newspaper reporter, and for slightly more than a year I covered the United States District Court in Nashville. Judge Frank Gray Jr. was the only district court judge hearing cases during 1970. He was a little bitty guy. He had been Kennedy's campaign manager in the 1960 election. Tennessee went Democrat, and that's how he got his appointment to the federal bench.

He was not thought of as a great jurist when he was elevated to the bench. He was thought of as what he had been, the mayor of Franklin, Tennessee. However, he proved to be a very fine judge and a wonderful storyteller. There are stories in Tennessee known as Hilldrop stories. Lawyer Hilldrop was a real person, and Judge Gray told Hilldrop stories because he had known lawyer Hilldrop, who apparently practiced in the courts of Williamson County, among others. Judge Gray said Hilldrop would come to work in the morning with the goal of making fifty dollars. If Hilldrop opened the morning mail and there was a check in there for fifty dollars, he had done his day's work and he would go home. He is legendary in Tennessee for his delaying tactics. Even today, lawyers honor his memory by pretending he wrote a text entitled "Hilldrop on Continuances."

Judge Gray remembered seeing Hilldrop in the clerk's office of the Williamson County Criminal Court after a pretty hotly contested murder trial one afternoon. Hilldrop had defended and lost. Judge Gray, who was also a lawyer, not a judge, at the time, was wandering through the office and heard Hilldrop on the phone talking to his wife. They were making a grocery list. Judge Gray swore that he heard Hilldrop say, "A head of lettuce, yeah; a quart of milk, yeah; get some broccoli if it looks nice; a pound and a half of ground round, make it lean. All right. Oh, him? He got the chair. Anything else you need, dear?"

"Him" was his client. "The chair" meant the sentence was death by electrocution.

John C. McLemore, Nashville, September 17, 2002

153. "The Wheels of Justice"

This story has profanity in it but is no good without profanity. It is a wonderful story because it is a true story. I was a newspaper reporter for the *Nashville Banner*, covering the federal courts in the 1970s. One afternoon I was standing in the clerk's office when in came a Vanderbilt Law School professor and a young law student, Ashley Wiltshire.

Ashley wanted to file a lawsuit against Ms. Mary Farrell, the Davidson County registrar. She was in charge of the voting rolls. In his lawsuit he accused her of being prejudiced against Vanderbilt University students. He alleged she considered all of them "transients" and refused to register them to vote.

Judge Frank Gray Jr., who was U.S. district judge at the time, was a pretty feisty guy. There was a special rule in the federal court at that time. Vanderbilt law students could practice before the court if they had the supervision of a faculty member. Ashley had a professor to sponsor him, and he was asking for an immediate injunction directing Ms. Mary Farrell to cease and desist for refusing to register Vanderbilt students to vote.

I said to myself that this is going to be a lot of fun.

I knew Judge Gray pretty well. He was short on patience, and I calculated it would not take long for him to get fed up with this green law student. Sparks were going to fly, and I did not want to miss a minute of this performance. When the clerk said Judge Gray had agreed to conduct an immediate hearing, I rushed into the courtroom.

The law professor introduced Ashley Wiltshire to the court. Judge Gray looked down at Ashley and very nicely, very gentlemanly, welcomed him to the U.S. District Court, "We're so glad that you're taking this opportunity to practice before us." I knew that this was just a mild wind before the storm. The Frank Gray Jr. I covered every day had a short fuse. An inexperienced law student like young Wiltshire was just the man to light it.

"I understand you have a witness, Mr. Wiltshire," Judge Gray said like a cat charming a canary.

"Yes, sir, I'd like to call Dr. Jones," Wiltshire replied, eager to proceed.

This doctor did not have on a suit and tie; he was dressed like a doctor. He had on green jumpsuit-type clothing. It was obvious he had come straight from the hospital.

Judge Gray told the bailiff to show him around to the witness stand and administer the oath. The doctor was sworn in, and Wiltshire began his line of questioning. This poor student doesn't realize he is walking in a minefield, I thought to myself. "State your name," Wiltshire began. "Could you tell the court your background?"

The doctor did not require a great deal of direction from Wiltshire. He just told his story. "I grew up in Kentucky, and I came to Vanderbilt as an undergraduate student about eight or nine years ago."

"Did anything happen while you were an undergraduate student at Vanderbilt which changed your life?" Wiltshire asked.

"Yes, during my sophomore year, my parents were killed in an automobile accident back home."

Then Judge Gray, wanting to get to the meat, jumped in with a question, "What did you do?"

"I stayed at Vanderbilt and continued to go to school there. But more than that, I stayed there. I got summer jobs at Vanderbilt. I lived in dorms at Vanderbilt. I lived on campus not just during school year but all year long. I cut grass in the summer and did anything I could do to make a little money."

"Where did you go to medical school?" Wiltshire asked.

"Vanderbilt."

"Now, when you reached voting age, did you attempt to register to vote in Davidson County?"

"Oh, yes," the doctor said. "When I became eighteen years old, which was also during my sophomore year, I went down to Ms. Mary Farrell's office and asked her to allow me to register to vote. Now, I did that for a specific reason. My father had been involved in Kentucky politics, and he just thought that the democratic system was the most wonderful thing in the world, and that a man's right to vote was something that was sacred to him. I went the first time on my father's birthday, I believe."

"Were you successful?" Wiltshire continued.

"No, I wasn't. She said I was a transient and that I could not register to vote," the doctor explained.

"Did you ever try again?"

"Yes, every year on my father's birthday I would go down and attempt to register to vote," the doctor said.

"Have you ever been successful?" Ashley asked.

"No."

"How long were you in medical school at Vanderbilt?" Wiltshire asked.

"Four years."

"Where did you do your internship?" Wiltshire continued.

"At Vanderbilt."

"How long did that take?"

"Oh, a year or so," the doctor said.

"Did you attempt to register to vote that year?"

"Oh, yes, every year," the doctor said.

"Where do you live?"

"I continue to live on campus. As a matter of fact, I have never moved off the Vanderbilt campus since my sophomore year. I have always lived on campus. Even when I was in medical school, and an intern, I found jobs that would pay me something. I was a dorm daddy, or supervisor, while I was in medical school. I lived in a dorm."

"What is your job now?" Wiltshire asked.

"I am chief resident of such and such a service at Vanderbilt Hospital."

"Where do you live?" Wiltshire asked.

"I live in the married quarters over here on Vanderbilt campus."

"Do you continue to attempt to register to vote?"

"Oh, yes."

"How old are you?"

He said twenty-six or twenty-seven, something like that. Then Judge Gray, obviously agitated, jumped back in, "Why can't you register to vote?"

"Ms. Mary Farrell tells me every time she sees my address that I live on Vanderbilt campus, that I am a transient and I can't register to vote," the doctor said.

That was the end of the proof. "Excuse me, we'll take a recess at this time," Judge Gray said and left the bench.

Judge Gray had very specific rules about the way he conducted himself in chambers, especially in dealing with the press. If he was to be quoted, I had to make an appointment with his secretary and meet with him in his office while he was sitting behind his desk and I was sitting in front of his desk. That was the rule. But I was free to roam around his court chambers and listen to anything I wanted to listen to within earshot and participate in any conversation, as long as I didn't quote anything that was said.

So, I thought to myself, something was about to happen behind the scenes. Judge Gray had left the bench for some reason, maybe just to look at a law book, but I didn't think that's the case. I ran out the doors of the courtroom, down the hallway to Judge Gray's chambers, stepped into his law clerk's office, and waited.

William Lamar Newport was Judge Gray's law clerk at that time, and he was seated at a typewriter typing up some decision they were working on. Judge Gray, with his robe on his shoulders like a cape, came to the door between the law clerk's office and his secretary's office. He looked at us and shouted, "Newport, I have just heard the goddamnedest testimony you can imagine! There is a young lawyer in my courtroom who has presented a doctor who has lived on the Vanderbilt campus for about ten years and has been refused the right to vote by Ms. Mary Farrell because she thinks he is a transient!"

Newport slowly turned around in this chair and looked at Judge Gray and said, "Yeah, that sounds about right. Do you remember the day you came out to Vanderbilt and picked Sarah [his wife] and me up to take us to dinner to celebrate my new job as your law clerk?"

"Yes, I remember that," Judge Gray said with a look like "What does that have to do with the price of eggs?"

"That was the day we knew we were finally going to move off campus and find a place to live in Nashville," Newport explained very calmly. "I had a little time that afternoon before you arrived. I went down to Ms. Mary Farrell's office and tried to register to vote. She turned me down because I was a transient."

Judge Gray's jaw dropped. "God damn!" he yelled aloud and swirled on one foot, his robe furling out behind him like Batman. As he walked out the door back toward his chambers and the bench, we heard him loud and clear: "I'm going to fix this shit!" And he did.

John C. McLemore, Nashville, September 17, 2002

154. "JUDGE KNOWS IT ALL"

I had this DUI case in Gainesboro, and we were there in general sessions court. I announced to the court that we would like a preliminary hearing to see if there is probable cause to bind this man over to the grand jury. Well, Judge Anderson is notorious about maybe knowing a little more about the case before it gets to court. And he stayed in the courthouse all the time and would hear everything about the case before it went to court.

I said, "Judge, that's a preliminary hearing on this DUI case."

Well, he starts to go through it, so he pulls out the warrant and reads it. Then he pulls out what is apparently the blood test. He looks at the blood test results, then looks at me as if I'm the utter moron of the world and says, "Have you seen this blood test?"

I said, "Yes, I have, Judge, but I still think we're entitled to our hearing."

"Well, whatever."

Of course, my client was bound to the grand jury, and I knew what the result would be, but that was it.

I think Anderson is the one who listened to a particular testimony in another case, then commented that's not the way he had heard it. He always knew more about the case than the state attorney, the state's witnesses, the defense, and the defense attorney, because he would call around to find out exactly what had happened. He could give you a summary of the case. You didn't need to try it, just say, "How have you heard it, Judge?"

James White Jr., Celina, August 27, 2002
(final paragraph stated by Bruce E. Myers, Livingston)

155. "PUBLIC ATTITUDES TOWARD CRIMINAL JUDGE"

I remember something that happened when I was teaching at Vines Ridge Elementary School, between my college and law school days. My uncle, Hillard Roberts, was the criminal judge back then. And all the people up in the mountains around the coal-mining area always called him Hillary Roberts.

One day, two or three big roughneck guys took the balls away from the kids that were playing out on the playground at the school where I was teaching. It was a one-teacher school.

I would go out there and try to get these fellows to let my kids play with the balls, and to go on about their business. I asked them to leave the balls on the porch there at the school, so the kids could come back to play if they wanted to.

One of these big roughneck fellows looked at me and said, "What is your name?"

I said, "John Roberts."

Then he asked me, "Are you any kin to that Hillary Roberts?"

I said, "Yes, he's my uncle."

Then he said, "Well, he put me in the penitentiary."

I thought for a minute, then responded, "Well, he's a very distant uncle!" [Laughter]

John M. Roberts, Livingston, August 27, 2002

156. "Drinking the Night before a Court Case"

Judge Hillard Roberts was a super Christian. He wanted John Hunter Smith to ride with him as company to Nashville to argue a case before the court of appeals. They stayed in some little hotel in downtown Nashville. Judge Roberts had a little sleeping gown and a funny hat that he wore when he went to bed.

John Hunter could not see just going to bed in the big city at seven thirty or eight o'clock that night. There was a little honky-tonkying to be done, and he wanted to do some of that. So he said, "Well, Judge, you go on to bed. I'm going to get a coffee, and I'll be back in a little while."

Well, at five or six o'clock the next morning, there was some rapping on the door. Of course, Judge Roberts wakes up with a sleepy look in his eyes that looks terrible. He slips the door open, and there's John Hunter, not drunk but pretty close to being drunk. Judge Roberts so eloquently says in a squeaky, sleepy voice, "How was your coffee, John Hunter?" [Laughter]

When they get to the court of appeals, John Hunter has got the shakes and is sweating profusely and looks real bad. The court calls the case in which Judge Roberts is involved. Judge Roberts stands up and says, "If it please the court, let me introduce my young friend, John Hunter Smith, recently admitted to the Overton County Bar, who will be arguing the case for our side." [Hearty laughter]

Bruce E. Myers, Livingston, August 27, 2002

157. "JUDGE ARRESTED FOR SPEEDING"

Howard Phillips was the chief Sixth Circuit judge. He had a daughter who was in school at the University of Tennessee, Knoxville. During the construction of I-40 in the Kingston, Tennessee, area, they would open a portion of it, then they would close it. They had barrels all around, along with all the other stuff. Judge Phillips was racing to Knoxville late to pick up his daughter. Lieutenant Stinnett of the Roane County police force stops the good judge for speeding. He calls someone to tow the car and carries the judge to jail.

I can't remember the sheriff's name, but he was sitting in the kitchen eating chicken and dumplings, which was his favorite meal. He did not want to be disturbed by Stinnett or any other person. He is hearing Stinnett question this gentleman, and the gentleman says, "My name is Harry Phillips. I am the chief judge of the United States Sixth Circuit Court of Appeals in Cincinnati.

The sheriff bellows out, "Goddamn it, Stinnett, if you've gotten us sued in federal court again, I'm going to kill you."

Bruce E. Myers, Livingston, August 27, 2002

158. "JUDGE SUPPORTS YOUNG TRICKSTER"

I was the general sessions judge here for several years, 1974–82. I'm the only general sessions judge this community has ever had who could read and write, or knew something about the law, or the Constitution.

Well, Billy Abbott was sort of a thorn in one side. He never had a driver's license, and it could be because maybe the sheriff didn't like him. The sheriff brought him in frequently due to the fact that Billy did not have a permit to drive a vehicle. Finally, I decided that I'd had about all of Billy that I could tolerate, so I told him that in order to get out of jail, violating every right the young man had, he was going to have to sell his vehicle.

I had not been back to my office more than fifteen minutes after court when some deputy calls me and says, "Judge, Billy sold his car. Can he go?"

I said, "Yes, that was the deal." Then I made the fatal mistake of asking the deputy to whom he had sold the car.

The deputy said, "Why, his mother!"

I said, "Well, the little rascal tricked me, but that was our deal, do turn him loose. Let him go."

Bruce E. Myers, Livingston, August 27, 2002

159. "Judge Wants to Testify"

Garland Anderson over here in Jackson County was one of the funniest general sessions judges around. I was hired to represent this poor young man in Jackson County who was charged with driving under the influence. The case was called in court, and Garland had written the warrant. So being the great jurist I am, I said, "Well, Judge, I guess you'll just have to recuse yourself. Since you've written the warrant, you've already found probable cause in this case, and that would not be in my client's best interest."

Garland kinda stickered up a little bit, not too happy with my remarks. He turned around to the sheriff and said, "I think he's right, Mr. Sheriff, let *me* be your first witness." [Laughter]

Bruce E. Myers, Livingston, August 27, 2002

160. "Judge Fines Himself"

My husband, Mack, who is also an attorney, tells about a Judge Crawford over in Blount County, whom he used to practice in front of all the time. Judge Crawford was very no-nonsense, very rule-bound, and all those good things. One day, Judge Crawford was late to court, and he found himself to be in contempt of court, so he fined himself fifty dollars, which he later paid tender to the clerk.

See, he walked in, said, "I apologize for being late, and I'm going to enter a fine on the record that the judge is in contempt of his own court and is assessed a fifty-dollar fine." And he paid it!

You don't hear of that too often. A lot of time the judges will make you wait. You're on their time, see, and you can't say a word about it.

Sarah Cripps, Smithville, May 8, 2001

161. "Women in Law School Back Then"

When I was a female student in law school, it was quite interesting and very challenging. A lot of the fellows had been in the military and were back in school. So, really I like to think and still say it was like being in the family. We went to school together from August 1946 to August '48. We went summer and winter all the way through. I always respected the men and felt like they respected me. I don't think

I was ever discriminated against, and I certainly tried not to discriminate against them!

My advice for young women starting to law school now is to always wear the same size hat, regardless of whether you're young or old; never get the big head; try to be yourself. A lot of us used the advice of my father. As far as men are concerned, he always said, "Try to listen to them, do your best to listen without interruption, and if they have an idea, listen. And if you don't agree with them, just try to present yourself so maybe someday, or someway, you can put them back into your thoughts and the way you are thinking."

It's good to have missions and goals, and that's really what life is all about. But I also feel that we've got to realize that since women are now almost in the majority, not only in law but in many other phases of life, that to present yourself well, try to be understanding and compassionate in society. That applies to all of us, whether it's the law or anything else.

Shirley B. Underwood, Johnson City, September 25, 1998,
provided by the Tennessee Bar Foundation, Nashville

162. "Classmate's Campaign"

Bill Russell was one of my classmates, and here's a story about him. He never did move up to be a federal judge as he really wanted to be, and I'm sorry. Anyhow, Bill came up in our neck of the woods seeking reelection to the court of state appeals. He stayed a couple of nights at home with my husband and me. I went out campaigning with him up in Johnson County, which is probably the most Republican part of the state then, and I think still is.

We went over there, and I took a bunch of cards, and I went over to ask some man who was working in a ditch if he'd vote for my friend and law school classmate, Bill Russell, for reelection to the Criminal Court of Appeals of Tennessee.

The man looked up at me and said, "Well, is he a Republican?"

I said, "Sir, I'm not sure what he is, but he is an American, and I want you to vote for him."

I don't know what ever happened with the man, but I just thought it was very interesting that he would ask that.

Shirley B. Underwood, Johnson City, September 25, 1998,
provided by the Tennessee Bar Foundation, Nashville

163. "Serving as Judge Ralston's Secretary"

I took the bar exam after my husband and I married, and we then moved to Marion County and lived in South Pittsburg. When we moved there, we were very short of funds because my husband was in his second year of practicing law with this firm. The senior member of the firm certainly didn't believe in paying much money to the junior partners. So I personally did not have a job. I had been there about two months when my husband came home one day. I was reading the paper. That's about all there was to do. I'd read the paper and walk up and down the street. I was really wanting to work. My husband said to me, "Well, Judge Ralston's secretary was at work last night, but today she's not at work. She left with her boyfriend."

He went on to say that the judge was desperate in need for a secretary. The judge was about seventy-five and still had a pretty good practice. They had two offices, one of which was in Jasper where my husband was located, and the judge's office was in South Pittsburg.

Judge Ralston had been the presiding judge of what we refer to as the [Scopes] monkey trial—evolutionary trial—up in Dayton, Rhea County, in 1925. He was the circuit judge and presided over that case. That was probably the high point of his whole life. He was a real celebrity but was defeated when he ran for the circuit judge's office. He came back into the practice of law. He was a well-known lawyer before he became judge, and he had a very distinguished practice from 1925 to 1950. During that time he acquired a lot of property. He was generally thought of as being the richest man in the county, or at least one of them, and he represented the people who could afford to pay a lawyer. But he also represented people who couldn't. He was also counsel for the Tennessee Coal Iron and Railroad Company, and that was the last case he ended on. And that was the last case I worked with him on. By that time, I had passed the bar and had become a colleague, and we really signed off on the same page.

When I went to work for him as his secretary that first day, I went down to see him to get a job. I just wanted a job. I had not passed the bar at that time. I just wanted something to do. He asked me if I could type. I said that I'd had typing in high school and that I could, but actually I couldn't type. I could get the paper in the machine, and I had the rudiments of typing. Fortunately, he didn't ask me how fast I could type.

One of the things we talked about was what he would pay me. He asked me what I would need to have, so I asked, "Well, what did you pay your last secretary?"

He said, "Well, $125 a month."

I said, "Well, I'll work for that."

He said that she had worked there for several years before she made that much money, and that would be all I could ever make. He would never pay more than that amount per month.

I said, "Well, if that's all I'm going to ever make, I just might as well start with that."

So we got along very well. Judge Ralston was well recognized. People in town looked with some awe up to him. He wore beautiful tailored suits, stiff starched collars that had to be attached to his shirts. He wore black Stetson hats. He drove an old Chevrolet car, but his wife drove the biggest, blackest, longest Buick in town. So everybody knew Judge Ralston. I worked for him for two years. I'm sure I would not have passed the bar had it not been for Judge Ralston. When we were not busy, he had a room that he didn't use very much, but he had a really nice office in there, so in case he wanted to impress clients, he would take them in that office. And he would make me go back to that room so he could talk to me about what I needed to know on the bar exam. He was very supportive, very encouraging.

Claude G. Swafford, Jasper, June 8, 2001,
provided by the Tennessee Bar Foundation, Nashville

164. "Elderly Man's Commentary in Court"

I remember trying a railroad case against attorney Thad Herndon in front of Judge Taylor down in federal court in Greeneville. It was a difficult case. Two children got knocked off the trestle and killed by the train. We never could get the train speeding, so we were latching on to almost anything. Well, they had a greaser, which is an instrument of a railroad track that they used. They'd put grease on the train car wheels to cut down on the wear and tear. We found it about two miles upstream from the bridge, and I thought, "Boy, if we can get that jury believing they greased these wheels!"

So, I started talking about the greaser, and Thad kept blocking me pretty well, but I was beginning to get a little of that in there, and I got a picture of it in there. There was an older gentleman sitting there at the table, and when the judge let that picture go in, then the old fellow said, "If you don't stop him, Thad, he'll have that train skidding all the way from Bluff City to Knoxville."

That man talked loud. The jury heard him; the judge heard him; the whole courtroom heard him. But he put into proof things I couldn't get into proof. He said exactly what I would like to have said. So you get some unusual help along the way, and we've laughed about that through the years.

Martin Lacy West, Kingsport, August 10, 2001,
provided by the Tennessee Bar Foundation, Nashville

165. "LADY JUROR OVERWHELMED"

Walter Garland was a very dignified man and a very good judge. And Bob Green over in Johnson City can really work on you when he's hitting on all fours. We were trying a jury case down in Jonesboro, and Bob had absolutely ruptured me. He'd whip me up one side and down the other in that courtroom. And it was time for me and my argument. And I knew if I was going to save that case, I had to do it then. So I put on a show!

I was begging and pleading and almost down on my knees trying to convince that jury. And all of a sudden, a woman juror threw her pocketbook straight up in the air and yelled out, "I can't stand it. I can't stand it. I'm going home." And sure enough, she came out of that jury box, picked up her pocketbook, and out the door she went. [Laughter]

Well, that's a hard way to get a mistrial, but I sure was glad to get that one. [Laughter]

And as I said, Judge Garland was always very formal. He was so shocked that he looked down and said, "Well, boys, what are we going to do?"

Martin Lacy West, Kingsport, August 10, 2001,
provided by the Tennessee Bar Foundation, Nashville

166. "TRIP TO AUSTRALIA AND NEW ZEALAND"

There's a great story about the trip taken by the International Academy of Trial Lawyers. When I was president, we went to Australia and New Zealand. The United States ambassador invited us to come by for a reception and so forth. Then after we did Australia and the outback and other places, we went over to New Zealand, a charming, delightful place. It's not next door to Australia but is somewhere up the ocean. That's where they invented the bungee jump.

An International Academy of Trial Lawyers is heavily populated by plaintiff lawyers, which means they have a lot of money as opposed to defense lawyers. Well, when we got to the bungee jump, over a great gorge there was a tumbling river underneath it, and with a spectator's platform. That's where you do the bungee jump. I've got a picture of that.

The story is told that my Jean was there with the spectators and all the other members of the academy, and I'm up there getting ready to bungee jump, which is a piece of cake for me, an old ex-paratrooper. They saw Jean wiping her eyes, so one of the ladies walked up and said, "Jean, don't be upset. I'm sure he's going to be all right."

Jean is reported to have replied, "You don't understand."

Her friend, who was trying to comfort and reassure her, said, "What do you mean, I don't understand?"

Jean said, "I am not weeping because of him killing himself, but because the old fool forgot to renew a life insurance policy before we came on this trip."

That's a true story.

Foster D. Arnett, Knoxville, July 21, 1999,
provided by the Tennessee Bar Foundation, Nashville

167. "The Uncle Lem Story"

Uncle Lem Owenby was born and reared in the Great Smoky Mountains, just north of the cottages at Elkmont, Tennessee. He was a mountaineer from the word go.

About twenty or twenty-five years ago, or whenever it was, the Sixth Circuit Judicial Conference—Ohio, Kentucky, Tennessee, and Michigan—was being held at Gatlinburg. That involved 170 or thereabouts federal judges, magistrates, U.S. district judges, court of appeals, and supreme court justices, at least one. I've been a life member for many, many years.

We were meeting up there, and I had been invited to host Potter Stewart and someone else. Stewart had been on the U.S. Supreme Court. I approached them and said, "Gentlemen, Thursday afternoon in this conference is an open date. It is my responsibility to look after you, and I'd just like to throw out an idea. Would you and your ladies like to go up to Elkmont, Tennessee, where the seeds out of the Great Smoky Mountains derived? Would you like to go up there and visit around?"

They said, "That sounds great." So Jean and I and the two justices and their wives got in the car in Gatlinburg and went up to our cabin at

Elkmont and had a toddy or two and stood out on the deck over the creek as it was tumbling down. Then we got ready to go back to Gatlinburg, where they were going to have a big dinner that night. As we got ready to leave the cabin, I said, "Gentlemen and ladies, one last thing before we go back to Gatlinburg to the conference. There is an old man who is in his nineties, Uncle Lem Owenby, who is one of the original park people, and the last member of the park denizens who is permitted to live in the park. He's got his beehives up there. Would you like to go up and meet him?"

They said, "Sure."

I never will forget, Potter Stewart had on some sort of crazy darn kid T-shirt. So we got up on the outside of Uncle Lem Owenby's cabin, on which the word "modest" is an exaggeration. It was just a tiny little place with a little, narrow porch. I knocked on the door, and although it was in June, I could just visualize Uncle Lem sitting down in there with his hat pulled down over his ears, smoking a corncob pipe.

I knocked on the door, and he said, "Who's that?"

I said, "Foster."

"What do you want?"

I said, "I want to see you."

"Why do you want to see me?"

"Well, because I have some friends here that I would like for you to meet, and them to meet you."

He asked, "Who are these folks?"

So I told him the names of the two United States Supreme Court justices.

Then he said, "Them fellers from Washington?"

I said, "Yes, sir."

He said, "Tell them to go back home. I ain't got no use for them and never did have. I'm not coming out." And he didn't.

For years after that, we'd get Christmas cards from those justices, saying, "Tell Uncle Lem hello."

They said, "We're not used to being treated this way. It's very wholesome and refreshing."

Foster D. Arnett, Knoxville, July 21, 1999,
provided by the Tennessee Bar Foundation, Nashville

168. "Taking a Drink of Moonshine Whiskey"

Senator McCarthy was making waves all over the country. This is a story about his first appearance in Jefferson County, Tennessee's political gathering. We had set up the proceedings to be at the football field in Dandridge, Tennessee, I believe at two o'clock in the afternoon. We were to pick him up at the airport in Knoxville at eleven. We did, and we were taking him to Swann's Millstone Grill, which was a real fancy restaurant for our county. It was on Douglas Lake. The restaurant was being operated by Alfred Swann III and his brother-in-law. They lived right next door to the restaurant.

So we took the senator into the restaurant and sat down. They came around to take our order, and the senator looked up and said, "Don't you have a drink?"

That kindly stunned all of us. He went on to say, "I've got to have a drink."

I didn't know what we were going to do, but Alfred Swann's brother-in-law, Willard Carter, spoke up and said, "Well, I've got something right over here in the house. We'll just go over."

So we excused ourselves from the table and went over to his home. When we got there, Joe McCarthy said, "I want a drink."

Carter said, "Well, the only thing I've got is moonshine."

Joe said, "What's wrong with that?"

Carter reached up there and got a quart jar and set it down. He handed Joe a glass that held eight to ten ounces, then he poured the glass full. Joe, or Senator McCarthy, turned it up, never batted an eye, and just drank it right on down like we drink water. He got up and said, "Let's go."

We went back over and ate lunch, then Joe went on and made the darndest speech you ever heard. You couldn't tell that he'd had anything!

Knowing the Swanns, the moonshine they had had to be good.

Chester S. Rainwater Jr., Knoxville, July 24, 2000,
provided by the Tennessee Bar Foundation, Nashville

169. "Judge Almost Elected as Bishop"

I suppose the most memorable case I had around 1950 was about the call Frank Clement, who was later elected governor, got from a friend one day. The friend told him he wanted him to talk with this woman, Bishop Mattie Lou Jewell, the true chief overseer of the "House of God, Which Is the Church of the Living God, and the Pillar and Ground of the Truth without Controversy," which comes from a passage in First

Timothy. Bishop Jewell was an interesting person, and I thought we could help her as we needed the money.

She'd been involved in litigation since 1933, litigation over who had the right to control the holy ground of the church, located on Hyman Street in Nashville. I could talk for two hours about this case without stopping. But I will tell about the fee.

Frank Clement and I had discussed what we ought to charge her. We were going to bring a case in the federal court so as to get it out of the chancery court. So, we agreed we would charge her $2,500 for taking the case in the United States District Court. That was a lot of money but seemed to me to be a reasonable fee in 1950.

So, we were sitting there after we'd discussed the case. And Frank says, "Now, Bishop, of course we'll have to charge you a substantial fee in order to take on a matter of this complexity."

She says, "Yes, lawyers, I know about lawyers."

So Frank says, "I think an appropriate fee might be $5,000." He'd just doubled what we had agreed on! I just about fell over.

Bishop Jewell said in her slow voice, "Do you want it all today?"

Skipping over to the end of the story, the end of it was that in the 1960s, when I-40 went through north Nashville, they took the back end of the property on which Bishop Jewell had built a school. We'd kept it in possession all these years. The result was that we were back before Judge William Miller in the federal court, and he ordered that Bishop Jewell allow the other claimants to the chief overseership to come to the property.

She was outraged with that. Finally, she said, "That judge is gonna take over this church. We'll just elect him chief overseer!"

Well, I've always regretted they didn't do that, because I could see this delegation of black, very dignified bishops, calling on Judge Miller to advise him that he had been elected the chief overseer.

William Val Sanford, Nashville, December 6, 2000,
provided by the Tennessee Bar Foundation, Nashville

170. "Women Jurors and Lawyers in Court"

I'll never forget trying a case against Fielding Atchley Jr. We'd just gotten women on the jury, and I was so proud of them. And, by the way, they turned out to be so hard on women. They made my life miserable until I learned how to handle it. Women were jealous of women in business. They didn't want to be on the jury; they wanted to be home. They didn't like the fact that women were working, so the women jurors were tougher on me than male jurors.

I had a field day in front of the men! I was fairly attractive, and I was young, and I played sex to the hilt and having a great time, but then they put women up there. They didn't like seeing a young woman practicing law. They felt like I should be home.

So, Fielding loved it with that handsome profile, so I started playing the equal game with the men. I'd wear sweater suits, and Fielding would be working the women with his beautiful profile, and I'd be working with the men, taking off my cardigan, on and off, on and off. Finally at the end of the second day, he said, "Listen, I'll quit playing games if you will."

I said, "You've got a deal, Fielding; we'll just try the case from now on."

When I started practicing law, it made a lot of difference what we wore. I wore only suits, dark suits, suits that looked professional. When pantsuits first came out, I'll never forget that, because I went to speak to a women's group at the University of Tennessee. They were young women studying to be lawyers. They wanted to know what I thought about wearing pantsuits to court. I said, "I don't know about pantsuits. My theory about what you should wear to court: I wear whatever I think the judge would like. If he wants me to be naked, I'll be naked! But I don't think he will."

So the next time I got to playing with that idea, Judge Wilson was trying a case for me, and I went in and said, "Judge, I have a question. What would you think about my wearing a pantsuit to try a case in your court?"

He said, "You do what you think you need to do, or should do."

Just the way he said it, I knew he didn't think very much of that idea, so I did not. But years later, when pantsuits were pretty well accepted, I did wear a pantsuit with a long jacket to Judge Kelly's court. He was a bankruptcy judge, and I knew he didn't like it. He turned to me, and before he could say anything, I said, "Now, Judge, I didn't know I was coming to your court today. I would not have worn a pantsuit." I went on to say, "If you prefer, I will take off my pants."

Well, he reared back, as he could do, and said, "Never let it be said that I asked a woman to take her pants off—at least in court."

Well, that shows how much the judges paid attention to what women wore, and I think the jurors did also.

Selma Cash Paty, Chattanooga, July 16, 2002,
provided by the Tennessee Bar Foundation, Nashville

171. "Did the Judge Really Decide?"

Judge Lytle of Columbia was the chancellor when my grandfather was involved in a lawsuit over who owned part of the property which is now where the VA Hospital is located in Rutherford County. It was part of the old Rucker land way back before then. My grandfather's portion of the heirs that claimed they owned it were insisting that they had title to the land.

A lawyer from Watertown was representing the other group, and we'd tried a long, long lawsuit before Judge Lytle over which title and which group of heirs was supposed to get this land. Well, while we were doing that the government came up in 1939 and condemned the land, paid for it, and took it over and converted it to the VA Hospital.

Well, the lawsuit sat there for some time, and then finally my grandfather got hold of the lawyer in Watertown and said, "Now, listen, we've been talking about this farmland being worth $6,000. The government has paid $12,000 in the court. Why don't we talk with each one of our clients and say, 'Let's settle this thing. You take $6,000 and we'll take $6,000, and you'll get what you thought you were going to get in the first place.'"

That's the way the case was settled, and Judge Lytle had taken the case under advisement, and he'd had it under advisement. This was a year later! So, the next time he was here from Columbia, we went in and stood before the judge, and my grandfather stood up and said, "Judge, we've settled that old case."

Judge Lytle reached into his pocket and pulled out some paper, tore it up, and said, "You'll never know how I decided that lawsuit."

I honestly believe he was just kidding, but he may have decided it.

John Richardson Rucker Sr., Murfreesboro, March 31, 2000,
provided by the Tennessee Bar Foundation, Nashville

7

Sexual and Physical Abuse

Perhaps the most traumatic court cases involve those related to rape and other forms of mistreatment committed against little girls by their fathers, stepfathers, brothers, or other family members. It is of considerable interest to note that some of these stories tell that the guilty men subsequently committed or attempted to commit suicide, perhaps in an attempt to wipe away their guilt. Equally sad is the stated claim that numerous persons commit sexual abuse and that some mothers ignore their abused daughters' plight.

The first account of physical abuse in this chapter provides a detailed summation of reasons for divorce cases across the years based on physical abuse. Such matters apparently are a much worse problem today than in past years. Child abuse by a parent is another crucial matter in today's society, as is abuse of adults by a nonrelated adult. Although only two physical abuse stories are included in this chapter, there are numerous domestic accounts in other story categories, such as homicide and divorce and adultery, that deal with physical and verbal abuse.

172. "Sexually Abused Little Girl"

I worked on a case two or three years ago here in Smithville. This was one case that was upsetting to me. It involved the Department of Human Services. They were seeking to remove a child from her mother's home. I was appointed to represent the mother, which didn't thrill me at all.

It was a failure-to-protect case. What had happened to this little girl was that she had been raped and gotten pregnant by her father because he had forced the little girl to have sex with him. She was about twelve years old at the time. Her father was charged. He was unable to make bond, so he was in the county jail awaiting trial. He hanged himself there in jail.

By the time we get the child a couple of months later, the mother has remarried and was a basket case. She was overmedicated and basically would not comply with court orders to care for the child. I was concerned for the child because she would have to go through pregnancy, then abortion, and deal with the fact that her father committed suicide based upon the earlier rape. I just don't see how she dealt with pregnancy.

The mother married this guy about three months after the father committed suicide, and she was living with this man whom she married. They were in court periodically because of domestic squabbles, et cetera. Truthfully, I think the mother is mildly mentally retarded. I've seen several of her sisters, and I think the same thing about most of them, too. I don't know whether it's genetic or not, but I do know that the mother is just not with-it.

The daughter that was raped, then went through pregnancy and abortion, is living with some relatives in Cookeville. Her mother was granted some visitation, but she doesn't go by to see her. Occasionally, she will call and say, "Oh, I'd like for my child to come back home." But the living arrangements aren't such that that could happen.

By the way, this little girl's brother started trying to have sex with her. Then, so did her cousin. These people lived in government-assisted housing—inadequate bedrooms, et cetera. So not only did you have the father who was forcing her to have sex with him; after he was out of the picture, her brother and cousin would come in and make advances toward her after she'd had the abortion. They didn't actually have sex with her, but they were trying to. So I would tell the mother, "If you want to have your daughter at home again, you have got to get this brother of hers out of the home."

"Well, I hate to kick him out," she would say.

So the mother did not ever grasp, did not care, and she never wanted to make any positive life changes so as to have any kind of relationship with her daughter.

Sarah Cripps, Smithville, May 8, 2001

173. "FATHER AND DAUGHTER'S INCESTUOUS RELATIONSHIP"

There was a court case at Greenfield in which I represented a fellow in his mid-thirties. He had three daughters, and he was having incestuous relationships with all three of them. He would take them out on country roads.

One of these daughters comes to mind because it all came out in another case in which I was involved. I just represented a woman in a divorce case in which this same thing had happened. I was representing a mother who was seeking a divorce from the father of their daughter. The father was a heavy-machine operator and worked for a construction company. He would take his daughter up to this shed on the clay pits and have sex with her. Then he would make her get down on her knees and pray that this would never happen again. When all this started, she was around thirteen or fourteen, but it continued for several years. She was never willing for this to take place, but she did give in to him. Her father was a rather threatening character, so she would just never tell anyone what was happening.

She did finally relate this to her mother that it was happening, and so they arrested the man. He went to court, and the court set the bond so high that he couldn't make the bond, so he was in jail. While in jail, he attempted suicide by hanging himself, but it wasn't successful. Then, under threats by some family members on his side, the daughter recanted the story by stating that it wasn't true.

Their incestuous relationship then continued, and she never went back to the authorities again with testimony. The father is still living, and the mother is still living. The divorce was final just a few months ago. Their daughter is now in her mid-twenties. According to the mother, the daughter has admitted that her father was still coming up to see her in the recent past to have sex with her. He is using money to procure this relationship. He gives her money, and since she doesn't want the money cut off, she submits to his demands.

James H. Bradberry, Dresden, June 7, 2001

174. "LITTLE GIRL ABUSED BY HER FATHER"

I've tried a sackful of sex abuse cases. The worst one I ever tried, insofar as my getting involved in it, and I shouldn't have let myself do it but I did, I was the prosecutor, and this was back about 1974 or 1975. It involved a little girl whose father had been sexually abusing her. When she came forth to me, she was about ten years old. He started doing this when she was about six. It was horrible, and she said the reason she came forth was that her aunt and her aunt's daughter moved into the house with them. The little cousin was six, and she was afraid that her daddy would start abusing her cousin.

Well, she told a teacher about it at school, and then the teacher told somebody else. The girl's father was a very arrogant man. He was retired military. She didn't trust adults at all, especially male adults. Well, I got the case as prosecutor, and I had to really gain her confidence, so it was necessary that I spend quality time with her. I spent too much time, and I got too personally involved, but she needed my attention. I took her up to the courtroom and showed her where everybody would be sitting, and all that stuff.

At that time, my office was just behind the big courtroom upstairs. Well, the morning of the trial we were in the office, and it was about time to go to court. Judge Ingram was on the bench. The girl's name was Windy, and I said, "Windy, it is time to go in there. Remember what I told you."

So I reached and opened the door, and I felt this tugging on my coat. I turned around, and it was Windy. She was a little blonde-headed girl. I said, "What is it?"

She said, "Mr. Hamilton, I just want you to know that every time Daddy did that to me, I took off my clothes real slow, hoping he would change his mind."

Well, you could have hit me in the face with a baseball bat, and it wouldn't have hurt me worse than that. Well, when I went into the courtroom I was emotionally distraught. Judge Ingram could tell something was wrong. We were getting ready to start picking the jury when he looked over at me and said, "Are you all right, Mr. Hamilton?"

I said, "Yes, sir." So he got to talking to the jury, and I kindly got hold of myself.

At that time, we didn't have the sex abuse laws that we have now. Now, we have rape of a child and all these sexual battery statutes that are designed to protect children. What prompted the legislature to do that was when all of a sudden we got a bunch of these cases coming into court, not only from this county but from all counties.

We picked the jury in this case, and I put the little girl on the witness stand. What's the hard thing about those cases for a prosecutor like I was at the time, your whole case depends on some little ten-year-old blonde-headed girl being able to sit in a courtroom full of adults, none of whom she trusts, and talk about her sex life with her daddy. But that's the way it has to be. So I put her on the witness stand, and I'm telling you, she sat there and—of course, she'd already asked me if she had to look at her daddy. I said, "No, you don't have to look at him. You look only at me." And she did, and buddy she really told it! I mean, she told it like a champ. You could hear a pin drop in that courtroom.

Well, they put her daddy on the witness stand. Like I said, he was military, arrogant as hell. His lawyer asked him some questions, and he just denied that it ever happened. He said, "She has made all this up. It never happened." So we cross-examined him, and I just asked him one question, and that was "Mr. So-and-so, you are telling me in the court and before this jury that what this jury heard your daughter say a few hours ago is stuff she made up—the times, the places, and the way it was done; that she made all that up, and that you did not sexually abuse her. Is that what you are telling us?"

He kindly straightened up in that chair and said, "Well, it all depends on what you mean by sex abuse."

Well, he shouldn't have said that. I said, "All right sir, I'm going to go over here and sit down, because I'm sure this jury, and I know I am, and I imagine the court is very interested in how you define sexual abuse." I went over there and sat down.

He straightened up, leaned back in his chair, and said, "I pinched her on the titty a time or two." With that, he stopped.

Well, buddy, when he said that, Judge Ingram came up off that bench and said, "Have you got any questions for this witness?"

I said, "No, sir. I sure don't."

Well, back then all we had to charge him with was rape. That's what we had indicted him for. That jury stayed out about an hour and came back in. (That's when the jury sentenced. Judges sentence now, but back then juries did.) They gave him ninety-nine years in the penitentiary.

When he got to the pen, this child's mother came to me just a few years before I got on the bench as judge. He would write her letters and told her things such as he had found Jesus, and Jesus had promised him that he would get her for what she had done to him. Finally, I got that stopped. I got the Department of Correction involved, and they began to monitor his mail. They weren't supposed to do that, but they did.

I was standing over there in the courthouse two or three months ago, and this lady walked up to me and said, "Judge Hamilton, you don't know who I am, do you?"

I said, "Well, no, ma'am, I really don't."

Well, it was this little girl. She's about thirty-five now; married, has a couple of children, is going to college. She hugged my neck and said that everything is fine, that she was happy, and is about to get out of college.

Jim T. Hamilton, Columbia, December 10, 2001

175. "STEPFATHER ABUSES LITTLE GIRL"

We had one case in which a little girl's stepfather was abusing her. And the last time he abused her, when she told about it, she told her teacher. The teacher said it was the day the little children all marched in the March of Dimes parade. Her stepdaddy picked her up at the parade and took her somewhere. She was able to show me and one of our investigators where it all took place. He took her out on a country road. But we nailed him because we had the exact time. All we had to do was to get the date of that little March of Dimes. But not being able to determine the exact time and place is the problem in most of those cases.

It's amazing the people that commit those crimes. They are all the way up and down the socioeconomic ladder. I've had college graduates, colonels in the military, and the list goes on.

Jim T. Hamilton, Columbia, December 10, 2001

176. "SEXUAL ABUSE AND THEN SOME"

This is something that deals with children, perhaps in the "lessons learned" category. I was raised in a large family. I had grandparents that lived close. My father had six brothers, and my mother had three sisters, so I had all kinds of aunts and uncles. Growing up, there was never any insecurity in my life. I was always loved and cared for. I'm about to cry thinking about my wonderful childhood. But lawyers don't cry, do they! I never really knew growing up that there were children different from me.

When I'd been out of law school for about three or four months— the new lawyer in town, the youngest lawyer in town, is the one that gets appointed to indigent cases. We're the ones judges look to when they need to appoint a lawyer for that kind of service. But then the other attorneys are getting paid, and the young attorneys don't have enough to do, so the judges appoint cases to us. And those are the ones for which you don't get paid, or you bill the state and get paid at a very low rate. It's always a joke around town when we'd love for a new attorney to come into town. The younger, the greener, the better, because that relieves our responsibility to take appointed cases.

When I'd been practicing for just a few months over in Rhea County, the juvenile judge appointed me to represent this young girl that was in juvenile court. And I was about as green as they come. They tell you that you learn a lot in law school, but when you get out of law school you don't hardly know how to find the courthouse. Now, that's about the truth! [Laughter]

So I went over to juvenile court and was appointed to represent this twelve-year-old girl. The charge against her was for running away from a group home placement. I sat down with this little girl. She had actually been in custody for a while. I sat down with her in the courtroom, and she was wearing an orange jumpsuit for prisoners. I started talking with her, and she was so charming, intelligent, and probably a bit of a con artist. She was probably a little smarter than I was at the time. She knew the court system better than I did. But I asked her why she ran away from home and was shocked that she was in a group home. I would assume that this was a young girl that had committed some criminal offenses in the past to have been in the place that she was in. That feeling was something that came from my childhood, I guess. I didn't realize that children could end up in those circumstances unless they did something wrong to deserve it. But in talking with her, I learned that she had been sexually abused by her stepfather and initially removed from her mother's home as a young child at the age of seven or eight. She had been placed in different foster homes and kicked out of one or another for other reasons. She probably did have some behavioral problems going on.

I asked her, "Well, you've run away from the group home, you've run away from these foster homes, so where is it that you're going? What do you want?"

She said, "Well, I really want to be with my family." And she went on to tell me that she had an uncle that was willing to take her in, and that she really wanted to go live with this uncle. So I got pen and paper out and wrote down all the information. I got his address, and I got his telephone number, then I said, "I'm going to contact this uncle. We're going to do all we can to see that you get to go live there."

Then I went into the clerk's office and sat down with the social worker, and I was all vim and vigor. I had figured out a solution to this girl's problems that nobody else had thought of in the past five years. So I set down with my pen and paper and said, "I've found a place for this girl to go live." The older social worker just kind of looked at me and said, "Okay, where?"

I gave her the man's name, and she closed up her file [relative to this girl], and I think the file must have been three or four inches thick. She looked at me and took a deep breath and said, "Boy, have you got a lot to learn." Then she said, "Do you think if there had been a family member out there appropriate for this girl that we wouldn't have put her there?" She went on to say, "That uncle has been in and out of jail on drug charges for the past five years. I don't know if he's out of jail right now, but if he is, she's not going to get to go live there."

Well, I was shocked and felt like maybe I'd been taken in, and I said, "Okay, maybe that uncle's not going to work. What about grandparents?"

She shook her head and said, "No." Evidently, the grandmother was a local bootlegger.

I said, "You can't tell me that there's not a family member out there that would take this girl in. That's what she wants, to be with her family." Well, I was totally shocked. I was twenty-five years old, but I had no clue that there were children that lived that way.

Anyway, I worked with that young girl but don't remember where we ended up sending her through the system. But over the next ten years, I saw her on a regular basis through the juvenile court system. Eventually, she did start committing crimes. I think she started having children by the time she was sixteen or seventeen. She's one of the classic stories around here. Now she's in the adult criminal system, but she never had a chance.

Lynne Swafford, Pikeville, December 4, 2003

177. "A RAPE CASE IN KNOXVILLE"

I tried what maybe was the most widely notorious rape case in the history of Knoxville, and that was some years ago. I would get calls at night while I was special prosecutor in this case from the defendant's friends telling me what they were going to do to me and my family. I'd say, "Hold up a minute. You're going to do these terrible things to me, so just tell me where I can meet you, and I'll be down there."

I went out four or five times to meet these people, but they never showed up. George Balitsaris was the judge in this rape case involving some very very prominent people. All these threats that were given to me, and after the jury came in and convicted the defendant in this case, everybody streamed out except two people. One was me, and I was deliberately taking my time to put my file together, and the other was Judge George Balitsaris. I finally got my briefcase packed, and I said, "George, what are you doing here?"

He'd been down there, and he knew all about these threats, and that they had passed word to me that they'd be waiting for me outside. George was a well-known University of Tennessee football player. He said, "Well, you and I haven't had a chance to talk. I just thought I'd stay down here."

After that kind of monkey business, I said, "George, you're down here because you heard these people are going to jump me."

He said, "No, no, no, I just wanted to walk up the street with you."

I said, "Don't give me that stuff. I can handle it; I can handle it."

"Oh, no," he said, "you and I are going to walk up the street together."

So he accompanied me from the old criminal courts building all the way to the Hamilton National Bank to be with me in the event that gang of hoodlums was going to jump me. Very few people would do that. But in any event, the foreman on that jury that convicted that guy I was prosecuting in this very prominent rape case was a man by the name of Andy Holt. Andy was a legend in his own time. He had a curriculum vita as long as your arm. Andy ended up as president of the University of Tennessee statewide, not just the Knoxville campus. He was one of God's great creatures.

Foster D. Arnett, Knoxville, July 21, 1999,
provided by the Tennessee Bar Foundation, Nashville

178. "DOMESTIC ABUSE CASES"

When I first started law practice in 1961, divorce was a sort of hushed thing. People were looked down upon and ostracized to some extent by society if they got a divorce. Today, people don't think any more about it than taking a drink of water, as six out of every ten marriages end in divorce. That is one of the most revolutionary changes in society. Ironically and sadly enough, many of the people who need a divorce the most are those who don't get it. These are the abused and mistreated spouse, usually the woman but not always. There are men who are terribly henpecked, mistreated, and abused, even physically sometimes by the wife. But in the overwhelming majority of the cases, it's the alcoholic and abusive husband who beats the wife up on Friday and Saturday nights, and then by Sunday afternoon and Monday he's all remorseful and promises never to do it again. All black-and-blue in the face, she may have already borrowed the money from some relative to put down for a divorce fee, then she dismisses it on the first of the week, or a week or so later, because he has promised to do better. But she is mistreated and abused in the near future, and that cycle goes on and on.

People who need a divorce the worst are those who are physically and mentally abused by the other spouse, but many times they don't follow through with it for psychological and economic reasons that they may have. I've handled many domestic relations cases in the last forty years, and what I've just said is repeated over and over in those cases.

Nathan Harsh, Gallatin, May 8, 2001

179. "Brainwashing"

I believe this happened in the court of appeals, or it could have been the supreme court. A lawyer whom I didn't know very well at that time, but who has since become one of my closest friends, the Honorable Lew Connor, was arguing a case with another attorney. The issue was a child custody, a question of child abuse, et cetera, and the case went on and on. The other attorney was arguing to the court that one could not program a child of tender years to believe to testify as to something that was not true. That argument went on and on and on. Finally, Mr. Connor stood up for his rebuttal. The court asked him, "What do you say to that proposition?"

Conner looked out over the top of his little reading glasses and said, "Apparently, counsel has never heard of the story of Santa Claus." One of the greatest false stories programmed into small children.

John Acuff, Cookeville, November 7, 2001

8

Courtroom Misbehavior and Jury Justice/Injustice

⚖

Various types of events occur in the courtroom, some of which involve physical attacks typically instituted by the accused, curse words uttered in loud tones, or guns pointed at someone on the opposition's side. Although curse words were and are rather commonly used in some instances, physical attacks and other forms of misbehavior are not common in modern times, especially among lawyers in the courtroom. On the other side of the picture, clients have been known to thank their attorneys by hugging and/or kissing them in the presence of others in the courtroom. Interesting, uncommon incidents took place during courtroom sessions described in the category of courtroom misbehavior, such as a client's misunderstanding the meaning of a certain word, a woman exposing her wounded breast, and a young man appearing in court dressed in inappropriate attire.

In public opinion, and among attorneys as well, the jury system has its ups and downs. Thus, opinions differ as to the fairness of this facet of the legal system. Some legal professionals believe that jurors often act in accordance with what they feel should be done, rather than on facts presented and illuminated during the court procedures. Personal opinion and belief may thus play a role in the way a jurist votes, yet some persons who serve on juries will do everything possible to vote on the "right" side. Judges typically firmly support the jury's decision.

180. "Drinking before Going to Court"

In one of the first cases I ever had, my parents had come down from North Carolina to watch me. I was representing a fellow who had clubbed another in the head with a baseball bat. My client was a little bit mentally defective somewhat. His name was Raymond Whitaker, and I'll never forget him. His face looked paralyzed on one side, like he had had a stroke, but he hadn't. He was young, but he looked old. He was still in his twenties, but he could have passed for the forties. Life had not been kind to him.

I took him up to the arraignment, and the judge says, "Mr. Fraley, your client is charged with aggravated assault. How do you plead, sir?"

I said, "To please the court, I waive the reading indictment and enter a plea of not guilty for my client." This was my first case, the first big case to be tried at some other point. Well, my client looked at me, and he thought when I pled him not guilty, the case was over. He reached around and grabbed me by the neck and gave me a big kiss right there in the courtroom!

Well, my dad broke down. He just couldn't help laughing at me with this client kissing me right there in open court.

I said, "Judge, looks like my client is quite enamored with me. I hope he still is after he spends some time in jail."

He didn't go to jail. He was sentenced. I talked the victim into having a little more compassion for the poor fellow who had lost his temper over this thing, and he agreed with me. As it turned out, the victim wasn't afraid to take a little drink himself, and he was drunk two or three times when he showed up in court. So it made it a little bit easier that they were afraid he would be testifying drunk and I would eat him up, so that worked out well.

Raymond Fraley, Fayetteville, September 20, 2001

181. "Teenage Lad Inappropriately Dressed for Court"

I came into juvenile court one day here in Dresden, and my youth services officer came up to me and said, "Judge, there's a young man in here who will be coming up before you in just a minute. He's got on a long trench coat, and he's got a chain around his neck with a bullet on the end of it. And he's got a stuffed monkey hanging around his waist."

So this young man came up before me, but the tragic thing was that his parents were with him. They were also very responsible people. And their son was dressed like the officer said.

I told the officer to get that young man out of my courtroom until he had dressed himself appropriately for an appearance in court. The young man was quite taken aback at my observations of him because he knew that I was blind. But they took him out and dressed him properly and brought him back in.

He really didn't say anything, but I'll bet he wanted to.

James H. Bradberry, Dresden, June 7, 2001

182. "Unethical Events in Court"

I wasn't there to see this, but I've been told this story about a lawyer that practiced here in Columbia for forty to fifty years. He is now deceased. He and this other lawyer got into a fight in Franklin in court. They actually came to blows, fist fight in the courtroom.

I've had lawyers that I thought were about to fight in court, but they never got beyond just shouting at each other. There are so many ethical things floating around these days that you'd get in trouble right quick if something like that took place. Lawyers kinda watch themselves.

I've had defendants to cuss me in court after I've sentenced them. I never will forget one guy down in Lawrenceburg; I sentenced him to a lengthy term in the penitentiary. They were taking him out of the courtroom, and as he walked by my bench, he called me a son of a bitch.

Jim T. Hamilton, Columbia, December 10, 2001

183. "Female Prosecuting Attorney Points Gun in Court"

This wasn't a court blunder. I think people were really worried about it. It was a preliminary hearing in an aggravated assault case that Frank Buck and I were trying here in Smithville. The defendant was accused of pulling a gun on two juveniles. The defense attorney was trying to say, "Okay, it wasn't a real weapon you saw; it was just an empty holster that he pulled out, and you just imagined out of thin air that it was a gun."

So we had the gun brought over from the evidence room. So I thought that I would just demonstrate to see if I could get her to see what really happened. Well, I think that Frank and the judge both got a little nervous because I was a blind person wielding a .38 revolver.

It was fairly comical because from what my paralegal assistant said, the judge tried to duck behind the judge's bench. The judge yelled, "Is that gun unloaded?"

I said, "Well, I'll check the chamber. I'll go ahead and do that, for I was taught in school how to check a revolver."

I held the gun up, turned toward the defense attorney, Frank, because he was saying what I was doing was objectionable, then I asked, "Is this what the defendant did?"

But I forgot that I still had the gun at the same angle, because I turned sort of in the direction of the defense attorney. So it appeared that I was just pointing the gun at Frank, and he was a little taken aback. [Laughter]

That was kinda funny because they didn't know what to do. I think they thought that I was inept with a pistol and didn't know what I was doing. That led them to believe that I didn't know what I was pointing at and that they didn't know what was going to happen.

Sarah Cripps, Smithville, May 8, 2001

184. "On Time"

I remember many years ago I was defending a civil case in Jackson County. Buck Hagan was the judge, and because he was the judge, I made sure that I was there at least on time. I walked in about five minutes till nine o'clock; it was supposed to start at nine. There were twelve people in the box. Judge Hagan looked up at me and said, "Mr. Acuff, your advisory has already done his voir dire. Would you like to do one?"

John Acuff, Cookeville, November 7, 2001

185. "Woman Exhibits Her Breast in Court"

Judge Bryant, who was kind of a big, heavy guy, more massive than heavy, had a case with Chancellor Vernon Neal, who was a young lawyer appearing before him. The allegation was that the overly endowed lady, who was in front of him, had injured a breast in a traffic accident or whatever. The judge apparently was a little skeptical of this whole injury, whereupon before anybody could say anything, she removed it from her blouse and her bra and flopped it right out on the edge of the bench.

The judge, being a very modest man, didn't really know how to deal with that. I think that ended the case, for in those long-ago days no judge or lawyer would have examined closely the evidence.

John Acuff, Cookeville, November 7, 2001

186. "MAN FALLS DEAD WHILE ON STAND"

I had an unusual thing to happen to me, probably back in the early 1960s. A party had sued Columbia Transmission because it had laid a third line across his property, and we had a trial as to damages. Willard Hagan, who is still living now in Lebanon, Tennessee, was on the bench, and it was a nonjury case. There weren't but five or six people in the courtroom. Bob Johnson from Gainesboro was representing Mr. Walton [who had brought a damage claim against the pipeline].

I had just started my examination, and Mr. Walton slumped over. I said to Mr. Johnson, "You'd better see about your client. I believe he is sick." Well, by the time they got him out and laid him down, he was dead.

The judge said, "I declare a mistrial," and he took off. But the man died on the stand. I didn't know it, but he had a very serious heart condition. His own lawyer didn't know it either. I later learned that Mr. Walton's family did not want him to get on the stand because his heart was really bad. The strange thing was that none of his family was in court with him. The poor man just died, probably in his late sixties.

I was cross-examining him. By the way, I got the transcript back later. I couldn't remember what I was asking him when he died, but I hadn't been on his case any. I was just asking him questions for factual answers, and he was giving them to me. I didn't get into cross-examining him. I was thankful for that.

The family didn't blame me, thank goodness.

James W. Chamberlain, Lafayette, November 5, 2003

187. "DISAGREEMENT OVER COURTROOM EXHIBITS"

I had one case in which I was trying a murder case, and as a prosecutor, I had to keep up with exhibits in the courtroom. In that court, the defense didn't care about the exhibits. We didn't have a court reporter, and the clerks didn't really care about the exhibits, but I tried to keep up with every exhibit in case the case had to be appealed. At least they would know what the exhibits were and what the numbers were. And I had approximately 130 exhibits as part of my prosecution duties. I also had to keep up with the exhibits with a special pad. And I had to write "exhibit number one," and I had to mark "exhibit number one" and write it down and describe what it was so we could keep up with it.

Well, the lawyers I was trying the case with took all kinds of pictures of the scene, and this one lawyer was so engrossed with the photos that he took that he told us—the jury—what type of camera he used, what the shutter speeds were. He was really pumping himself up as to what a photographer he was. He brought a projector and a screen on his own so he could show them to the jurors. Of course, every time he would show a picture, I'd say, "Your Honor, let the record reflect that the picture is number so-and-so and that it reflects whatever it was." So the defense attorney was full of himself with pictures, and when he finished with all of his pictures, I said, "Your Honor, the court of appeals will probably want to look at these pictures, so what I would like to do is to make the projector number such and such as an exhibit, and the screen as number such and such as a part of the exhibits."

Of course, that lawyer was walking around proud of his pictures. The judge says, "Fine." So when we got through, and the case was over, I think I got a conviction. The other lawyer got ready to fix his screen and projector to take them home.

I said, "Wait a minute. You can't take those home."

He said, "I just brought these to show the jury."

I said, "No, no. They are exhibits into the courtroom lab, so therefore they are property of the state." I knew he wasn't paying any attention to me, and that was just one way of getting back at him.

He said, "Well, I paid for those. They're my personal property."

I said, "No, they are an exhibit to the state."

About two or three days later, we had to enter a special order allowing him to withdraw these exhibits, thus let him have his projector and screen.

The way I did to him was just the way I did to some of the defense attorneys.

Don Dino, Memphis, January 7, 2004

188. "THE REAL PURPOSE OF LAWYERS"

Chris, a buddy of mine when I was in law school, had a girlfriend who got a traffic ticket and didn't appear in court when she was supposed to. So the clerk issued her a notice that they do when people don't appear for a driving ticket. The notice says that if you fail to appear, a judgment will be taken against you for fines and cost and executions may lie.

So she came down to me and just showed me the notice. I didn't bother reading it because I knew what it was. So we went down there to court, and I talked the prosecutor into dismissing it. I came out into the hall and told her that it was dismissed and she could go on her way. Well, she threw her arms around me and started hugging on me. I mean, she slung herself on me like a wet sheet.

I said, "I was glad to help you out, but it's not really a big deal."

She looked at me and said, "I was so afraid they were going to kill me."

I said, "What do you mean?"

She says, "Look here; that's what it says on the ticket—if I don't get down here, they're going to take a judgment against me, and executions may lie."

"Execution may lie" means that they may issue a writ to get money from you. But she thought they were getting ready to haul her up to court square, put a bullet in her head, and dump her body into the city fountain.

So I looked at her after she was so thankful to me and said to her, "Ma'am, that's what lawyers are for."

Yes, I took full credit for having saved her life, but I know doctors who have done the same thing.

Larry Rice, Memphis, January 7, 2004

189. "JURORS NOT ALWAYS ACCURATE"

I have a story to tell about this nursing home case I was trying in Nashville, Tennessee, two or three years ago. My client had Alzheimer's disease, and he had gotten out and wandered around and fell into a ditch and hurt himself. We sued the nursing home. The nursing homes in this country make a lot of money, and they are understaffed, and they pay so little that they get people who are not really qualified to work, and they are not very nice people either.

After this case had been turned over to the jury, they came back and wanted to know if they could give more than had been asked for.

Well, at that point, the lawyer on the other side said, "Look, we haven't offered you money. We'll offer you $120,000."

I said, "Oh, let's just let the jury say what they're going to give."

When the jury came back, they left me $100. So I left $50 on the table.

Every lawyer who has ever tried enough lawsuits has probably experienced where the jury has come and asked some inane question, then when you ask them at the end, "Why did you ask that?" they'll say, "Well, we were just curious."

Raymond Fraley, Fayetteville, September 20, 2001

190. "Having Sex during Court Process"

A few years ago I was trying an aggravated assault case. I was representing a man in his seventies, who was a bondsman in Pulaski, Tennessee. He was accused of having stabbed a one-arm fellow coming out of the bank. And the bank was located right across the street from what was then the jail. A witness observed this from the second floor of the jail looking down across the street at the bank's opening door.

My client, Mr. Woods, was accused of stabbing this fellow, and as it turned out, the altercation arose over some money that was owed to the bondsman by this deadbeat one-arm fellow. He had a reputation of being a deadbeat. I held a preliminary hearing, and the case was bound over and then set for trial by the great judge over there whose name is Jim T. Hamilton. He is my friend and my buddy.

Jim was trying this case, and during the course of the trial I had to have subpoenaed the fellow who had witnessed it from the second floor of the jail. He was then in the penitentiary, and we had to transport him from the penitentiary and bring him down to the trial.

Unbeknownst to me, during the course of the trial I had to bring this fellow in to testify. But at lunchtime, unbeknownst to me, this prisoner had to go to the bathroom. The prison guard stood outside the bathroom. The women's bathroom was close to it. You could almost walk into both of them. They let him go to the bathroom by himself. While he was in the bathroom his girlfriend had slipped in there, and he had her up on the countertop of the lavatory and was pouring it to her. I mean, absolutely pouring it to her! About that time, Judge Hamilton had to go to the bathroom before he went back onto the bench. And he walked right in on this guy with his drawers dropped down to his knees, and this gal straddle-legged on top of this lavatory. The judge watched for just a minute, then went, "Gosh!" and turned around and walked out.

Well, the first witness to testify that afternoon was this prisoner. And Jim Hamilton was on the bench. I called the witness, and Jim wasn't paying attention. I said, "Judge, call the witness."

This fellow went up and stood there in the witness box, which was right there by the side of the judge. When this fellow turned, the judge went, "Uh-h-h-h, that's the one! That's the one! Ray [the lawyer], what have you done to me?"

I said, "Judge, what's going on here?"

He called me to the bench and told me that he had seen this guy having sex with this woman.

The jury found the man innocent, not guilty, because the witness was important. He had described what happened. This one-arm guy that claimed that he couldn't do anything was as dexterous with one arm as you and I could do with two. But that was a great case for Jim Hamilton.

Raymond Fraley, Fayetteville, September 20, 2001

9

ILLEGAL SALES

One of the stories in this category is not about illegal sales per se, but it does portray a man who intentionally placed his cows in the road in hopes of collecting payment from the assailant's insurance company. Although there are only three stories relative to illegal sales in this chapter, such sales were very common in earlier times, and court cases about illegal sales frequently occurred. However, back then many persons who made moonshine whiskey were never captured and brought to court, as they typically were hill country or mountain farmers whose available crop acreage was often too small to produce enough farm products to get family members through the forthcoming months. And, as indicated in the final story in this category, local people were often in sympathy with persons who had been caught and jailed for making moonshine whiskey. Those were the days prior to the arrival of marijuana and other present-day illegal products.

191. "FEMALE AFRICAN AMERICAN SELLS MOONSHINE WHISKEY"

One of the more archaic cases as it would seem today was a standard type of petty criminal case in the early 1960s when I first started practicing law. It was about the illegal sale of alcohol. I represented a very elderly African American lady who was charged with selling moonshine liquor. Her case was tried before a jury of twelve here in Gallatin. She was found guilty of selling alcohol to this undercover Gallatin policeman and was sentenced to thirty days in jail.

The testimony of the policeman was that when he understood she sold some, he went and asked her to fill up this half-pint container that he brought with him. He said that she took him out the back door of her house and on through her chicken yard and into an outdoor toilet, then she raised the lid to the toilet that was still in use. And suspended by coat hangers down in the outdoor toilet hole was this big jug. She pulled it out of the toilet hole and began to fill his bottle. Then he arrested her for the sale of moonshine liquor.

These were the marijuana- and cocaine-type cases of the early days, and as recently as the 1960s. So times have changed, but possibly they haven't changed all that much.

Nathan Harsh, Gallatin, May 8, 2001

192. "Farmer Purposely Lets Cows Get Killed"

I was driving home one afternoon, and as I turned a corner and started down another strip of road, I hit a cow. I mean, I never saw the cow. She came right out in front of me. I was driving a Volvo, with the windows cracked and the top open. And I was sitting there. My glasses had fallen off, and I had cow doo all over me—in my ears and my eyes.

Well, the farmer was very worried about me and the cow both. I saw the cow had died. So, some time passes, and he writes me and asks me if my insurance is going to voluntarily pay for the cow.

I thought, well, I'll give it to my insurance company. They can do whatever they want to. About the same time I was getting ready to make a hike from home to Sewanee, where my boys went to school, and for each of them I did a pilgrimage. It's about ninety miles there. And I went into the podiatrist office to have my corns trimmed, and all that. His assistant said to me, "Did you kill the cow?"

I said, "Yes."

And she said, "My husband killed one at the same place, and there's been another one or two killed there."

And I said, "*Pardon* me?"

And she said, "Yeah."

So I guess I wrote my insurance company and said, "Apparently, the guy has found a very unique marketing tool that is kindly the same as it used to be when we had the railroads. You know, you could take an old cow that ain't worth much and put it in front of the train, and suddenly it is a prizewinning milk cow.

John Acuff, Cookeville, November 7, 2001

193. "Caught Making Moonshine Whiskey"

Back in the early 1970s, we had at that time ABC [Alcoholic Beverage Commission] agents who were revenuers. Still occasionally, they would find a whiskey still in Blount County. I was the assistant district attorney here, and the supervisor called me one day. The elected district attorney general lived in Kingston. He called me and said, "I found something I want you to see. It is a groundhog still."

Well, I didn't know a groundhog still from anything else, but I agreed, and they picked me up and drove way up into the mountains, near Allegheny Loop. We walked through the fields and through the woods and came to this groundhog still. And they had the guy whom they thought was running the still; he was still there standing around. His .22 rifle was propped up against the tree, and he wasn't wearing handcuffs or anything. All of them were just standing there.

It turned out that a groundhog still is a still that is pretty well buried in the side of the mountain. In other words, it's concealed, with as much of it as possible located underground. They were all friendly. This fellow was going to jail, and they were going to destroy his still. The agent said, "Crank it up; he was making whiskey, so show him how it works."

So they turned on the gasoline and started it up, and some whiskey started dripping out. He was proud of that.

Anyway, we had a nice conversation and went on. The man was ultimately convicted, but I don't think he served any time after that.

At that point, most of the judges felt that there were a lot of things worse than a man making a little bit of whiskey. And this was a small operation. It wasn't any kind of a commercial or industrial still that you've heard about that turned out gallons of poison in the inner cities. This was a local still for local people.

Ed Bailey, Maryville, December 4, 2001

194. "Smartest Man in Clay County"

This is a true story according to Albert Williams, who was a very fine lawyer and circuit judge in this area. It has to do with a moonshiner in Clay County whose name was Rad Long. And I know there was a Rad Long, for before they both died, they told me about Rad Long. He got caught in the act of moonshining during Prohibition, still working in the mash and the whole nine yards. Well, Albert Williams was on the bench, and the first day in court they indicted Rad. At that time the penalty was pretty severe, so it was a penitentiary offense. So Rad came to court with his wife and four or five children. He answered to the indictments, said, "Yeah, I'm guilty." He didn't have a lawyer, so in order to expedite things, the state just said, "He's pled guilty, so let's just go ahead and give him a sentence." So they sentenced him to the penitentiary.

During the lunch break, the sheriff came to Judge Williams and said, "Judge, there's been a gospel meeting going on, and Rad's been listening to the preaching." See, the jail was pretty close to where the preacher was preaching, so Rad heard him. The sheriff went on to say, "Rad wonders if he could be baptized before he goes to prison?"

The judge says, "Why certainly, certainly." So he took him down to the Obey River, near the confluence of the Obey into the Cumberland. So that afternoon after lunch the sheriff said, "Judge, he's kinda got the sympathy of the town, and people are giving him food, clothing, and just a groundswell of opinion in his favor. We need to do something about this case."

The judge said, "Well, I could grant a new trial, I guess, but he doesn't have a lawyer to make a motion."

The attorney general said, "Well, it's getting close to election time, so just let me make a motion." So he made the motion, and the state granted Rad a new trial. Then the state said, "Well, we ought to dismiss this case, Judge."

The judge said, "Well, who's going to pay the court costs?"

"Well, he doesn't have anything, so I reckon the state will just have to pay the costs. And, by the way, there's such a groundswell of opinion in his favor that a local fellow here in town donated a wagon and team of mules to put all this stuff on to carry him home." Judge Williams gave five dollars.

The judge said, "Well, that's good. I'm glad to see the community responding to the needs of this man's urgent situation."

Well, the long shot of it was, Rad borrowed his team of mules and wagon and got his provisions—groceries, clothes, and everything—and piled them up on this wagon. They took him down to the ferry that crossed the Cumberland River where the bridge now is. They ferried him across to the other side on the road to Tompkinsville. And just as the ferry was about halfway across the river with Rad facing the Celina side, Rad stood up on top of this wagon with all his provisions, took his hat off, waved it in the air, and yelled out, "I'm the smartest son of a bitch in Clay County." [Laughter]

James W. Chamberlain, Lafayette, November 5, 2003

10

POLITICAL ELECTIONS

⚖️

Stories in this category are interesting and very informative. Of significant note is that the political division between Democrats and Republicans was and still is of major importance across the state, even between husbands and wives in some instances. Stories herein describe a man who campaigned in the wrong state, another who campaigned for Congress while drunk, and still another who was advised to identify himself as his opponent in order to obtain more votes. These accounts, regardless of the theme, tell us that political campaigns are very serious, but in some instances also humorous. One thing is for sure: political campaigns and elections will likely be the source of many more stories in forthcoming years.

195. "CAMPAIGNING FOR OFFICE IN WRONG STATE"

Hughie Ragan, a lawyer, was campaigning for public service commissioner, a statewide office. Hughie had come back from his campaign travels and was explaining to one of the local lawyers here in Jackson, whom he routinely talked with, about where he had been during his campaign while riding on his motorcycle. And he said, "I got on my motorcycle this day up and around Bristol, and I went east and I went on out in there."

After about two or three minutes the lawyer said to him, "Hell, Hughie, you were campaigning in Virginia!"

Hughie didn't stop at the border. He just kept going seeking votes for the Public Service Commission, and he never knew the difference. He didn't know where the state line was, but that didn't bother Hughie.

David G. Hayes, Jackson, August 8, 2001

196. "UNCLE DAVE MACON HELPS YOUNG CANDIDATE"

I knew Uncle Dave Macon, the old-time musician. This story is about him. It begins with a young war veteran from Lawrenceburg, Tennessee, who came back from the war. In 1948, he was running for Congress against an incumbent named Alex Brown [pseudonym]. Brown was absolutely a brilliant man, had a great educational background. Had gone to Princeton, or to Harvard or Yale Law School. But he had a serious drinking problem. Back in those days, people weren't as familiar with their congressman as they are today. In reality, a congressman would send out calendars and garden seeds to their constituents. That way, he was pretty sure of being reelected.

Well, because of Congressman Brown's drinking problem, he was absent from Congress. And his opponent, this war veteran, was a young, vigorous, handsome young man.

Uncle Dave Macon was traveling with this veteran, drawing crowds for him on courthouse squares. He picked the banjo. One day, Uncle Dave, with Sam and Kirk McGee, who were old-time fiddling brothers, were playing together. [Anywhere they played,] the veteran, who was running for office, would be in front of the crowd, and he'd call off such-and-such a bill and say, "Where's Mr. Brown?" Uncle Dave would say, "He's drunk!"

Well, the young man won that election by, I believe, forty-eight votes. It was a tight election.

William J. Peeler, Waverly, June 14, 2001

197. "HOW TO WIN A POLITICAL CAMPAIGN"

There are a lot of Hughie Ragan stories around here. He was good friends with a local legendary lawyer, Carmack Murchison, whose son is still practicing law here in Jackson. Hughie was quite a famous criminal lawyer. Years ago, he ran for the Public Service Commission against Buck Avery, a man who was later a judge on the court of appeals.

Hughie went in to see his friend Carmack one day and told him that he didn't think his campaign against Avery was doing very well.

You've got to know, too, that Hughie wore coveralls and rode a motor-cycle around while campaigning.

Carmack said, "Well, I'll tell you what I think you could do that will help your campaign."

Hughie said, "Well, what is that?"

Carmack said to him, "Everywhere you go, tell people that your name is Buck Avery [his opponent's name], and you'll win this election." [Laughter]

Alan Highers, Jackson, August 8, 2001

198. "SWITCHING RELIGIOUS AND POLITICAL AFFILIATIONS"

About 1963, I decided to run for a position on the school board. So I began to inquire as to how it is you run for the school board. And I found out you had to qualify to run for political office, and you qualified under a party. In Marion County, my husband came from a long line of Republicans, so I'll tell how I came to be a Republican.

I grew up in Greeneville, located in east Tennessee, but my father was from Virginia and was born in 1863. Thus, he was much a part of the Old South and the Civil War theme. He lived it until his dying day, and he felt a great loyalty to the Democratic Party, and a great loyalty to the South and to the Lost Cause. Because of that I thought, well, if he's a Democrat, then I'm a Democrat. I was twenty-two years old when I got married, but had never voted.

So, when my husband and I married, he was very gallant. We had a wonderful honeymoon in New York City, but we argued about politics later on. I said, "Well, I'm a Democrat."

He said, "You can't be a Democrat and be married to me. I'm a Republican." [Laughter]

I was emancipated enough by that time that I wasn't going to be told what to do along political lines. So, we had another bone of contention. I had been reared in the Methodist church. That was my life growing up. My parents were very strong-willed people of the Christian faith. Well, I couldn't imagine going any other place to church. So, finally I said to him one day, "I'll tell you what. If you'll go to the Methodist church, I'll be a Republican."

He said, "You've got a deal."

So, after that, I became a Republican. Then I started reading what the Republican Party was all about, and I said, "Well, really, I believe in that. I am a Republican." I believe in the work ethic, and I believe the government should not do for you what you can do for yourself. And by that time, I qualified as a Republican to run for the school board. I was elected in 1966 and served in that capacity for twelve years.

Claude G. Swafford, Jasper, June 8, 2001,
provided by the Tennessee Bar Foundation, Nashville

199. "WORKING ON WOMEN'S RIGHTS"

When I graduated from Vanderbilt Law School, a student who was one year behind me pulled a group together and came to see me and told me that I was running for the state legislature. I told them I'd lived in Nashville only approximately three years, had no experience in politics. But they brought a petition, filed it, and I ran for the legislature. At that point in time, the city of Nashville had a ticket, and the county had its ticket. I ran as an Independent between them, although this was a Democratic primary. I was a solid Democrat and still am. I'm a true, New Deal Democrat—a yellow-dog Democrat. That means that the person would vote for a yellow dog before he would a Republican.

I was elected by eighty-one votes . . . and was appointed chairman of the Labor Committee in the House of Representatives. I had lived in California for a short while when Warren was governor, and I was somewhat surprised at what I saw was going on in the state of Tennessee. Women were not being able to serve on juries. They were legally prohibited from serving on juries. So, a lady by the name of Underwood, a good Republican, was working in the field of women's rights, and not many people at that point in time were working for women's rights or discriminations of all sorts. I proposed a bill that women would be permitted to serve on juries but not required to do so. If they were subpoenaed for jury service, they could simply say over the phone, "I choose not to serve." But that was the best we could get at the time. This bill only passed by a very few votes. We did get it passed, and from that it has grown along with other participants in women's rights activities, such as pushing for equality in many areas.

During the Vietnam period, three hundred women were sitting in at the War Memorial Building in Nashville, and all were arrested and taken to city court for trial. Three hundred stood several deep around the edges of the courtroom, in the aisles and any other space that was available. Andrew Doyle was city judge at that time, and he asked if there was anybody there to represent them and what they were charged with. I told the judge that they were protesting the Vietnam War, and they pled not guilty. To his everlasting credit, Judge Doyle said this case is dismissed and told his clerks to be sure that these people are courteously escorted out of the courtroom.

Some other cases of interest in which I participated:

1. I represented Jimmy Hoffa when he was charged in Nashville with a misdemeanor which later got converted to several felonies, and

2. Judge Charles Galbreth, a state court of appeals judge, who was charged with tax evasion in federal court. He was acquitted.

Cecil D. Branstetter Sr., Nashville, November 16, 1999,
provided by the Tennessee Bar Foundation, Nashville

200. "WRITING THE FUTURE GOVERNOR'S SPEECH"

When I was future chairman of the Tennessee Law Revision Commission, Frank Clement was going to have to make a speech in December 1962 to the Nashville Bar Association. Frank was going into office as governor in January, so the Nashville Bar Association asked him to be the principal speaker at the annual meeting in December.

Frank turned to Doug Fisher and me and said, "You boys write me a speech."

So we flipped, and I lost; so I had to write the speech. Well, I had a lot of ideas about what I would propose if I were going to be governor. So I wrote him a fi-i-i-ne speech, and one of the things in that speech was when we were going to raise judges' pay; we were going to have an executive secretary at the supreme court to help in the administration of the courts; to create a law revision commission; study reforming the corporation code, the rules of practice and procedure, and a court reform. All of these things were in the speech, closing with the great quotation, "Caesar Augustus found Rome a city of bricks, but he left it a city of marble." I went on to say how much more noble it would be to find Tennessee a state where the legal system was in disarray and to lead it to where we had brought into being a legal system worthy of our people.

Well, you know, the Nashville Bar Association thought it was a great speech! I don't know whether Clement had read it before he gave it, but anyway he was then committed to it, and he followed through.

He put it in his legislative package, and in those days the governor's legislative package was passed.

We proceeded to do many of these revision things.

William Val Sanford, Nashville, December 6, 2000,
provided by the Tennessee Bar Foundation, Nashville

11

Thievery

Theft is typically a difficult crime case involving many attorneys. It is generally not an easy charge to defend nor to prove the accused is guilty. Occasionally, jurists may also have trouble voting to convict the accused because they, too, may have been guilty of theft one or more times across the years. The following stories are related to animal theft, car theft, armed robbery, music theft, and even religious conversion while in jail. As is true in most other story categories, humor plays an occasional role when theft is illustrated in story form.

201. "Fingerprints Not Available While Wearing Gloves"

This is what a lawyer told me on the criminal side. He may have heard and repeated it from other sources, but I've always attributed it to him. It's Charlie Miles, who was a great defense lawyer. He was in a jury trial one day, and his client was seated next to him. In those days, you really didn't know what was going to develop in a trial, because you didn't have these "rules of discovery." You went into a trial, and they called it "trial by ambush." You didn't know what was going to develop. But, today, the trials are so orderly and orchestrated now, that's what has taken the humor out of trials. . . .

Well, here Charlie Miles was, back in the 1950s or '60s. He had this fellow seated next to him, and the guy's on trial for larceny—theft of property in a house. Things were looking pretty good, since he'd assured his lawyer, Mr. Miles, that he was innocent of all charges and of all wrongs. Well, all of a sudden the state announces unusually that the next witness will be a fingerprint expert. Miles cringes and looks over at his client. The client kindly said, "Don't worry, Mr. Miles, I was wearing gloves." [Laughter]

Miles has told that many times, but I'm not sure that it's true.

Alan Highers, Jackson, August 8, 2001

202. "THIEF GETS CONVERTED IN JAIL"

Back when they were pirating music, I represented a guy whose name I can't remember just now. He was at a hearing in Nashville that didn't directly involve us. But somehow or another he was on the stand and started telling how I had cheated him, and so on, and on, and on. Val Sanford, who was just a pillar of the community and the legal community, stood up, and Judge Morton said, "Sit down, Mr. Sanford, I know Mr. Acuff."

I went wild, as I was probably, when I was practicing criminal law in the Upper Cumberland. I could plead that the guy had a jailhouse conversion and be listened to, because the judge knew that I knew the difference between a true conversion and a conversion for convenience.

John Acuff, Cookeville, November 7, 2001

203. "CONVICT STEALS JUDGE'S CAR"

At general sessions in Clay County, back two or three years ago, perhaps in the year 2000, we had a day when the district attorney was there for prosecuting criminal cases, and we had a Mr. Henry as defendant. He was not a Clay County person and was sitting over where the convicts, the people in custody, sit in their little orange suits. It was quite a lengthy day, and I noticed Mr. Henry there that morning, but I didn't think anything about it. However, I didn't see him after lunch. But on the docket I saw his name, and late that afternoon he was the only one that I had not marked off. I said, "What happened to Mr. Henry?"

One of the deputies said to me, "Judge, we think he has escaped. He went to the bathroom and didn't reappear."

Well, about four thirty, I get through with the court session and go over to the office. The girls are gone. It was Friday afternoon, and the square is getting a little abandoned. I was getting ready to close up, so I walked out the door and walked to where my car was parked. But it wasn't there. I thought, "Well, where is my car?" I thought maybe my

wife had come and got it, that she needed it for some reason. In my
mind I go through what might be the explanation. And about that time,
one of the ladies from the antique store walked out. I said to her, "Do
you know if they came and got my car?"

Of course, I had left the keys in the car. The lady from the store
said, "Why, I'll bet the convict, the escapee, got it."

I said, "Surely not."

So I go back in the office and call home and asked, "Did you all
happen to get my car?"

My wife said, "No."

Then I called down to the jail. One of the deputies answered, and
I recognized his voice. I asked him, "Did Henry escape?"

"Yeah."

I said, "I believe he got my car."

When the deputy turned to the sheriff, I heard him say, "Ha, ha,
he got the judge's car!"

Well, Henry drove on to Nashville and wrecked the car down
there three nights later. So, I got my car back.

I've had much ribbing about having him in court and him stealing
my car.

James White Jr., Celina, August 27, 2002

204. "ACCUSED MAN CONFESSES"

When I first started practicing law, it was customary for new lawyers to
be appointed from time to time to represent indigents. My first appointment was to represent a black citizen who allegedly had stolen a
ham of meat from his employer. Judge Hart, who was the presiding
criminal judge, said, "You are appointed. Take him outside, talk to him,
and be back in five minutes."

So I came back in five minutes, and the judge said, "Have you
reached a decision?"

I said, "Judge, I haven't had time to give this man any information
about what to do, or how to do, or how to plead."

He said, "Well, he wants to plead guilty, doesn't he?"

After becoming somewhat concerned, my client said, "Well, I did
take the ham at Christmas." [Laughter]

That man got eight years in the penitentiary.

Cecil D. Branstetter Sr., Nashville, November 16, 1999,
provided by the Tennessee Bar Foundation, Nashville

205. "Accused Man Acquitted"

Back in 1956, as prosecuting attorney, I was trying a case in a neighboring county involving an armed robbery of a gentleman at his home, a very wealthy gentleman who was known by everybody in the county. We developed that the defendant had been convicted of a couple of other felonies. We didn't have anything but circumstantial evidence. We tried the case for three to four days, and I was convinced that he was guilty. I prosecuted him hard. The jury came back eleven to one in favor of the state.

One man stopped that conviction. So we reset it for trial, and before it could be tried again, we discovered that the man was not guilty and found the man who was.

That case had a well-nigh paralyzing effect on me to think that I could have made such a mistake. This man took the witness stand, which is unusual in criminal cases, and denied that he had done the robbery. I referred to several states in asking him, "Where were you at such and such a time?" And everybody knew there was a big penitentiary in each state I asked about. The jury picked up on the fact that he had been there, and I got away with it.

I thought to myself, if I use that talent or ability as it were to convict an innocent person, I don't think I'd ever get over it. So I thought, in view of the fact that I had almost done that, that the best thing for me to do was to get out of the prosecution game and go back to where you can't hurt somebody.

Another element entered into that case. Criminal court judge John R. Todd called to my office one day and said, "General, if you think you're going to educate those three children, you'd better get out of office, you ain't going to make it there." And those were pretty strong words. But all that together convinced me that I was in the wrong end of it, and so I did not run again, though I was unopposed. I haven't tried a criminal case since that day.

Martin Lacy West, Kingsport, August 10, 2001,
provided by the Tennessee Bar Foundation, Nashville

12

EXECUTIONS AND RACE RELATIONS

⚖

The following account of a legal public execution, the first story in this chapter, is the only one available for inclusion in this book, although in early times public hangings were rather common in Tennessee and other states in the Upper South.

The second story in this chapter provides a description of the historic Highlander Folk School and the racist activities that occurred during efforts to revoke the school's charter. The next story is related to typical Ku Klux Klan activities in the South up until the 1950s.

206. "PUBLIC HANGING IN TIPTON COUNTY"

Do you remember the public hanging of the Negro Andrew Sanders? I was present that day. I was also in the courthouse and heard Attorneys Blackwell and H. S. Young argue the motion for a new trial, which Judge Flippin overruled, pronouncing the death sentence. There have been only three legal executions in this county since the Civil War. Sanders was the only public one. L. P. Reaves, who was sheriff, executed Sanders. The other executions were held in enclosures in the jail yard. Now, the death sentence is executed in Nashville, at the state penitentiary. To the credit of the good citizenship of Tipton County, it can be said that we have never had a lynching in the county. Judge "Lynch" has never held jurisdiction here.

Written by Judge William A. Owen, Covington,
and published in the Covington Leader, *April 9, 1931;*
provided by Russell B. Bailey, Covington mayor and Tipton County historian

207. "THE HIGHLANDER FOLK SCHOOL"

I have been an advocate of equal protection against all race or other types of discrimination. In the late 1950s and early 1960s, I represented the Highland[er] Folk School located in Monteagle, Tennessee. Myles Horton, who was president [founder] ... started an adult education program near Monteagle to educate coal miners and help them in that geographical area. Later on, the school undertook to educate and to assist in the field of equal protection, civil rights, women's rights, and the education of like nature. The adult education program continued in the field of civil rights, and people that were interested in that field would be taught to sit in protests where discrimination, in restaurants, for example, was taking place.

I recall that a black professor from North Carolina with a Ph.D. degree was teaching there when an effort was made to revoke the charter of Highland[er] Folk School. One morning very early he came to see me because the case was in progress. I asked him why he was getting up so early. He said he had to go back to North Carolina for a couple of days and that he had to get up real early to go because there wasn't a single restaurant, hotel, or motel between Monteagle and his home in North Carolina that would serve a black person. Martin Luther King came to Highland[er] Folk School as a teacher and participant. Rosa Parks, who refused to go to the back of the bus, and Septima Clark and many other black citizens either taught or were attending classes at Highland[er] Folk School, seeking to educate in the areas of methods and procedures, seeking to destroy the terrible discriminations.

At this time, the attorney general for Arkansas, Bruce Bennett (now deceased), and a group from Alabama was seeking to have the charter of the school revoked. The governor and the legislature, at the request of the governor, held hearings, and a resolution was adopted to direct the local attorney general to institute a proceeding to revoke the charter. The highway patrol, sent to the school, claims they were selling beer at the school and were letting blacks and whites sit in the same classroom. That was one of the specific charges. They raided the school but found nothing to justify the charges. The highway patrol then raided the school, checked out the library, and pushed the employees around. Septima Clark, who was well known in the area of civil rights and civil liberties, was hauled off to jail. Later on, a judge declared that the sealed warrant was void on its face.

Judge Chatten was the circuit judge at that time. He later became a justice of the Tennessee Supreme Court. I've often said that Highland[er] Folk School got him promoted, and it did! They did, however, revoke the school's charter. Black students were not permitted to go into town, and as one witness testified, no blacks were to be permitted on the mountain. They could not go into town. In fact, anyone that did was arrested. So someone would make a list of the things they wanted, put money in a cigar box along with their names and the things that were wanted to be bought, then send a white person in to get what they wanted by paying for it. The white person would then take the items back and give them to the black individuals. The sale of beer was legal in town, and they would buy beer, so that was one of the bases for the claim to revoke the charter. They were also charged for letting blacks and whites sit in the same classroom. The state law of Tennessee said that blacks and whites could not sit in the same classroom. So the school's charter was revoked on the basis of the complaint of selling beer and letting blacks and whites sit in the same classroom.

The Tennessee Supreme Court got smart and knew that couldn't stand since *Brown v. the Board of Education* had been decided. But Highland[er] was a private school, hence that decision applied only to public schools. They revoked the Highland[er] charter on the basis of selling beer and letting blacks and whites sit together in the same classrooms.

> *Cecil D. Branstetter Sr., Nashville, November 16, 1999,*
> *provided by the Tennessee Bar Foundation, Nashville*

208. "KKK Posted Warning Sign"

I defended a black man once, tried his case on the rape of a white woman, and the jury hung for me. The state never retried the case again, but in my old office the windows were shot out and a card was posted. It read, "The Ku Klux Klan is watching you."

When I was interviewed about it, I said, "I don't mind them watching; I just don't want them to shoot me."

> *Raymond Fraley, Fayetteville, September 20, 2001*

13

Bad Words in Court

Dirty words and curse words used in court are not typical, but on occasion they are uttered, sometimes shouted. It is rare for lawyers to use abusive words during court procedures, but occasionally they do, as indicated in one of the stories in this chapter. In other instances herein, a prisoner used a dirty word when responding to the judge, and a convicted person cursed the judge verbatim. Two other accused men also cursed the judge, and one of them tossed feces at him. Lawyers occasionally use curse words against opposition lawyers. Such instances are rare, but they have occurred across the years and still do, however infrequently.

209. "Dirty Word Uttered at the Judge"

I've heard a story about a dirty word in court that came during a case in Hohenwald, where this guy came down there as a witness. They brought him down from the penitentiary as a witness. They had him on the witness stand, but he wouldn't answer any questions. The DA, or whomever had subpoenaed him, finally said to the judge, "Your Honor, I wish you'd instruct this man to answer these questions."

The judge looked at this man and said, "Mr. So-and-so, I understand that you are in the penitentiary. What sentence do you have?"

He said, "Well, I got two life sentences."

The judge said, "Well, you realize, don't you, that if you don't answer these questions, you could be held in contempt of court and could get up to ten days in jail?"

Said the guy looked at him and said, "Bullshit." [Laughter]

Jim T. Hamilton, Columbia, December 10, 2001

210. "YOUNG CLIENT CURSES JUDGE"

TLH

In my early years, we had a judge who was a Scotch-Irishman, a very stern gentleman. In his later years on the bench he suffered from arthritis and wasn't in a very good mood. We had a young lawyer from here who was fresh out of law school and wanted to make his mark. He was appointed to represent an indigent defendant, who was charged with some kind of theft. In those days, a person convicted of a felony almost invariably went to the penitentiary. As a matter of fact, it was a foregone conclusion you had to have a special motion for probation. So this lawyer came in and said, "This guy is poor and can't afford a lawyer, and this court system treats people like that as meat on the hook. I want to try to do something to defend him. I have found a young minister who would like to talk with this boy to see if he can't change his life. But the sheriff won't let him see him but once a week during visiting hours, and it's going to take more than that."

At that time we had term courts. Courts only met four times a year in this county. So this guy was going to be in jail for quite a while before trial. I said that I didn't think that anything was wrong with that, so I talked to the sheriff and said, "Why don't you let this preacher come in and talk to him?"

Well, he did, and he was very well received, not only by that defendant but by the combined Felony A and Felony B sections of the jail. He pretty much converted them. Well, the day the sentencing hearing came up—the judge wasn't from here—and they called the defendant to the witness stand, and he told about how he had found religion, was a changed individual, and was determined that he was going to do better.

And then they called his mother. She said that she loved him, didn't want him to go to prison, didn't think he was really a bad boy, and that she had seen a big change in him. Then they called this minister. And the minister said that he had worked with him and talked with him and counseled with him, and he felt that he was a genuinely converted individual.

The lawyer just didn't know the judge very well. The old judge believed in work, and he believed that everyone should have a job and work at it hard every day. And that was his religion. So after he heard all this, he called that boy back up to the stand. He said, "Bring that boy back up here."

I remember he pointed his crooked finger out. It never really pointed at you but he thought it pointed at everything he wanted. Said, "Bring that boy back up here." Then said, "I want to ask you one question. If you walked out of here today on this probation they are talking about, I want you to tell me what you want to do for the rest of your life."

Well, right at that moment I knew that if the boy said that he wanted to get a job and work at some honest profession, that he was a free man. He said, "I want to carry the message of the Lord to as many people as I can."

The judge said, "Well, I'm sending you where there are more people who need that message than anywhere else, because you are going to the state penitentiary at Brushy Mountain."

The boy looked up and said, "Why you hypocritical old son of a bitch."

The judge, of course, let that slide right over him. Said, "That's all right, young man. Mr. Sheriff, take him away." Out the door he went, and the judge looked down and said, "Well, I guess I've saved that soul!"

Ed Bailey, Maryville, December 4, 2001

211. "Penitentiary Inmates Tried for Rioting"

Here's a story about a dirty word in court that happened to me. Down at Waynesboro, we've got two penitentiaries down there—state pens in that little county. They had a riot down there one time, and several inmates got indicted for aggravated riot, aggravated assault, arson, vandalism. There were twelve or fifteen of them. So I called the DA and said, "Look, Mike, hell, if we bring these people up to the courthouse at Waynesboro, we'll have to get the national guard up here." I said, "Why don't we go to the penitentiary and arraign them?"

In arraignment all you do is advise them what they are charged with and make sure they've got a lawyer to defend them. I said, "Hell, me and you and the public defender and the court reporter can go to the penitentiary."

So I called the warden down there. He thought that was a great idea because he didn't want to have to transport that many prisoners. So he set us up a little makeshift courtroom. It had a table for my desk, a table for the DA, a table for the public defender, because none of them could hire a lawyer, and court reporter. So we went in there, and they started bringing them in, one at a time. And they were all very courteous. They'd bring one in, and I'd say, "Mr. So-and-so, you've been indicted here for aggravated arson. Do you understand the charge?"

"Yes sir, I do."

I said, "I don't suppose you have a lawyer?"

"No, sir."

I said, "Well, I'm going to enter a plea of not guilty for you here today and appoint a public defender here to represent you."

"Thank you, sir."

We got down to the last one, and they brought this guy in there. They had him chained every way you could chain a prisoner. He had hair down to the middle of his back; he was a good-sized guy. They had a guard on each side of him. They brought him in and stood him up there at the podium in front of my desk. I said, "Your name is (whatever; I don't remember his name)."

He said, "Yeah."

I said, "You've been charged with two counts of aggravated arson, two counts of aggravated assault, two counts of aggravated riot. Do you understand those charges?"

He said in a shouting voice, "Why of course I do, dickhead." [Laughter]

When he said that, those guards came after him, but I said, "No, that's all right." I appointed a public defender to represent him, and they carried him on out.

After that was all over, I asked the warden, "That last guy, what kind of sentence does he have?"

He said, "Aw, hell, he's doing about six hundred years for all kinds of things."

Jim T. Hamilton, Columbia, December 10, 2001

212. "DEPOSITION OF UNTRUTHFUL WITNESS"

John Jones, who was probably the best deposition taker I've ever seen, bar none, was taking depositions. When the group broke for lunch, the guy he had been pounding on all morning stopped by him and said, "You are nothing but a son of a bitch!"

And John said, "You know, sir, that's the first time you've told the truth all day."

John Acuff, Cookeville, November 7, 2001

213. "HUMAN FECES THROWN AT JUDGE"

I had a case some time ago where the fellow whom I had represented in the past was in the courtroom in the circuit court in a criminal case charged with a crime that was something terrible. However, he was charged. I noticed he looked like he was wet. I also noticed that he had a Mohawk-looking haircut. He was seated at the counsel table in shackles, and as I approached him, he smelled, I mean very malodorous. I spoke to him at a distance and found out that he was up there for a bond hearing, and that the judge wasn't about to give him a bond because he thought he might be just a little bit deranged.

Well, we had a brand-new lawyer in town by the name of Steve Broadway. To this day, Steve has never gone back into that criminal arena. He searches titles and does quite well doing that. I told Steve that he had been appointed to represent this fellow, and that I was going to introduce him. Well, as it turned out, this fellow was a little deranged on this particular day anyway. He had been in the toilet, and he smelled awful. And Steve was trying to stay close to him and talk to him about his case, and you could see that he was just appalled. About that time the judge came in and said that he was going to deny the bond. Well, this fellow jumped up and called the judge a "motherfucker." Just hollered at him, "Aw, you a motherfucker."

As he did that, the judge said, "Somebody restrain that man." Someone said, "Well, judge, he's in shackles."

"I mean take him out of the courtroom," the judge said, "for I'm not going to put up with this."

As they came to get this fellow, they had to kinda go past the judge. The fellow reached into his pocket and pulled out some feces and threw it up there on the judge's bench, where it splattered! I mean, it was just hilarious. It wasn't funny at the time, but later on it was.

Raymond Fraley, Fayetteville, September 20, 2001

214. "Lawyer Uses Curse Words in Court"

There was a lawyer in Jamestown by the name of Jim Blaine Reagan, and I didn't know him until he was up in his seventies. He used to come to Nashville occasionally and talk with Judge Williams. They were cronies from way back. Well, Reagan was a very intelligent fellow, and he carried mail in the morning and practiced law in Jamestown in the afternoon. He was also clerk and master. The clerk and master was an odd office. They have clerks and masters where they have chancery court. We still have chancery courts in Tennessee. Mississippi does, too. Other states use the term "equity" instead of "chancery." Anyway, Reagan was a clerk but a glorified clerk, a clerk with several judicial responsibilities.

He was also a hard-nosed lawyer. He was a tough old bird. Anyway, one time they were taking depositions, and Jim was on the other side. His opposing lawyer asked his client a question. Well, Mr. Blake and Mr. Reagan objected, and the judge said, "What are the grounds of your objection, Mr. Reagan?"

Reagan said, "Well, it's hearsay. He's quoting somebody else. It's irrelevant, doesn't have anything to do with this case, and it's a goddamn lie."

Some lawyer stories have got a little rough note to them, but they do happen. The lawyers up in that district still talk about Jim Blaine Reagan.

James W. Chamberlain, Lafayette, November 5, 2003

14

ANIMALS IN COURT

⚖

Animals typically constitute valuable property, whether they are raised for commercial purposes or simply beloved pets. The first story, which received national and international media coverage, is about an already divorced couple that received joint custody of a pet dog. Court cases are often the only means of settling disputes relative to ownership or custodial care. The animal stories herein thus provide descriptive accounts of pet dogs, including the one just mentioned and another that belonged to the judge, a pet deer that was shot and killed, a mare that was accidentally fenced away from her colt, a humorous story about a cow that didn't sweat, and commercial cows and chickens that were viewed by neighbors as offensive. All these stories are very personal and tell us much about local life in Tennessee.

215. "Dog Custody Case Attracts Nationwide Interest"

I went down to Pulaski one day and looked at my docket and noticed a case on there listed as *Lanier v. Lanier*. I asked my clerk, "I assume that's a divorce case."

She said, "No, it's not. They've already had their divorce. They want you to determine who gets custody of their dog."

I said, "Well, all right. Do they have a lawyer?" She said, "Oh, yeah, both of them have. Howell Forrester represents one of them, and Joe Fowlkes represents the other." Hal has been a lawyer for about fifty years, and Joe is a lawyer there and is state representative, and is about to run for Congress.

Anyway, we finally got through that case, and they were dead serious. The dog was a mixed breed—part Doberman, part Labrador retriever. They had the dog tied to a dogwood tree out on the lawn of the courthouse. They presented evidence, with Mrs. Lanier going first. She testified that she should have custody of the dog because she had kept that dog away from "ill-bred bitches," and that she had a Bible class in her home every week, and the dog attended and always sat there and listened attentively to the ladies' Bible class. She wouldn't allow anybody to drink alcoholic beverages in the dog's presence. Because of all this, she testified that she should have custody of the dog. She presented two or three witnesses, and two of the ladies that were in her Bible class talked about the dog being there.

Well, Mr. Lanier testified that he should have the dog because he had taught it a lot of tricks, that he never drank any beer in front of the dog because he knew that his wife didn't want him to, and that the dog had learned to ride on the back of his motorcycle with him, so he should have the dog.

I pondered on it a little bit, then said, "I'll tell you what I'm going to do. You all are already divorced, and you've divided up everything else." Mercifully, they didn't have any children. I said, "So I'm going to grant joint custody of the dog. We're going to let Mrs. Lanier have custody of the dog the first six months, so Mrs. Lanier in June you are to come here with the dog at high noon to the gazebo out on the courthouse lawn. You bring the dog with you, and Mr. Lanier you be here to take custody of the dog for your six months."

Well, I forgot about that. I did the rest of my docket and left. I got in my car and drove back to my office. My secretary at the time asked me, "Did Channel 5 get hold of you?"

I said, "Well, no. Why?"

She said, "Well, it is something about a dog that you've been in court about."

I said, "Well."

She said, "Here's the number," so I called this guy. He said, "Oh, yeah, we'd like to come down and interview you."

I said, "Well, come on." So they did. Well, the next night, I was on Channel 5 about custody of this dog.

I had to go up to Clarksville later that week to try a case. That's out of my district, but the Supreme Court sent me up there because some lawyers had been sued, and those judges up there didn't want to fool with it.

Channel 2, I think it was, called from New York City and said that they'd like to come and interview me about this dog.

I said, "Well, I'm going to be in Clarksville."

"Where is Clarksville?" they asked.

I said, "It's close to Nashville. If you want to come to Clarksville, I'm going to be up there for a week." Well, they came to Clarksville.

Then I got a call from a talk show in Nova Scotia. It was a telephone talk show. I was on that show. Of course, the newspapers all had feature stories about that dog custody case. My mother called me from Selmer and said, "Jim Travis, what on earth are you into down there?" Said, "People are calling me, something about a dog." And a friend of mine from California said he was sitting there watching the news, and it showed this interview by this station in New York. He said to himself, "My God, there's Jim T." He and I were at Middle Tennessee State together.

A few years went by, and I got a call one day from the *20-20* television show. The guy introduced himself and said, "We're doing a segment on pet custody cases, so we'd like to come and do a film of you."

I said, "You've got to be kidding!"

He said, "No."

I said, "Well, where do you want to do it?"

He said, "We want to do it in Pulaski, in the courtroom."

Well, we met down there, and they did about a two- to three-minute clip. They had a special on divorce cases that end up with pet custody being one of the issues.

Unbeknownst to me, some of the lawyers who were on this show specialize in this type thing—getting custody of the dog or the cat or monkey, or whatever it is.

But back to the case. What happened is that Mrs. Lanier never showed up six months later with the dog. This boy came to see me, and I said, "Well, do you know where she is?"

He said, "The last information I had on her was that she was seen in a beer joint in Amarillo, Texas, with a Mexican piano player and the dog." So, I said, "Well, what I suggest you do is to get a copy of this decree certified and go to Amarillo and get you a lawyer and see if you can get that enforced."

Well, lo and behold, the *20-20* people had found her, and she was indeed in Amarillo, Texas. They had some film clips of her with the dog. They showed them to me, and they were on that *20-20* segment.

That was an amazing case. I thought to myself, of all the murder cases I've tried, the one for which I get all this publicity is the case involving the custody of a dog. It just goes to show, I guess, that people eat that sort of thing up.

Jim T. Hamilton, Columbia, December 10, 2001

216. "THREE YOUNG FELLOWS FINED FOR SHOOTING PET DEER"

When I was a very young lawyer, I was approached by these two or three guys to represent them, I believe, for the charge of illegally shooting a deer, or something similar. They were from Louisiana and were in Cookeville to put a new artificial surface down on Tennessee Tech's football field. And they decided to go deer hunting while they were up here. I think they had the correct license and all that.

As the tale unfolded, they were out in a particular area of the county, and they saw this deer in this pasture. So they saw this farmer and said to him, "Can we shoot that deer?"

The farmer said, "Well, somebody is going to sooner or later."

So they shot the deer. The problem was, it wasn't in the farmer's pasture. And the people who had the deer considered it a pet and were very ticked off. So a case was called, and I stood up and said I was representing the defendants. Basically, what they wanted to say was that they did not intentionally shoot somebody's pet deer. It was interesting. The case was called, and the judge said, "All I know about this is what was in the paper."

Well, the story in the paper was that somebody had shot Bambi. But the fellows came to court simply to prove that they were not bad guys. They paid a fine for shooting the deer, however.

John Acuff, Cookeville, November 7, 2001

217. "CHICKEN HOUSES DECLARED AS WINNERS"

In a rural area, representing farmers is quite common, but I am known in this district as the farm animal expert. I am; I kid you not! I represent Farm Bureau Insurance Company, and they insure farmers, so I have been involved in more than a few cases about farmers and animals. And when someone has a question, they can call me and ask what type of fence do they need to construct so that they're not liable if their horse gets out. I've got answers to those questions, because I've been involved with it so much.

This was back perhaps in the year 2000, when I was contacted to represent the Malone family. They operated a chicken house, and I became an expert in chicken houses in a really short time. They were located in the northern part of Hamilton County, and that area of Hamilton County had historically been the rural area of the county. There were farms—horse farms, cattle farms, dairy farms, everything in that part of the county. It's called the Harrison area. The Malone I'm talking about was David Malone, who was probably in his mid- or late fifties. His father had originally had a chicken house on their farm, about a ninety-acre farm. David Malone's father's chicken house was one long building. They bring in baby chicks and raise them to a certain age until they're sellable, then the producer comes and picks them up. This had been going on on that farm for many, many years.

The Harrison area began to become developed for residential homes. Because it's such a beautiful area, and because of the acreage involved, there were some fairly expensive homes being built there. Basically, Chattanooga just grew out and out until the residential areas were taking over what was left of farms in Hamilton County.

The Malones were running their farm, and running that chicken house that was owned by David's father, when a doctor purchased a home that was basically located right in the middle of their farm. This doctor bought a tract of about ten to fifteen acres, and there was a home constructed there—a beautiful, expensive, big home with a pool outside. The old chicken house was very close to where the doctor built his home. Well, David Malone's son, Tommy, was also getting into the farming business. He had an outside job that the farmers call a public job. To them, you're either a farmer or you have a public job. Tommy had been a part-time farmer for a while, but he wanted to be a full-time farmer. So the Malones decided to build new chicken houses because the old ones were becoming so run-down that that business was not going to operate long. The Malone family then went into debt to build new chicken houses. These are expensive structures. I think they borrowed over $300,000 to construct two new chicken houses. They started construction on the new chicken houses, and they were located behind the doctor's property. And the doctor's house was back quite some distance from the road. He had a swimming pool, and he had a lot behind that where he kept horses. Well, right behind that horse lot was where they built the new chicken houses.

There is some odor that comes from chicken houses. So the doctor objected to these chicken houses being built, but the problem was he didn't really say anything to the Malone family until after the construction was getting to the point it was almost complete. And the Malone family was $300,000 in debt with their chicken houses.

The doctor sued them to basically close down their chicken houses, which would have caused the Malones to lose their farm. There would have been no way they could have shut down those chicken houses and paid the $300,000.

I went over to look at the situation, and we brought in experts to look at the situation. We were able to show in court that all of the modern technology had been used to minimize at best the odor or problems from the chicken houses. There was a slope between the doctor's property and the farmers. They also had fans that blew down into the ground so that some of the odor is absorbed downward. They did all kinds of things like that.

We tried the case, and it took three days in Hamilton County Chancery Court. It was a very, very emotional case for this family that faced losing a farm, as they were the third generation on this farm. It was a very frightening situation for them. They spent quite a bit of money, went farther into debt to protect their farm, but we won the case. I was really impressed with this chancellor that tried the case. He is Frank Brown in Hamilton County. His manner and demeanor and just the way he conducted his courtroom was very impressive.

The judge then wrote a twelve-page opinion going through the law and the facts of the case. His report is most, most interesting.

I need to add that when this doctor and his family initially moved into the area, they became very close friends with the Malone family, even to the point that the doctor's children loved playing at the farm. My clients had visited with the doctor's elderly father-in-law and were really fond of him. They think the doctor didn't file the lawsuit until after his father-in-law's death because he wouldn't have approved of what they did. They were just really, really close neighbors, and you could tell during the trial that the doctor's wife was sad and disappointed that this litigation had ended a friendship for her and her children. I think she would have probably tried to find some other way to solve their problem other than what happened.

Anyway, we won, and in the judge's legal opinion, which he wrote later, he cited other cases and not only wrote his legal opinion, he also put in a whole section of suggestions on how these neighbors could repair their problem, which is going above and beyond his duty. All he had to do was decide the case. In his written opinion, he starts out,

"Often, it is as difficult to restore good neighborly relations as it is to repair a cracked egg," and then he cites Humpty Dumpty, but underlines it like you would a case. . . .

The doctor placed his house up for sale while the lawsuit was pending, and he appealed the local judge's decision, and we had to go through the court of appeals. But the Malones still won. I've not heard from them recently, but not long ago they were still neighbors with the doctor's family. . . . I don't think the men ever repaired their relationship, but the women did.

Lynne Swafford, Pikeville, December 4, 2003

218. "The Innocence of Youth"

When I was appointed trustee in bankruptcy for the Circle W Dairy, Lawrenceburg, Tennessee, the owner, Willard Weaver, was supposed to have on hand more than 2,000 cows. He had only 35. Ultimately we found 427 cows, two bulls, and assorted progeny.

The cattle had been spread out all over Lawrence, Giles, and some of the other counties in southern middle Tennessee. They were being hidden from me. I did some detective work, found them, and got them hauled back to the farm. Then the question arose, "Could those cows be the nucleus of an operating dairy farm, or was this an impossible situation?"

I knew nothing, I mean nothing, about dairy farming. But when you are a bankruptcy trustee, you can't just say that you know nothing, and therefore you're not going to do anything. You've got to do something. So we got in touch with the agriculture department at Middle Tennessee State University and put together what we loosely termed an evaluation team. Professors came on a Saturday to evaluate our farming operation. Their job was to tell us whether we should continue milking or sell the cows. Of course, a trustee never wants to quit. If at all possible, the trustee wants to bring the business back to life. That was a very important day for me.

Our son, Will, was about ten years old. I encouraged him to go with me. I assured him there was nothing as much fun as visiting a dairy farm, and I was pleased when he agreed to go.

We got in the pickup truck and drove down past Lawrenceburg, past Leoma, Tennessee, to the farm, where we met with the evaluation team. These professors were 100 percent business. They were not interested in sitting around and talking to a man and his boy. They had work to do. So off they went to evaluate the silage, to look at the feed mixture, to poke the cows, and do all manner of things that needed to be done.

While they were inspecting and evaluating, I took my son on a tour of the farm and explained to him what operating a dairy farm was all about. The fact I didn't know much did not inhibit me; I'm creative. I explained more than I knew about almost everything. Any question Will had, I could answer. We had a wonderful time! I talked about milk production, feed mixtures, and the importance of cleanliness. I took Will to the manure pond, which held great fascination for a ten-year-old, and went into great detail about how the manure is collected, saved in this pond, and eventually used to fertilize the fields. I told him the fertilizer was so potent we had to watch out about the fence posts sprouting leaves.

Every time I explained something, my son's eyes just gleamed. He soaked it all in. I think he knew my presentation was total bull. He was accustomed to my hyperbole. Will told me he did not like the smell of the cattle, but other than that he seemed to enjoy his adventure on the farm.

Shortly after noon there came one of these freak thunderstorms that suddenly drenched everyone. One minute, there was a slight sprinkle, then thirty seconds later we were being inundated with rain—a gully washer. When it started to pour, men ran from all over that farm to get to shelter.

We all gathered in the area of the barn where the doctoring of the cows was done. There was a big red steelhead stall there, and cabinets where medications were kept. We stood and watched out a glassless window, as the rain fell. Sitting right in the middle of the floor was a stainless steel container marked "Liquid Nitrogen."

My son wasn't tall enough to look out and see the rain, so he was occupied by investigating the container on the floor. "What is this, Daddy?" he asked.

"It's a big container of liquid nitrogen," I replied.

"What do you do with liquid nitrogen?" he wanted to know.

"It keeps things very, very cold," I said.

"What do you keep cold in this container of liquid nitrogen, Daddy?"

All the agricultural experts turned from the window and the door and the rain and looked straight at me to find out what the answer was going to be. I thought for a second, then said, "Bull juice, Will."

He looked right back and asked, "What do you do with bull juice, Daddy?"

You could have heard a pin drop. Every eye was on me. "You put it in a cow, and the cow has a calf."

Will looked up at me with an expression of disappointment, "Aw, come on Daddy, you can do better than that!!"

John C. McLemore, Nashville, September 17, 2002

219. "Jurors Express Human Concern"

This is a story about people and juries. I've always respected juries, but I have seen times when I could shoot them! But after I thought about it for a while, I realized that they were right. Jurors want to do the right thing and want to be helpful.

I was trying a case down in Rogersville, Tennessee, in front of Judge Wilson. We had a little farm down there, and we had a mare that was going to deliver. And Julia, my wife, was out at the farm. Well, about halfway through that lawsuit, in came the clerk waving this note. Julia had called and said the mare had had a colt. The colt had rolled underneath the fence away from the mare and could not nurse, and the mare was about to go crazy. Julia's message said, "You've got to come." So I said to Judge Wilson right there in open court, "I need about a thirty-minute intermission here so that I can go take care of some private matters."

He said, "Well, Mr. West, what are they?"

So I told him, and he said, "Well, you've got to do something about that."

The jury stood up, almost all of them, and said, "Let's go with him and help him." [Laughter]

Now that's the way it ought to be. But Julia called again, and somebody else had got the colt back, so we didn't go. Things like that get close to your heart. And the plaintiff's attorney wanted to go, too.

I think that's what it's all about. When it's business, it's business; when it's something else, it's something else.

Martin Lacy West, Kingsport, August 10, 2001,
provided by the Tennessee Bar Foundation, Nashville

220. "Cows Don't Sweat"

This story is about my first case in court that I had to try. It was before a magistrate. Back then we didn't have general sessions judges; we had magistrates who held court, and the way they got paid was on fees. They took care of all the minor misdemeanors and the small civil cases.

Well, I got involved over the custody of a cow. My client claimed that the cow that was out in the field was his cow. The other man claimed, no, the cow was his cow. I was arguing with the magistrate, "Now this man can't be sure about that's his cow," because it was in the summertime, and it was hot, and he was identifying the color of the cow.

I said, "Well, you can't do that because cows sweat and get hot, and it will change their color."

The magistrate leaned forward and said, "Mr. Rucker, cows don't sweat." [Laughter]

I lost the case, my first one ever.

John Richardson Rucker Sr., Murfreesboro, March 31, 2000,
provided by the Tennessee Bar Foundation, Nashville

15

DOMESTIC RELATIONS

⚖

Domestic relations is a broad story category related to family matters. These stories describe serious episodes, ranging from physical spouse abuse to threats to kill a spouse with a gun, adultery as appropriate cultural behavior, custodial cases, failure to pay child support, unsuccessful attempts to verify parentage, bankruptcy, changing a probate will, a young man flirting with an elderly woman in order to obtain her money, and typical domestic problems that appear in court. Humor is not a factor in these stories, which portray serious domestic problems that are typically settled in court. Divorce and adultery, also related to domestic relations, are separate categories included elsewhere in this book.

221. "KNOW YOUR JUDGE"

I had a case that was a removal case. People call them move-away cases now. The mother had custody of a child and wanted to move down to Austin, Texas.

I had one case in which I was representing a kid whose brother I had been to Methodist youth fellowship with when I was growing up. We went to trial, and the opposing counsel was an overly aggressive female with a wonderful sense of humor. Well, we were in court, and we started trying the case. She stood up and began telling the judge how her client needed to move because the mother was living in a bad place in a run-down part of Memphis, and that her father was going to buy her a house in Austin, Texas. She pulled out this Polaroid picture of the current apartment and handed it up. It looked like a cave. All you could see was a light at the door. Everything else was dark. She said, "Your Honor, this is the Oak Acres apartment complex, and you know where that is."

The judge looked over and said, "Yes, Counselor, I know where that is. It's about three blocks from my home, and I don't live in the ghetto."

Well, she's tough. She took that in stride and says to the judge, "Well, Your Honor, there's another reason, and that reason is that this husband, the father, is undermining the mother's custodial authority just like you'd have in a joint custody situation."

The judge started listening to her, then she said, "What this man does, he's undermining the mother's custodial authority because every night he calls his daughter on the phone, and he talks to his daughter for ten to fifteen minutes. He doesn't cuss anybody. He isn't derogatory about the mother, but he is such a part of that child's life every day on the phone that it undermines her custodial authority."

The red drained out of the judge's face, and he said, "Go ahead, Counsel, put your proof on."

At that point, I turned and stood up and raised my arms up like a choir director, and I had about ten people to stand up. I pointed out the door, and they headed out the door. The judge said, "Mr. Rice, what is that?"

I said, "Your Honor, the rule is going to be called for, and this is the family that this child has in this area, and I don't know which ones I will call."

Then he said, "I'm not going to listen to all those witnesses."

I said, "I don't know which ones I'm going to call. I do have an economic geographer that's going to be able to compare the two cities. But he's an expert witness, and I'm going to put all these people out in the hall."

Well, this has made that point of how much family there is for this child in the area. The judge just watched them go out.

So they are out in the hallway, and I'm really feeling confident because I know what's going on.

The opposing counselor gets up and calls her first witness, which is the child's grandfather. He was currently living in Connecticut; he was retiring and moving to Austin. He was six feet tall, had white hair. He is *the* corporate grandfather. He got on the stand, testified on as to how much he loved his daughter, and he was going to buy his daughter a house. They went on to introduce a picture of the house, and it looked like they cut the picture out of *Southern Living* magazine. They then introduced a picture of the proposed school in Texas, and an interesting thing about this picture of the school was that there was an arch around the school. They asked what the arch was, and he said that it was the front door of the house he was going to buy for them. So she was going to be able to basically walk straight across the street to school. Mind you, he wouldn't make any down payment on the house; he was buying the house.

So we get started and the next witness is called, and it's the grandmother. She is about five feet tall and about five feet wide. She's white haired, sweet, and she gets on the stand and starts testifying about when her daughter and granddaughter visit her, and this and that. I start making notes of that. Then the daughter gets on the stand and testifies, and I can't resist cross-examining the daughter because according to the daughter's testimony, she's able to be both in Connecticut and Memphis on the same day, which I thought was pretty impressive. That's just one of those court things you can't resist doing!

So they got finished with that, and here I am. It's looking pretty bleak from my side, you might think. So I called my client and put him on the stand and asked him a few questions about his daughter, about how he loves his daughter, what he and his daughter do, and I finally get around to asking about the family of friends in the community. Then I ask him, "Is it true you call your daughter every night on the phone?"

He said, "Yes, sir, it is Mr. Rice."

I asked him, "Why do you do that?"

He said, "Because I love my daughter, and I can't stand to be away from her."

I said, "Thank you." Then I sat down.

In the movie *Alien*, there's this monster that just jumps right out on this person's face and they can't get it off. Well, that's what this other lawyer did. She wound up, and boy she let the father have it every way she could! She did everything short of crawling up on the stand and biting him on the neck.

But he just answered every question pleasantly. The female lawyer got finished, and the judge asked me if I had any redirections. I said, "No."

The judge said, "Mr. Rice, you can call any of those witnesses you got."

I said, "No, Your Honor, I don't think so."

She made her final argument. I made my final argument. Then the judge proceeded to figuratively rip her head off with his ruling. The other lawyer was in a bad mood and didn't want to talk to me. So I didn't get to tell her that about six months before I was on program with the judge, he and his wife and me and my wife were out at dinner. The judge was telling about his son up at the University of Tennessee and how much he loved his son, and how the most important thing for him every day was to call his son on the telephone.

Larry Rice, Memphis, January 7, 2004

222. "MOUNTAINTOP RULE APPLIED"

We are trying an adultery case; the wife has committed adultery with a next-door neighbor. A friend of the family was on the stand testifying that on the night the husband found out about the affair, he called up and said, "My heart is broken. I've just found out that my two best friends are having sex with each other."

The lawyer on the other side representing the wife stands up and objects.

I replied, "On what basis?"

She says, "Hearsay."

So I stand up and say, "Well, Your Honor, hearsay often has to be offered for the truth of the matter asserted. It is obvious in this case, this is not offered as a truth of matter asserted, because the wife is not her husband's best friend. And obviously this neighbor guy wasn't his best friend either because he was having sex with his wife."

So in this same case, the next day we were trying to put proof in that the wife has committed adultery, and we have a witness that testifies the wife and her boyfriend went into his apartment and went into the bedroom and locked the door. She came out twenty minutes later in just her underwear.

Her lawyer stands up and objects, says, "Wait a minute, that doesn't prove they committed adultery."

So I stood up and said, "Well, Your Honor, I think Tennessee law on that is an old equity maximum; it's an old mountaintop rule."

I knew this judge. She knew me, and she looked up at me and said, "Mountaintop rule, Mr. Rice?"

I said, "Yes, Your Honor, the story has long been known in Tennessee as part of our law. It was a case where the husband and his girlfriend go up on top of the mountain in East Tennessee and spend the night there. They come down off the mountain, and it comes up in trial, and he admits, 'Yeah, we were both on top of the mountain, but I deny anybody had sex up there.'

"The old trial judge looks at them and says, 'Well, divorces are heard as matters of equity, and one of the equitable maximums is the court assumes those things to have been done which ought to have been done.' Therefore, Your Honor, I'm arguing that the mountaintop rule applies here."

So the judge agreed.

Larry Rice, Memphis, January 7, 2004

223. "Persons Born out of Wedlock"

I participated in a case some years ago in which we created some new law in Tennessee in that a person born out of wedlock could only inherit from its mother. You knew who the child's mother was, but it was difficult before the days of blood testing to determine who the father might be. We were successful in creating some new law where an illegitimate son was able to inherit from his father, even after his father's death, with the appellate courts in Tennessee ruling that an illegitimate child can inherit after the father's death if he can prove clear and convincingly that the deceased through whom he claims was in fact his father. We were able to do that.

Many of the interesting cases through the years have involved forged wills and traced signatures and that type of thing. These cases are always very interesting where you have handwriting experts, one swearing one thing and one swearing another, there on the witness stand.

Nathan Harsh, Gallatin, May 8, 2001

224. "Family Disputes Residential Matter"

I happened to be in federal magistrate Julian Griffith's court in Nashville a few years ago when they were moving a bond hearing for a gentleman on a bankruptcy fraud charge. The U.S. attorney was demanding that bond not be given. The dialogue between the U.S. attorney and the defendant continued. "And you say this person that you're talking about is your son-in-law?" the attorney said to him.

"Yes, sir."

"That's your daughter's husband, right?"

"Yes, sir."

I walked out into the hall where the U.S. marshal and all the other people were, and I said, "Would anybody like to bet $1,000 whether or not this guy will show up for his hearing?"

One of them said, "You're crazy. He'll skip."

I said, "Look, he's a graduate of the University of the South, has a Ph.D. from the University of Tennessee, and he is a former marine officer. He may play all kinds of games with you all, but if he tells you he will be somewhere, he will be there come hell or high water."

The defendant claimed he couldn't remember his social security number, so I said, "Well, why doesn't someone ask him for the serial number of his rifle in boot camp?"

Well, when they asked him at the door when they came to the house where he was living, "Is this your residence?" he responded, "No, it is not." He explained in court that it was not his residence, that it belonged to his mother-in-law.

I asked on a break to speak to him. His lawyer looked askance at me, but he agreed. I told him that his humor appealed to me, but that the feds had little sense of humor, and he would do better if he put his humor on the shelf for now.

John Acuff, Cookeville, November 7, 2001

225. "Failure to Pay Child Support"

I've always loved the situation where the deadbeat father, who won't pay child support, gets his come-up short and sweet. I saw Judge Bobby Cathers in court in Carthage one day. The guy didn't have any money to pay his child support, et cetera, so Judge Cathers said to him, "Well, pull out your billfold."

This fellow pulled it out, and the judge said, "How much money is in it?"

The fellow counted it out and said, "Two hundred and fourteen dollars."

The judge said, "Okay, hand her that money. And if you can come up with so much more before Saturday, you won't go to jail."

I've seen variations of this same thing in Judge Chuck Hastings's court in McMinnville, and in Muriel Roberts's court in Nashville.

John Acuff, Cookeville, November 7, 2001

226. "Changing the Family's Will"

I had a situation with a will a few years ago when a daughter brought her father into my office. She laughed, and I said, "What do you want to do?"

The father told me how he wanted to leave everything to his children, that he was getting remarried and that he didn't want to leave everything to his second wife, except what she was entitled to legally.

So that's the way I prepared the will. We executed it. A week or so of time passed, and he walks in and says, "Can I see Mr. Acuff?"

I said, "Sure."

So we went back to my office, and he said, "That will we did the other day, can I change that?"

I said, "Yes, sir, until you die you can change it any way you want to."

He said, "Well, I want to change it."

I said, "Well, what do you want to do?"

He said, "I want to leave everything to my second wife, as she will have to put up with me when I get old and feeble."

So I did. But it was in another county, and I didn't probate the will, but it should have been interesting.

John Acuff, Cookeville, November 7, 2001

227. "Gender Mistreatment"

One of the saddest things to come about, and I've seen two or three of these situations in my lifetime, is where some elderly lady with some money will allow herself to be taken advantage of by a young man who promises affection for her love and attention, even to the point of marriage sometimes, even though there is an enormous disparity in age. So, the almighty dollar is at the bottom of it.

Most of those cases don't get into court. The man has already pauperized her by her susceptibility and gullibility to his attentions, and he's gone, and the way she acquiesces in it, there is really no criminal thing involved. It is not a matter of criminality so much; it's just a matter of being duked.

We try many cases in which the elderly are financially abused by their own children and grandchildren, nieces and nephews. The child will take the power of attorney when a parent or relative becomes not quite as aware as they once were, and place their money in their own name and do away with it. The elderly person will be in a nursing home on Medicaid and in a room with numerous others, when they could pay privately if the relative or child by virtue of the power of attorney had not taken the money. We've got some laws to protect the elderly now, but it's a constant source of white-collar crime. I always tell my elderly clients to keep their own money in their own name until they die.

Nathan Harsh, Gallatin, May 8, 2001

228. "DEALING WITH DOMESTIC PROBLEMS"

When I was with the prosecutor's office back in the days when boyfriends and girlfriends used to get into fights, or husbands and wives got into fights, that was before the domestic relations that they have nowadays. The defendants usually were working, and if you locked them up they usually would lose their job. The female would be on welfare, so it would cause a lot of trouble.

So what we would do is dismiss or nolle prosequi [drop prosecution] those cases. But before we did, we had to bring the victim into the office and make sure the victim wanted it and was not a part of being forced.

I was always kinda like the play, so what I would do in the office there, which was right outside the courtroom, was bring the victim in. Then I would stand up and have the victim stand up and raise her right hand. It was always a female. Then I'd raise my hand and say, "You want to drop these charges. Am I correct?"

She would say, "Yes," and I would say, "Under oath, in a court of law, swearing before God, tell me, do you want to drop these charges?"

Most of them said, "Yes," except one time I had this female, and I swore her in, then asked her did she want to drop the charges. She started crying and said, "Since I'm under oath, I've got to tell the truth. He told me that he'd beat me up if I didn't drop the charges."

So, the oath did have some effect where I was doing this more as a joke. Of course, we dismissed the case anyway.

Don Dino, Memphis, January 7, 2004

229. "AFRAID OF BEING SHOT"

Lieutenant Stinnett was a deputy sheriff in Roane County. He often caused more difficulty than he saw. One afternoon, he was sent to the Mousy Marlow residence in South Harriman, Tennessee.

Mousy was chasing his wife with a revolver. He had told numerous people in that area that he was going to kill his wife because she had taken some of his money. So Lieutenant Stinnett was instantly dispatched to the Marlow residence to block the driveway so that we could arrest Mousy before he gets into the house. Several minutes go by, then the dispatcher calls back to my friend, Lieutenant Stinnett, and says, "Clint, have you seen him?"

"Yes."

"Where is he?"

"He's in the house."

"Well, how did he get into the house, Clint?"

"He drove into the driveway and got out of his car and went in."

The dispatcher says, "You were supposed to block him."

Clint came back with the words, "Didn't you say he had a gun? I might get shot."

Bruce E. Myers, Livingston, August 27, 2002

16

BANKRUPTCY

The New American Heritage Dictionary defines "bankrupt" as "an individual or corporate debtor, who, upon voluntary petition, . . . is judged legally insolvent and whose remaining property is therefore administered for the creditors or distributed among them in accordance with the law. . . ." The three stories in this category, all told by the same attorney, fit nicely within this definition. The first focuses on a goat brokerage company whose owner paid for nonbusiness, personal items with checks written against the business account. The lawyer's advice on how to handle monetary matters worked things out successfully. The second story begins by describing the steps taken to collect money owed to a bankrupt hospital and ends by looking at the deeds of a young man. The third account deals with a bankruptcy trustee account working with a family estate. All these are very serious accounts, although humor enters the picture at the conclusion of the final story.

230. "STUMPED BY THE OBVIOUS"

As every lawyer knows, there is no better way to see what is happening in another lawyer's case than to attend the motion docket. One of the things I have to do as bankruptcy trustee every month is go to Cookeville for the motion docket. For several months, I watched hearings in the matter of D & R Livestock, Inc., Sparta, Tennessee, a goat brokering company.

Donnie Richards ran it, and it seemed as if he could not do anything right. Creditors were pouncing on him every month about something he had done, or not done. They pleaded with the judge to make D & R follow appropriate bankruptcy procedure. After three or four months of Donnie Richards almost being tossed to the wolves, I walked into court one morning to find D & R Livestock first on the docket. Donnie Richards rose one more time to try to explain to the court how everything he was doing was just and right. He attempted to convince the court creditors were losing patience for no reason. The judge looked around, pointed to me, and said, "Mr. McLemore, I'm appointing you as trustee of D & R Livestock"; then with emphasis he said, "Straighten this mess out!"

At least that temporarily blocked all the attacks on D & R. "I'm continuing everything that's on the docket for today until Mr. McLemore can familiarize himself with this case," the judge added and moved directly to the next matter.

I was a young lawyer, and this was an opportunity to be a trustee in a real Chapter 11 reorganization. As soon as court was over, I drove to Sparta to see Donnie Richards and to take control of the goat brokering operation. I didn't really know what to do. I knew nothing about buying and selling goats. Before we left the court, I had told Donnie to be in his office shortly after noon, that I would meet him there, and that he had better be on time. He was. I stood on one side of his desk. Donnie sat on the other. "I want to see your books and records," I began. That seemed like a good place to start.

Donnie chewed a little on his tobacco and spit. "All right," he said, pulling out a desk drawer and placing two checkbooks on the desktop. I took the first one—a great big daddy checkbook with three checks on the right-hand side and the stubs of checks already written to the left. I looked through the stubs. There I found the stubs recording the purchase of fifty goats; another for thirty-five goats; another for feed; and others for electricity, Kroger, a contribution to the local Catholic church, and his wife's car payment. I had very little experience at what I was doing, and I certainly was not an accountant, but I knew Donnie was not supposed to buy groceries and give to the church out of the business account.

I picked up the other checkbook, and check 101 was still in it, never written. "Donnie, explain these books to me," I said, sincerely interested in the ridiculous answer I knew was coming.

"This one is my business checkbook," Donnie said, pointing to the first book. "This one is my personal checkbook," he said, pointing to the checkbook that had never been used.

"Why are personal checks being written out of your business checkbook?" I asked.

"Because that's where the money is."

"But the whole idea is to find out whether your business is making any money—that is, enough money to support you, your wife, and your son. You are supposed to take an amount of money out of the business checkbook each week and put it in the personal checkbook," I explained. "You use the personal checkbook to buy your groceries and make your car payments and contribute to the church if you want to." I went on to preach a short sermon on how business success would be achieved when he could pay all of D & R's expenses from the first book and have enough left over each week to meet his family budget, which would be managed from the second book.

He looked at me as if the light had been turned on in his life. "Why, that makes sense," he exclaimed. "Nobody ever told me that!"

And that was the beginning of six years of reorganization. We finally wore the creditors down and turned the company around. D & R Livestock is still operating today.

John C. McLemore, Nashville, September 17, 2002

231. "SWIFT JUSTICE"

Very few lawyers ever get a case to the U.S. Supreme Court. I got one there, sort of.

When I was a young lawyer in the 1980s, maybe the late 1970s, a hospital in Trousdale County had to close. It left scores—hundreds—of unpaid bills, and I was contacted to see if our firm would be interested in collecting those accounts receivable. I was told that we would get one-third of everything we collected, and the quicker we got to work, the better. We took the job.

We began sending collection letters and had pretty good success. We're not talking about sending out one hundred letters; we're talking about sending out several thousand letters. Finally, we worked the accounts down to the point we either knew they were uncollectible or suits were going to be necessary to bring in the final dollars. We picked out what we thought were the best of those that were left and prepared civil warrants. It was clear that if we were going to have any impact at all, we needed to file the suits in Trousdale County.

I knew better than to file five or six hundred lawsuits in a rural county without first going and testing the waters. I called one of my lawyer buddies in Hartsville and told him what I was about to do. He strongly suggested I come to town and talk to the clerk.

That was a very good idea. My friend agreed to introduce me.

The meeting went well. I told the general sessions court clerk what I was about to do, and he said that he wanted to talk it over with Larry, the judge, before he gave me final word on how I was to handle what was going to be an enormous influx of business for the court.

The lawyer looked at me and said, "Larry is not a lawyer. Larry is one of the few judges still left in Tennessee who is a layman. And most everybody just calls him Larry."

"Well, whatever," I told the clerk. "Talk to him. I've got to bring these lawsuits. You all set the ground rules, and I'll do it your way."

A few days later I received a phone call from the clerk. "I've talked this over with Larry, and we want you to bring forty lawsuits at a time. We will call twenty lawsuits at the beginning of the general sessions court docket on Tuesday afternoon, and twenty at the end of the docket because we want to make sure that everybody has an opportunity to appear and defend themselves," the clerk explained. "If somebody shows up late, we want them to get a hearing."

In other words, for the next several months I was going to be spending all my Tuesday afternoons in the General Sessions Court of Trousdale County.

In the beginning, the proceedings were pretty stiff, as you might imagine. I had to call my own cases. For some reason neither Larry nor the clerk wanted to call them. As I expected, the defendants in most of the cases did not appear in court. In those cases I took default judgments. If someone showed up, I would negotiate with him or her in the hallway and reach a settlement. During the four months I worked those cases, I tried one lawsuit.

As the weeks went on, I became more and more friendly with Larry. He got to be a pretty good buddy. He was not a bad judge. He had studied. He knew that level of the law. Still, we had to do things Larry's way. I would call twenty cases. Larry would call any other civil cases on the docket. Then he would call the criminal docket. Finally, he would allow me to call out my last twenty cases. I would then take default judgments and go home.

One Tuesday Larry came in the courtroom, and I stood up in anticipation of being called to announce the cases that were going to be heard that day but was cut short. "Excuse me, John, hold up just a sec-

ond," Larry said, signaling with his hand for me to sit down. Then he
motioned for the deputy sheriff to approach the bench from the back
of the courtroom. "Where's Miss Maude and Mr. Bill?" he asked the
deputy.

"I don't know, Your Honor."

"You go get them. Get in the patrol car right now and go out
there and get them; bring them in here," Larry ordered.

I didn't know what to think. This was not routine procedure. As
the deputy left, Larry looked over at me and said, "Call your cases."

So I called out twenty cases, *Hartsville General Hospital v. Joe Jones*,
et cetera. I went out into the hallway to settle up with a defendant.
When I finished, I returned to the courtroom, sat down, and waited.
About forty-five minutes later, in the middle of the criminal docket,
Larry looked up at the deputy sheriff and said, "Go back there and get
him and bring him on out here."

A few minutes later, in comes a kid, who could not have been any
more than nineteen years old, wearing an international orange jail
jumpsuit furnished by the Trousdale County Jail. His hands were
manacled to a waist chain, and he was wearing leg irons.

"Miss Maude, you and Mr. Bill come on down here," Larry said.

An older woman and a man with a humongous band-aid across his
forehead came to the front of the court. Larry looked up at the woman
and said, "Miss Maude, tell me what happened."

"Larry, not a thing hardly at all, just a little spat, and there wasn't
anything to it," Miss Maude said, almost apologetically.

"Miss Maude, how did Bill get that big old band-aid up there on
his forehead?" Larry asked with a touch of meanness in his voice.

"It was just an accident," she said.

"Miss Maude, I know different. Now, you are before this court, and
you've got to tell the truth. Tell me what happened," Larry demanded.

"Well, Russell was in the front room with his girlfriend, and they
were doing some things that I just didn't approve of as a Christian
woman, and I went in there and told them that they were just going to
have to leave the house if they were going to act like that," Miss Maude
said. "And Russell sassed me, and I told him I was going to go back and
get his daddy and bring him in there. Well, he said I would not. Then
he reached over in the corner and got a baseball bat, walked back down
to the end of the hall where his daddy was asleep in bed, and whomped
his daddy over the head with that baseball bat. Then he come back
down the hall and said that he and his girlfriend would be leaving. He

took me by the arm and walked me out to the front porch and pushed me off the front porch. And that's what happened."

"Mr. Bill, what do you think? What happened?" Larry asked. "Tell me what happened."

"Larry, I don't know what happened. I don't know. I just woke up with my head split open. That's all I know." That was Mr. Bill's only contribution to what looked a little bit like a trial, but not much.

"Russell, tell me what happened?" Larry demanded.

"They ain't a word of truth to it, Your Honor," the accused said.

"Eleven twenty-nine on the county road," Larry said. "Take him away."

Then Larry glanced over at me as I sat dumbfounded in my regular front-row seat. "John, come up and call your cases."

I slipped up by the bench and got as close to Larry as I could. I turned around and said in a whisper, "I've heard about swift justice, but I believe that takes the cake."

Larry looked back at me and said, "Been laying for that boy for two years."

I had just seen some instant country justice. In a matter of less than five minutes Russell had been convicted of whomping his daddy with a ball bat and pushing his grandmother off the porch. The sentence was eleven months and twenty days at hard labor on the county work gang. I knew then, as a matter of fact and to a moral certainty, I did not want to get on the wrong side of Larry.

About three or four weeks later, I had to have a conference with a lawyer at the silk stocking law firm of Neal & Harwell in Nashville. They were way, way out of my league, but some of my legal business had intersected with theirs, so I had to talk with this lawyer—a very, very busy lawyer. We exchanged phone calls several times, but I could not get in touch with him. I talked to his secretary. Finally, after many attempts, I got him on the phone one morning. "We must talk," I said.

"I know we must talk, and I appreciate all the effort that you have made to try to get in touch with me, but the only way I can work you into my schedule is for you to come over here this afternoon," he said. "I'm going to have to take someone to the airport. I will let you ride in the car with me, and we will discuss the case while we are in the car."

"Is this how a real hotshot, big-time, highfalutin law firm does business?" I wondered. But when you're just a little lawyer like me, if you can get an opportunity to talk with one of these guys, you'd better take it. So, at the appointed time, I went over to the big offices of Neal

& Harwell. We went out, got in the car to go to the airport, and I looked over at the lawyer and said, "Now about this case . . . ," and got no farther when he held up his hand and said, "Excuse me, but our passenger is not a lawyer with the firm of Neal & Harwell. I cannot discuss this case in his presence. The attorney-client privilege would be breached if you were to begin talking in front of him. You will have to occupy yourself some other way until we get him out of the car at the airport."

"If that doesn't beat all," I thought. So, I turned around, introduced myself to this fellow and said, "If you're not a lawyer, what do you do for a living?"

"Oh, I am a lawyer," the passenger replied. "I'm in Nashville to interview with the great firm of Neal & Harwell. I am a clerk to Justice So-and-so at the United States Supreme Court."

"You are a U.S. Supreme Court law clerk?" I asked, somewhat amazed.

"That's right," he said cordially.

That was tall cotton! Those guys are bright. They are the best of the best! I could not resist.

"You know something; you are going to be a great big hotshot lawyer who is going to be earning a whole lot of money the rest of your life, but you don't know anything about what really goes on in the courts of this land. You don't have a clue," I said. The great firm of Neal & Harwell was yanking my chain, so I thought I would yank back a little.

"Let me tell you what happened to me about three weeks ago," I began and told him the story of Miss Maude, Russell, Mr. Bill, and Larry the judge.

He listened as well as any audience I have ever had. He was mesmerized by the story. We arrived at the airport just as Larry made his whispered confession to me about "laying" for Russell for two years. We said our good-byes. Off went the U.S. Supreme Court law clerk. On the way back to the great firm of Neal & Harwell, the lawyer and I had our conference. Finally, everything was fine.

Three weeks later, I was on the main banking floor at the Third National Bank in Nashville, filling out a check to pay my mortgage, when I was tapped on the shoulder by none other than James F. "Jimmy" Neal, the man who got Hoffa and handled the Watergate prosecutions— arguably the finest lawyer in the state of Tennessee.

I turned around; hardly got "Mr. Neal" out of my mouth, when he took me by the lapels and said, "What did you tell that boy that we were interviewing for a spot in our firm last week?" I knew he was talking about the Supreme Court law clerk. "I told him about something that happened up in Hartsville," I said as calmly as I could considering the circumstances.

"I will thank you, when you are in the presence of the staff of the United States Supreme Court, to KEEP YOUR MOUTH SHUT," Neal said. That boy went back to Washington and told that story to the entire United States Supreme Court. They have called me on the phone to try to determine if the story is true or not, which I doubt. But based on their comments, I believe they are about to grant certiorari.

John C. McLemore, Nashville, November 15, 2002

232. "Satisfying Maybelline and Her Mama"

I serve as the Chapter 7 bankruptcy trustee in Cookeville, Tennessee. My job is to examine the debtors and the documents they file with the court to determine if there is anything we can sell to raise money for distribution to creditors. Most don't have anything. So I go through dozens of no-asset cases to get to an asset case. Each debtor must appear before the trustee at a hearing, is sworn in, and answers questions.

One morning a man came in, raised his right hand, took the oath, and announced his name was Edward E. Rowlett [pseudonym]. He took his seat in the witness chair. I looked at his bankruptcy schedules, asked him a few questions, and concluded this man was as poor as Job's turkey. He did not have anything, but he had about $26,000 in debt. I asked if there was anyone in the courtroom who wanted to ask any questions of Mr. Rowlett. Up popped this young female attorney who was pleased to have an opportunity to try out her newly gained law school skills. She began to ask Mr. Rowlett questions:

"I have a deed here to a piece of property in Overton County, Tennessee, in the name of Ed Rowlett. Are you Ed Rowlett?"

"No, ma'am, I am not Ed Rowlett," the witness replied. "I'm Edward."

"Who is Ed Rowlett?"

"He's my daddy."

"Where is Ed Rowlett?" she asked.

"I don't rightly know," he said with sincerity.

"Is Ed Rowlett alive?"

"No, ma'am."

"When did he die?"

"1953."

This hearing was taking place in the 1980s. Laughter erupted in the courtroom.

"Do you have any siblings?" she asked him.

"Pardon me?"

"Do you have any brothers and sisters?"

'Well, yes, I have a sister, Maybelline."

"Is your mother still alive?" she asked.

"Oh, yeah, Mama is still alive," his face brightening.

"Did your father die testate?"

"Excuse me," he said in a dumbfounded voice.

"Did your father die having written a will?"

"I don't think so."

She concluded by saying, "I see. Thank you very much." Then she walked over to me and tossed the deed onto the table right in front of me and said, "I believe you've got an asset there."

Edward's father had died owning a piece of property, but he had no will. Therefore, the land passed to next of kin by statutory state law—descent and distribution. In the Rowlett situation, the property went partially to Mama and partially to Maybelline, and partially to Edward. Edward owned about one-third. The death of the father had occurred before the state legislature abolished dower and curtesy. That made the mother's share just a little bit more than that of the two children. The precise ratio had to be figured out.

I sent the deed to a lawyer in Clay County, Jimmy White, who I knew was very thorough. I told him we had to figure the puzzle out. I would get a death certificate for the father while he calculated how much Mama would get, how much Maybelline would get, and how much Edward would get. The property would be sold, and the bankruptcy estate would get Edward's share.

That's a very simple explanation. The bankruptcy trustee cannot just go and sell a piece of property that is owned by three different people. The bankruptcy trustee has to initiate a lawsuit in the bankruptcy court and have a judge approve the sale.

I thought, "Maybe I can avoid this lawsuit by getting Mama and Maybelline to agree to a sale of the property and a division of the money in accordance with the state law. Somehow I found Maybelline's telephone number and called her. Maybelline talked like magnolia blossoms. She had the most bizarre accent I ever heard. She said in the most extraordinary drawl, "Oh-h-h-h, Mr. McLemo-o-o-re, I could neve-r-r do anything without Char-r-rles's permission."

I asked her, "Who is Charles?"

"He's my husbun-n-nd," she said.

"Well, good. Get him on the phone, and I'll explain this to him. It's very simple," I said.

"Oh, we cannot do that," she said.

"Why can't we do that?"

"Well, Charles has been called to the Desert Storm, and you cannot telephone the Desert Storm."

"Oh, is he like in Saudi Arabia, or Iran, or somewhere like that? Kuwait maybe?" I asked.

"We don't really know," she said, "but we cannot call him on the phone."

"Really, I don't think you need to talk with Charles. When do you think he's going to be home?"

"Well, the Desert Storm is not going to be over until it's over," she said.

I was getting nowhere with this lady. Time marched on. I called her many times, and Charles would still be at the Desert Storm, and there was just no way to get her to do anything. Finally I said, "Maybelline, I must sue you."

"Oh, Mr. McLemore, do not do that. Mama and I would be just mortified if we were to be taken into a court of law. The people at the church, you know what they would say."

"I'm to the point, Maybelline, where I'm not that concerned about what they would say. I have *got* to get this property sold, and if you can't come to an agreement with me on your own, and Mama can't come to an agreement, then I'll have to sue you."

"Please do not sue me. Please do not sue me."

But I went on and sued her anyway. And I called her on the phone and told her when the trial was going to be held and that she could come down and plead her case before the judge.

"No, I'm not interested in doing that," she replied, then went on say that I had mortally ruined her reputation in the community by bringing her into a court of law. She was not going to come to court and compound the damage.

So, I got a judgment against her, and against Mama. Finally, I could sell the property and divide the money. Meanwhile, Jimmy White of Celina investigated the property. The deed clearly said that it was sixty acres, more or less. Jimmy was working on the title in his office when his father walked in and looked at some documents he had out on the table. "Jimmy, what are you doing?" his dad asked.

"I'm searching this title for the bankruptcy trustee," Jimmy replied.

"You'd better be very careful. Is this a survey of the property?" his dad asked, holding up a drawing.

"Yes, it is."

"I went to high school with this surveyor. He was an alcoholic by the time he was thirteen years old. After he became a surveyor, he would sit in his office and dream up real estate. He would not go out in the field, so there's a good chance that this drawing only remotely resembles what the property boundary looks like. You'd better get a new survey."

Jimmy called me on the phone, told me what his dad had said, and asked for instructions. "Please, I don't want this thing to get messed up," I told him. "Get us another survey."

Three or four weeks later, the surveyor reported we did not have sixty acres; we had more than two hundred acres. Jimmy White's daddy was right. Not only that, the land was contiguous with one of our state parks, which made it even more valuable. Potential bidders would know for certain the land on one side of the property would never be developed and, therefore, would always have its rural setting.

Sale day came, and that land brought a ton of money. We were stunned by the amount. We had no reason for concern. The buyer wanted the land; he had the money; the sale was going to close. It did close, and I ended up with a bankruptcy trustee account that was well into the six figures!

I paid all of Edward's debt and sent him a check for a lot of money. Then I prepared checks to Mama and to Maybelline that were in enormous amounts and put them in the mail. The next day the phone rang. I was in a meeting, and my secretary came to the door and said, "It's Maybelline."

"I don't want to talk to Maybelline. I've talked to Maybelline enough," I said, trying to put off one final confrontation.

"She says she must talk with you," my secretary said.

"Tell her that I've sent her a check, and that I don't want to talk with her until after she's gotten the check. There is no sense my talking to her today and then talking with her again tomorrow when she receives the check."

John C. McLemore, Nashville, November 15, 2002

17

Miscellaneous

The stories in this chapter are somewhat related to other themes in the book, but not closely enough to be assigned to any of them. Nevertheless, these accounts are interesting and insightful, providing information about local life and culture and attitudinal behavior. These stories present accounts of stolen whiskey, a lie, an anticipated duel, use of metal detectors, a city located on the state line, a humorous painting on the courtroom wall, the exorbitant cost of beer, medical malpractice, a potential increase in a teenager's automobile insurance rate, a teenage defendant who was reluctant to cut his hair, and two mentally disabled individuals who are featured in these stories as "well-thinking" characters.

233. "A Buford Pusser Story"

A friend of mine brought me some moonshine whiskey just the other day. I don't know whether it was made in this county or not. What I do with it, I give it to my ex-barber. He retired from barbering several years ago, and he just loves moonshine whiskey. I don't like it.

I practiced law and served as mayor for four years in Selmer, Tennessee, before I moved to Columbia. And Sheriff Buford Pusser of the *Walking Tall* movie, he was sheriff in that county when I was mayor. He and I were very close friends. My favorite Buford Pusser story is about the time when he got a tip that a U-haul truck was coming through Selmer heading for Corinth, Mississippi, at certain times, and it would be filled with Scotch whiskey that had been stolen from a warehouse in, I believe, Houston. So Buford set up a little surveillance, and sure enough here comes one of those big U-haul trucks. He stopped it. He arrested these two old boys in the truck. It was full of Scotch whiskey from this warehouse. The next morning when I came to my office, the phone rang. It was Buford, and he said, "Judge Treece wants you to come over here. We're going to appoint you to represent these boys I arrested."

So I go over there. I'd been practicing law for a couple of years at the time. They had them in jail, and I went up to interview them, and boy they were thugs. The only thing they were interested in was, "You get us a bond set, and when you do, you call this number right here." They gave me a phone number in Houston.

So we go down, and Judge Treece and the DA is there, and Judge Treece sets their bond at $10,000 to $5,000 per person. That was lots of money for 1967, so I called this number. A man answered the phone. I identified myself as Jim T. Hamilton and said, "I'm a lawyer in Selmer, Tennessee."

He said, "Where in the hell is Selmer, Tennessee?"

I told him, then I said, "I'm representing so-and-so." I gave him their names. I said, "They got stopped here last night with a load of stolen whiskey, and I've got their bond set at $10,000."

He said, "What's your fee?"

At that time, I didn't know how to set a fee. Anyway, I said "$2,500," which wasn't a bad fee.

He said, "Is there a Western Union office in Selmer?"

I said, "Yes, sir."

He said, "I'll wire the money." And about two hours or so, they called me from the Western Union office and said, "Jim T., my God, there's $12,500 over here for you."

So I went over there and got it. I took $10,000 and posted it as a cash bond, and got those old boys out of jail. We haven't heard from them since. I put the $2,500 in my right front pocket.

Of course, they didn't appear for their court hearing, but about a month or so later I forfeited that money to the county. Buford called me. He had that truck impounded with all that whiskey in it. He said, "These people from Houston won't come to get this whiskey. What am I to do?"

I said, "Well, hell, it's their whiskey, Buford, you've got to give it to them." Then I said, "But you've got to hold some of that whiskey out for evidence. What if those old boys show up and you haven't got any whiskey here to show what was in the truck?"

"Well, I hadn't thought about that," he said. "How much do you think I ought to hold out?"

I said, "Oh, hell, let's hold out a dozen cases."

He said, "That many!!?"

I said, "Yeah," and I think he ended up holding out about ten cases.

Well, I'm here to tell you that we drank Scotch whiskey around there till those ten cases were finally gone!

Buford was a real good friend of mine. But it wasn't long after that that he got shot so bad, and his wife was killed, in ambush. They never found out who it was that shot them. They blew the whole bottom part of his jaw away and blew her head off. He had a lot of enemies because he was a no-nonsense type guy, a great big fellow about six feet six, but just very quiet and neat. He was just the type fellow that you didn't fool with.

Jim T. Hamilton, Columbia, December 10, 2001

234. "Man Lies to Judge"

This happened in a general sessions court in Clay County. The office got a call one morning from the defendant, who said that he would not be able to be in court as he was having problems with his car. Without batting an eyelash, the judge told him, said, "That's no problem. The sheriff's department here has a service. He'll come out and pick you up to make sure you get to court on time."

Well, it turned out that the guy didn't need the sheriff's service after all! He came right on into court.

John Acuff, Cookeville, November 7, 2001

235. "Metal Detector in Courtroom Door"

We tried a case in federal court years ago in Nashville. The U.S. attorney, now the U.S. judge, was Aletia Arthur Trogger. Our judge was L. Clure Morton. My client had been accused of counterfeiting; to wit, he would cut two fives off a five-dollar bill and paste them onto a one-dollar bill. And as profound evidence of this, he was caught with a pocket knife on his person.

As part of my final argument, I took out my pocket knife and said that all of us as boys in the Upper Cumberland carried pocket knives, and we didn't do illegal things with them. The judge asked us to approach the bench and said, "If the jury doesn't cure this, I will."

Obviously, this was in the carefree days prior to the need for metal detectors. Not long ago, I was going in the Nashville Federal Court and feeling abused for having, as a lawyer, to go through a metal detector. I heard someone call my name. As I looked, I saw the honorable Robert Echols, federal district judge, waiting in line, so I got over my self-pity.

John Acuff, Cookeville, November 7, 2001

236. "MAIN STREET DIVIDED BETWEEN TWO STATES"

Just for the record, Bristol, Tennessee, and Bristol, Virginia, were on the state line, which was down the middle of State Street—the main street. This caused a problem for the policemen because they could only pick up someone that was to be arrested if the arrest could take place on the side of the street that the police were serving. They could not go across the street into the other state and arrest someone. Therefore, the drunks, or whoever, could run across to the other side of the street and not get arrested unless the policemen from the other side of town were there to make the arrest.

Craig H. Caldwell, Bristol, January 5, 2002

237. "HUMOROUS PAINTING BY JAIL INMATES"

This is a true story because I heard the judge tell it. Maybe it was back in the early forties when a judge from McMinnville, Robert Smartt, whose daughter married Joe Evans, a congressman from this area, used to come over here and sit as special judge. He came on this particular case because our regular judge, John Mitchell, was in service. I guess it was during World War II.

Anyway, Judge Smartt came up here when the upper room of the courthouse was badly in need of paint. Judge Smartt said to the sheriff, "Sheriff, don't you have some good painters down there in jail who can paint this courtroom? It looks awful dismal. Can't you get the county to buy the paint and get some people up here to do a little work on this courtroom?"

The sheriff said, "Oh, yes, Judge, as a matter of fact we've got two painters down there now who are good painters."

"Well, see if you can get the county to buy the paint and get them up here and paint this courtroom so it will look better."

So the judge adjourned court about noon, and in the meantime the sheriff had gone and got two inmates. One was named Smith Cole, and the other was Red Jones. The sheriff put them on the job to paint the courthouse, and he told them, "Now, boys, I'll come back and get you about five o'clock. So, do the best you can. Try to finish it up today, but if you can't, we can finish it up tomorrow."

The sheriff came back about five o'clock, and the painters were gone. And on the wall were their names, "Smith Jones, and Red Cole," and they were gone. They'd taken off, but he found them! [Laughter]

James W. Chamberlain, Lafayette, November 5, 2003

238. "Very Expensive Beer"

There was a man that had a restaurant here, and it was for charitable purposes. I think he paid either $30,000 or $35,000 for one bottle of wine. The money went to a charitable organization. It was on television and in the papers, and he had a special dinner where he invited some of his friends, and they tasted this $35,000 bottle of wine. It was an old bottle, very unique for whatever it was.

At that time I was representing a DWI client, who was a crane operator who worked construction work. And when he came into my office, I asked him how many beers did he have. Of course, when you represent DWI, they only had two beers. Nobody has more than two beers. So he told me the standard, said, "I only had two beers."

Of course, I looked at his reading for the blowing in the balloon, and of course he registered way higher than two beers. So I explained to him that the presumption at that time was .15, and anyone that registered over that was presumed, and he was like over .20. So, to make a long story short, he decided to plead guilty. I think he had a $350 fine, but there was no time assigned in those days.

After he had pled guilty, he and I were going back to the office. We stopped and had a cup of coffee. He thanked me for representing him, and I remember charging him $300 to represent him with a DWI charge, plus he had to pay a $350 fine, and the court costs were also added to that.

I asked him if he had seen in the paper where this man had paid $30,000 or $35,000 for a bottle of wine. And he said, "Yes, and boy that had to be some type of wine!"

I asked him, "In terms of money, what do you think that you make in a day?"

He then told me what he made each day for running a crane operator, and he made better money than I did! Then I asked him, "How many days did you lose as a result of this DWI?"

It came up to a total of around $3,000 as to what this DWI cost him. So, I told him that whenever he is sitting in a bar and they get into a discussion about the price of beer and things like that, mention that this fellow paid $30,000 for a bottle of wine. Then I said, "And you had two beers. Did you realize that they cost you $1,500 a bottle?"

He said, "I'll always remember that those two beers cost me $1,500 each!"

Don Dino, Memphis, January 7, 2004

239. "Experts in Medical Malpractice Cases"

You cannot imagine the social pressures put on doctors who agreed to testify in medical malpractice cases. I had one case I remember against a local hospital. They did not have an anesthesiologist on staff. My client had a severe reaction from an epidural during childbirth. One woman in a hundred is going to have some reaction, but she had a severe reaction. Because of some mix-up in scheduling, there was only one nurse on the whole delivery floor. The nurse couldn't find a doctor, and she panicked. A certified nurse anesthetist was giving the anesthesia. He didn't have the correct medication on his tray to counteract the epidural and stop the seizure. So here they were, the certified nurse anesthetist and the nurse, dashing this woman through the halls, pushing the bed and trying to get to a delivery room when they should have just delivered her wherever she was. They were worried about the baby instead of the mother. The baby is fine, but the mother ends up a vegetable. Twenty-three years later she is still living. The mother has no brain functions. She just exists.

That's a heartrending case. Because there was no anesthesiologist on staff, no training had been given the personnel for seizures during childbirth. The only nurses who might have known what to do were in a meeting on another floor. There was no one in labor and delivery who knew what to do. The OB was around the corner having coffee. So basically, the woman was unattended.

I persuaded a qualified doctor at Vanderbilt to testify about the negligence in not having anyone on the floor qualified to treat the reaction. He was almost hounded out of his own club because he had given a deposition in this case. I did settle the case, but I don't know how long the "expert witness" could have withstood the pressure. He told me, "Don't ever ask me to testify in another case like this." After that, Vanderbilt University put out a type of unwritten law that their doctors do not testify in medical malpractice cases.

Selma Cash Paty, Chattanooga, July 16, 2002,
provided by the Tennessee Bar Foundation, Nashville

240. "TEENAGERS' DRIVING PENALTY"

They passed an act when I was general sessions judge that said my kind of judge would handle all sixteen- and seventeen-year-old youngsters on traffic violations. We had another law that said a general sessions judge could not adjudicate a case in which we had a minor. So I got worried about that, and I said, "Well, what we will do is when you have a traffic case, speeding, et cetera, I would have the clerk bring the mother and father and the defendant in, and make them sit through my traffic court. I would set this case last, then I would make the officers swear the young man or woman in and have them testify."

The highway patrolman would say, for example, "Well, he was doing eighty-two miles an hour in such and such a zone."

Then, I would have the defendant take the stand, and he would look at his mama and daddy over there, because he had already told them that the highway patrolman was picking on him. He would say, "Well, my speedometer might have been broken."

I said, "Do you realize that you have tried to tell your mother and father that the officer was picking on you?"

"I guess I have."

I said, "I'll tell you what we are going to do. Now, if I fine you $25 in costs, you are going to get mad at me, and your daddy and mama are going to get mad at me. But I don't care; the highway patrol doesn't care, because we are paid by the state. So we don't have to worry about that, but in about six months when this record goes into Nashville, and your daddy's insurance rate jumps from $200 to $800, he's going to be mad at you. And it's going to be awful sad around that home, so what I am going to do is put your name right here on a card, and in ninety days if you don't have any other traffic offenses, you come back into court and ask me to dismiss this speeding ticket, or whatever it is, and if you haven't had another charge, then I'm going to dismiss it. But you've got to come back and ask me to. If you get another speeding ticket within ninety days, I'm going to double the fine. Do we understand each other?"

The mother and father liked that, but when I started talking about that increase in their insurance rates, it really got their attention.

Paul R. Summers, Somerville, July 9, 1999,
provided by the Tennessee Bar Foundation, Nashville

241. "Hippie Outwits Lawyer"

One of the funniest things I ever saw in court was back in the 1970s when hippies and judges didn't mix well. I was representing a Tennessee Tech student with hair down to his shoulders that they had arrested on a very minor drug charge. Well, they simply didn't have the evidence to make it stick. Baxter Key, who was the attorney general at that time, told me that if my guy would get a haircut, they would turn him loose. If he didn't get a haircut, that would force us to go to trial.

So late in the morning I told my client this. I said to him, "Look, I don't care if your hair hits your butt, but you've got a choice. You can get your hair cut and walk out of here, but if you don't get your hair cut, you can go through trial, and nobody knows what's going to happen."

I came back after lunch, and my client is standing there, and it took me a minute to recognize him because he no longer had hair down to his shoulders. So I said to the attorney general, "Is this good enough?"

He said, "Yes," so they dismissed the charges.

We walked over to the rail, and my client said to me, "Mr. Acuff, is it over?"

I said, "Yeah."

He said, "Then they can't do anything to me anymore."

John Acuff, Cookeville, November 7, 2001

242. "Mentally Retarded? Well, Maybe"

We had a fellow in town who was one of the best-hearted old boys in the world, but he was just really mentally challenged. And he would collect boxes and sell them. We had a man who would come out of the hotel coffee shop every morning, and he would see this fellow coming down the street. He'd call him over, and he'd hold a nickel and a dime out and say to this fellow, "You can have whichever one of these coins you want."

The mentally challenged fellow would reach and take the nickel. All the people there would laugh. That went on for several weeks, and finally one of the other fellows took this boy aside and said, "Look, he's making a fool of you. That little coin is worth twice as much as the big coin."

He said, "Hell, I know that, but if I ever take the little coin, he'll never do it again!" [Laughter]

F. Evans Harvill, Clarksville, July 3, 2001

243. "The Mentally Imbalanced Millionaire"

I had a fellow that I represented early on in my career that never realized that he was mentally imbalanced. His name was Claude Clanton, and I liked him. He was a big black fellow, who had been a former plumber. And he would come to the office every day, wearing a coat and tie, and would read the *Wall Street Journal* until they finally realized that he wasn't going to pay for it in a subscription, so they cut him off. He went on to run for sheriff, and he used his 1942 sailor suit as his poster, which was really hilarious. He didn't win, but I was his campaign manager.

He would always come in and tell us he was reading the big board, et cetera. He was just a real character. He thought he had a million dollars in the bank, so he bought a Cadillac one time, and the salesman brought it by the office. He lived in the projects, and when I got him out of bed to come down and look at this car, an Eldorado Cadillac, he kicked these tires a few times. He came to me and said, "Is my money still in the bank so that we'll be able to get it today?" Well, these salesmen knew by then that they'd been had, so they put me in the car and said, "You drive this, Mr. Fraley. You look real good in it."

I came back through town to my office. At that time, I had this old beat-up Volkswagen in front of my office. I said, "Can I trade in a German import for this thing?" He said, "Yeah, what have you got, a Jag [Jaguar]?" I said, "No, right there," as I pointed to this beat-up Volkswagen. Those two salesmen looked at each other, and both of them were overweight. One said, "Goddamn, let's get out of this town before we lose this Cadillac!" thanks to Old Claude.

One day, Claude gave me his business card. The cards were hilarious. I still keep them till this day. Claude used to drive me to the criminal court of appeals, and things like that.

He got sick one day later on in life. The doctor called me one day, said, "Claude's here and he needs to be seen. He won't take his medicine. You've got to tell him to take his medicine."

Claude said, "You know what they want? They're trying to get my money."

I said, "No, I'll take care of that. You've got to take your medicine and do therapy."

So all these years that he drove me, the next thing is that my secretary or I are driving him every day. We'd go to get him at the physical therapy place, and instead of coming out to the car and getting in the front seat, he'd get in the back seat, and we'd drive him back home. It was just hilarious.

Raymond Fraley, Fayetteville, September 20, 2001

BIOGRAPHIES OF STORYTELLERS

John Acuff was born July 20, 1940, in Chattanooga. He graduated from Red Bank High School in that city in 1958, then from David Lipscomb College in 1962. He served as an officer in the U.S. Navy, 1962–66, then enrolled in Vanderbilt University Law School, graduating in 1969. He was an attorney in Baltimore, Maryland, in 1969; served in an office position in Nashville for a few months; and then moved to Cookeville, where he has been involved in law practice from 1971 to the present time. He has served in numerous official legal positions across the years, including president, Putnam County Association (1984–85), and chairman, House of Delegates (1996–2000). He was a member of the Association of Trial Lawyers of America and of the Tennessee Trial Lawyers Association. Acuff has reviewed numerous books across the years.

Foster Deaver Arnett was born November 25, 1920, in Knoxville. He graduated from Knoxville High School, then served as a parachute infantry officer during the latter years of World War II and was awarded the Silver Star, Purple Heart, and Bronze Star. Subsequently, he graduated from the University of Tennessee in 1946, and from the University of Virginia Law School in 1948. He began practicing law in 1950 in Knoxville but did not retire until 1999. He has been a member of numerous professional and social organizations, serving as president of the Knoxville Bar Association, 1959–60, and as dean and president of the International Academy of Trial Lawyers, 1989 and 1992.

Ed Bailey was born in central West Virginia, but his parents moved around the United States when he was a small boy. In 1964, they arrived in Manchester, Tennessee, where Ed graduated from high school. He attended Middle Tennessee State College, subsequently taught school for a brief period, then served in the army for several years. He enrolled in law school at the University of Tennessee, graduating in 1968. Bailey has practiced law since then and has served as assistant district attorney in Maryville since 1974.

James H. Bradberry was born in the Gleason area in 1936. At age eighteen, he went to Michigan, where he worked and attended Michigan State University. While visiting his parents back in Tennessee in 1974, he was accidentally shot in the face by a young neighbor boy and lost his eyesight. Bradberry returned to Michigan and enrolled in Cooley Law School, graduating in 1979. Still blind, he returned to Tennessee that fall and has practiced law there since that time, primarily as juvenile judge in Weakley County.

Cecil D. Branstetter Sr. was born December 15, 1920, in Morgan County. He attended Sunbright High School, Lincoln Memorial University, Oxford University, and George Washington University, from which he graduated with a B.A. degree in 1947, then graduated from Vanderbilt University Law School in 1949. He has been a member, president, and fellow of many Tennessee bar associations across the years. He was also recognized in the publication *The Best Lawyers in America*, with listings under the categories of plaintiff's work, labor law, automobile collision, criminal defense, medical malpractice, and products liability. He was elected as state representative in 1950 and while in office sponsored and passed a bill allowing women to serve on juries. He is also a past board member of the American Civil Liberties Union.

Craig H. Caldwell of Bristol finished law school at the University of Tennessee in 1945, then actively practiced law from that time until 1991. He served as Bristol city attorney for thirty-three years. He is the grandson of a lawyer, son of a lawyer, nephew of a lawyer, and father of a lawyer.

John H. Caldwell, lawyer, realtor, and coal operator, was born in Athens in 1856. He attended King College and the University of Tennessee. He attended law school at the University of Tennessee, then practiced law in Bristol. (Information obtained from the book John Trotwood Moore, *Tennessee, the Volunteer State, 1769–1923* [Chicago: S. J. Clarke, 1923], 903–4.)

James W. Chamberlain was born in Lafayette in 1930. His father, James Madison Chamberlain, and his father's brother were also attorneys. James graduated from Castle Heights Military Academy, then attended David Lipscomb College, Nashville; Western Kentucky State College, Bowling Green; and Cumberland College, Lebanon, Tennessee, from which he earned a law degree in 1954. He practiced law in Nashville, 1954–58, then returned to Lafayette, where he has practiced since that time. He was city judge in Lafayette for thirty years and also served as Macon County attorney.

Sarah Cripps was born and raised in Smithville. She was the first blind person in Tennessee to go all the way from kindergarten through high school in the public school system. After graduation from high school, she attended Tennessee Tech University, from which she graduated in 1994. Ms. Cripps then attended Vanderbilt Law School, from which she graduated in 1997 with a J.D. She is presently a lawyer in Smithville, where she is also city attorney.

Don Dino was born in Memphis in 1932. He attended Christian Brothers College, Memphis Law School, and Southern Law School (the latter two subsequently merged with Memphis State University Law School). After passing the bar exam in 1964, Dino worked for seventeen years as assistant district attorney, then practiced nonspecialized law for three years, served as city prosecutor for the Traffic Division for four years until 1990, after which he practiced law again until 1998. He presently serves monthly as juvenile defender in juvenile court.

Raymond Fraley was born and raised in Fairfax County, Virginia. He attended the University of North Carolina, then served as a marine in Vietnam. After a brief span in a contract business, Fraley subsequently attended Cumberland Law School at Samford University, Birmingham, Alabama. Upon receipt of a law degree in 1973, he moved to Fayetteville, Tennessee, where he has practiced law across the years, including cases in other counties and states. One of his choice sayings is, "We live forward, but we remember backward."

Jim T. Hamilton was born in Selmer, McNairy County. He graduated from high school there in 1959, then from Middle Tennessee State College in 1963. He graduated with a law degree in 1966 from Memphis State University, then returned to Selmer, where he practiced law and served as mayor for four years. He closed his law office in Selmer, then practiced in Nashville for eighteen months. From there he moved to Mount Pleasant, where he was a lawyer and part-time assistant district attorney until 1982, at which time he was appointed as circuit judge, Division One, Twenty-second Judicial District, and has served as circuit judge since then.

Nathan Harsh, born December 26, 1937, has lived his entire life in Gallatin. He graduated from high school there, then from the University of Tennessee, Knoxville. Subsequently, he attended law school at Vanderbilt University, graduating in 1961. He began law practice in Gallatin and has engaged primarily in civil lawsuits—litigation, deeds, wills, estate, personal injury, workers' compensation, and so forth, in that location since then. His law firm gladly welcomed African American clients, beginning in the 1960s. Harsh has never run for public office.

F. Evans Harvill was born January 24, 1926, in Lascassas, Rutherford County. He attended public schools in Clarksville and subsequently graduated from Austin Peay State University in 1947 and Vanderbilt University Law School in 1949. He practiced law in Clarksville from 1949 to the present time. He has served in multiple Tennessee Bar Association committee leadership positions and is especially recognized as lecturer for the Tennessee Bar Association's legal education seminars. Harvill is a member of the American Bar Association and has served as a member of its Committee on Ethics and Professional Responsibility, 1983–89.

David G. Hayes was born August 22, 1943, in Cookeville. Later, he attended public schools in Obion County. He obtained an undergraduate degree from the University of Tennessee in 1964, then from law school at the University of Mississippi in 1970. He is also a graduate of the National Judicial College, Reno, Nevada, and the National College of District Attorneys. He was admitted to the Tennessee bar in 1971. Judge Hayes has been a member of the Tennessee Court of Criminal Appeals since 1994. Prior to his appointment as appellate judge, a position which he currently serves from his office in Jackson, he served as district attorney general beginning in 1978, then as circuit court judge of the Twenty-seventh Judicial District in northwest Tennessee, 1990–94.

Alan Highers was born and educated in Memphis. He graduated from the University of Memphis Law School, then practiced law in Memphis for many years. Highers subsequently served for five years as a referee, a type of judicial position, in the juvenile court. He was appointed to the circuit court in Memphis and served in that capacity for six years. In 1982, Judge Highers was appointed to the Tennessee Court of Appeals and has served in that capacity since that time.

John C. McLemore was born October 20, 1948, in Vanderbilt Hospital, Nashville. He received a B.A. in English from Virginia Military Institute in 1970 and a J.D. from the Nashville School of Law in 1974 while working as a reporter for the *Nashville Banner*. McLemore's private practice, which began in 1978, focuses on bankruptcy and business reorganization. He represents both debtors and creditors and is well known for his work as a bankruptcy trustee. He administers estates on a rotating basis with nine other trustees in Davidson and surrounding counties; he is also an active member of the Nashville Bar Association, for which he served on the board of directors during the years 1980–82.

Bruce Edward Myers was born January 10, 1943, in Portsmouth, Virginia. He graduated from Woodrow Wilson High School in 1961, then from the University of Tennessee in 1966. Subsequently, he graduated from the University of Tennessee Law School in 1970 and passed the bar examination in 1971. Since that time, Myers practiced law in Kingston and Livingston, Tennessee, and continues to do so in Livingston. He served as general sessions judge during the years 1974–78.

Judge William A. Owen was born near Covington on March 6, 1869. He attended the Covington Male Academy, then graduated from Vanderbilt University Law School. He practiced law in Covington until he was elected to the West Tennessee District Appeals Court in 1918. Judge Owen was serving his second term as a member of the court of appeals at the time of his death on February 4, 1933. (Information obtained from the *Commercial Appeal*, Memphis, February 5, 1933, provided by Russell B. Bailey, Covington mayor and Tipton County historian.)

Selma Cash Paty was born March 2, 1927, in New York City. She graduated from Chattanooga High School in 1945 and from Cumberland Law School in 1947. She began law practice that same year and expects to remain in legal practice until she dies. Across the years, Ms. Paty has served as president of the Chattanooga Bar Association, the Chattanooga Trial Lawyers, and the Altrusa Club. Additionally, she served as a board member of the Tennessee Trial Lawyers and the Juvenile Court Commission, and as a member of the Tennessee Commission on the Status of Women.

William J. Peeler was born November 27, 1927, in Humphreys County and grew up in McEwen. He attended the law school at Cumberland University, Lebanon, graduating in 1952, then moved to Waverly, Humphreys County, that same year. Peeler passed the bar examination in 1952 and has continued to practice law at Waverly since that time. He was a state legislator and/or senator during the years 1958 to 1974, and was senate majority leader for six years during that time.

Chester S. Rainwater Jr. was born January 4, 1919, in Dandridge, Jefferson County. He graduated from Maury High School in 1935, attended the University of Tennessee, and graduated from the University of Tennessee law school in 1940. He began the practice of law that same year and continued until his retirement in 1998. He served as chancery court chancellor from 1978 until 1998. He was state representative, 1951–53, and was also elected as delegate to the Constitutional Convention of the State of Tennessee in 1953.

Larry Rice has practiced law in Memphis since 1977. He graduated with distinction from Rhodes College, attended University College in Oxford, England, and subsequently completed the American Trial Lawyer Association National College of Advocacy. Rice is certified as a family law trial advocate and as a family law specialist. A master storyteller, he has also authored books and articles about divorce practice, has lectured at seven American Bar Association conventions, and is listed in three *Who's Who* lawyer and judge recognition books. He has remained married to his high school sweetheart and recently bagged an eight-hundred-pound grizzly bear in Alaska.

John M. Roberts was born in Fentress County on December 8, 1936, but grew up in Overton. He graduated from Livingston Academy in 1954, then from the University of Tennessee Law School in 1960. He served as attorney for the Tennessee Valley Authority, 1960–62, and practiced law from 1962 to 1977. Throughout the years, Roberts has served as general sessions judge, district attorney general, deputy state attorney general, and United States attorney for Middle Tennessee.

Senator John Richardson Rucker Sr. was born November 2, 1915, in Murfreesboro, Rutherford County. He graduated from Central High School in 1933 and from Cumberland Trace Law School in 1934. Subsequently, he graduated from Middle Tennessee State Teachers College in 1938. However, he passed the bar examination on September 14, 1934. At various times across the years, Rucker served on the Murfreesboro City Council, as general sessions judge, and as Tennessee state senator. He retired from all legal affiliations in 1992. His great-grandfather was a lawyer and judge, and his grandfather was also a lawyer.

William Val Sanford was born August 25, 1923, in Ripley, Tennessee, located in Lauderdale County. He graduated from Murfreesboro Central High School in 1940, then attended Virginia Military Institute (1940–43) and Vanderbilt University (1947). He graduated from Vanderbilt University Law School in 1949 and entered law practice immediately thereafter. He was actively involved in law practice until his death in 2001. Across the years Sanford served as president of the Tennessee Board of Law Examiners and as chairman of the Law Revision Committee; he also founded the Tennessee Supreme Court Historical Society. He was cited in a joint resolution by the Tennessee General Assembly's proclamation, which reads as follows: "No person alive has had such a profound influence on the statutory and procedural law of our state."

Paul R. Summers was born in Fayette County in 1923 and died in 2003. He graduated from high school in Fayette County, circa 1941, then attended the University of Tennessee and Cumberland University School of Law (now Samford University). He began law practice as a private attorney at age twenty-seven and remained in practice until he retired in 1982. He was elected as general sessions court judge, chancery court judge, and court of appeals judge. He served for thirty-five years in active duty and reserve in the Army Corps of Engineers, U.S. Air Force, and Tennessee Army National Guard. He also served as brigadier general and staff judge advocate for the Tennessee National Guard. His son Paul G. Summers presently serves as attorney general, Nashville.

Claude (Galbreath) Swafford was born in Greeneville on December 5, 1925. She graduated from Greeneville High School in 1944, then attended Tusculum College and the University of Tennessee College of Law. She passed the bar examination in 1949, then served as legal secretary to the famous Judge John Tate Raulston for two years. As a married person, she did some law work across the years, but primarily remained at home. Once her children had grown up, she practiced law in South Pittsburg from 1976 to 2000. Ms. Swafford was appointed by President Reagan to serve as a member of the National Legal Services Board (1984–92) and by President Bush to serve as a member of the Defensive Advisory Council for Women in the Military Services

(1989–92). Her husband is a lawyer, still in practice; their son is a lawyer, and their daughter is juvenile judge in Shelby County.

Lynne Swafford, born December 13, 1961, is a member of the sixth generation of Swaffords to reside in Bledsoe County's Nine Mile community. She graduated from Bledsoe County High School in 1980, from Tennessee Technological University in 1983, and from law school at Memphis State University in 1987. She initially practiced law in Dayton, where the historic Scopes trial occurred, then entered practice in Pikeville in 1992 as a member of Swafford and Swafford law firm. Lynne and her husband, David Emiren, who is a member of the Tennessee Bureau of Investigation, have two children.

Shirley Baumgardner Underwood, a native of East Tennessee, graduated from Bristol High School in 1939. She first attended East Tennessee State University, then graduated from the University of Tennessee in 1943, and from the latter's College of Law in 1948. She became the first female judge in Tennessee licensed to practice law when appointed to the bench. She was admitted to the Tennessee Supreme Court and practiced law from 1948 to 1958 in her father's law firm, then was admitted to practice law in the U.S. Supreme Court in 1964. Judge Underwood eventually did graduate work at the University of Edinburgh and the University of Glasgow, in Scotland. Among numerous professional affiliations, she was a member of Tennessee and National Council of Juvenile Court Judges, and in 1994 was named as the Outstanding Juvenile Court Judge in the United States. She retired as judge in 2002. Judge Shirley B. Underwood is listed in *Personalities of the South*, *The World's Who's Who of Women*, and *Who's Who in American Law*. In 2002, the University of Tennessee Law School named a large classroom in her honor.

Martin Lacy West was born March 6, 1927, in Raleigh, North Carolina. He graduated from Dobyns Bennett High School, in Kingsport, Tennessee, in 1943. He attended the University of Alabama, then enrolled in law school at LaSalle Extension University, from which he graduated in 1951. He began practicing law that same year and continues to do so fifty-three years later. He served as city judge in Kingsport, 1952–55, and as district attorney general, Twentieth Judicial Circuit, State of Tennessee, 1955–56. He was elected president of the Kingsport Bar Association for the years 1989–90.

James White Jr. was born March 25, 1957, in Virginia, while his father was in military service. His parents later moved to Clay County; thus James attended Celina High School, from which he graduated in 1975. He then attended and graduated from Western Kentucky University in 1979 and from the University of Louisville School of Law in 1982. He passed the bar examination in 1983 and began private law practice in Celina in 1983. Throughout the years he has served clients from many counties in north central Tennessee. He was appointed as general sessions judge for Clay County in 1998 and still serves in that capacity, along with maintaining his private practice.

119 - Ashley Wilmshin.
140 - Joe Fowlkes.
212 - Aleta Thornton.
Back cover - Charlotte Miles.
WL "Contributors e rene.